1067006?

LET'S COOK

italian & pasta

This is a Starfire book
First published in 2001

02 04 05 03

3 5 7 9 10 8 6 4 2

Starfire is part of
The Foundry Creative Media Company Limited
Crabtree Hall, Crabtree Lane, Fulham, London, SW6 6TY

Visit the Foundry website: www.foundry.co.uk/recipes

Copyright © The Foundry 2002

All rights reserved. No part of this publication may be reproduced, stored in a retrieval system or transmitted, in any form or by any means, electronic, mechanical, photocopying, recording or otherwise, without the prior permission of the copyright holder.

ISBN: 1-903817-08-0

Printed in China

ACKNOWLEDGEMENTS

Authors: Catherine Atkinson, Juliet Barker, Liz Martin, Gina Steer, Carol Tennant, Mari Mererid Williams, and Elizabeth Wolf-Cohen
Photography: Colin Bowling, Paul Forrester, and Stephen Brayne
Home Economists and Stylists: Jacqueline Bellefontaine, Mandy Phipps, Vicki Smallwood, and Penny Stephens

All props supplied by Barbara Stewart at Surfaces

NOTE

Recipes using uncooked eggs should be avoided by infants, the elderly, pregnant women, and anyone suffering from an illness.

LET'S COOK

italian & pasta

Contents

SOUPS & STARTERS

White Bean Soup with Parmesan Croutons 30
Rice Soup with Potato Sticks 32
Rich Tomato Soup with Roasted Red Bell Peppers 34
Bread & Tomato Soup 36
Arugula & Potato Soup with Garlic Croutons 38
Classic Minestrone 40
Cream of Pumpkin Soup 42
Lettuce Soup 44
Antipasti with Focaccia 46
Mozzarella Frittata with Tomato & Basil Salad 48
Fried Herring with Arugula Salad 50
Bruschetta with Pecorino, Garlic, & Tomatoes 52
Crostini with Chicken Livers 54

Italian Baked Tomatoes with Endive & Radicchio 56
Spaghettini with Lemon Pesto and Cheese & Herb Bread 58
Mussels with Creamy Garlic & Saffron Sauce 60
Peperonata (Braised Mixed Bell Peppers) 62
Wild Garlic Mushrooms with Pizza Grissini 64
Hot Jumbo Shrimp with Prosciutto 66
Mozzarella Pockets with Cranberry Relish . . .68
Fresh Tagliatelle with Zucchini 70
Beet Ravioli with Dill Cream Sauce 72
Gnocchi with Broiled Cherry Tomato Sauce . .74
Spinach & Ricotta Gnocchi with Butter & Parmesan 76
Tagliatelle with Brown Butter, Asparagus, & Parmesan 78
Pasta with Raw Fennel, Tomato, & Red Onions 80
Spaghetti with Fresh Tomatoes, Chili, & Potatoes 82
Pasta Genovese with Pesto, Green Beans, & Potatoes 84
Tiny Pasta with Fresh Herb Sauce 86
Louisiana Shrimp & Fettuccine 88
Salmon & Roasted Red Bell Pepper Pasta 90
Spaghettini with Peas, Scallions, & Mint 92
Fusilli with Tomato & Chorizo Sauce with Roasted Bell Peppers 94
Pasta with Walnut Sauce 96
Pasta & Bean Soup 98
Gnocchetti with Broccoli & Bacon Sauce . . .100
Penne with Artichokes, Bacon, & Mushrooms 102
Fettuccine with Wild Mushrooms & Prosciutto 104
Tagliarini with Fava Beans, Saffron, & Crème Fraîche 106
Linguine with Fennel, Crab, & Chervil 108

FISH & SHELLFISH

Pea & Shrimp Risotto 110
Stuffed Calamari with Romesco Sauce 112
Scallops & Monkfish Kabobs with Fennel Sauce 114
Red Pesto & Clam Spaghetti 116
Sardines in Grape Leaves 118
Parmesan & Garlic Lobster 120
Roasted Cod with Saffron Aioli 122
Foil-Baked Fish 124
Roasted Monkfish with Prosciutto 126
Mussels Arrabbiata 128
Tuna Cannelloni 130
Seared Tuna with Italian Salsa 132
Mediterranean Fish Stew 134
Flounder with Parmesan & Anchovies 136
Broiled Red Mullet with Orange & Anchovy Sauce 138
Broiled Snapper with Roasted Bell Pepper . .140
Pan-Fried Salmon with Herb Risotto 142
Sea Bass in Creamy Watercress & Prosciutto Sauce 144
Marinated Mackerel with Tomato & Basil Salad 146
Seafood Special 148
Farfalle with Smoked Trout in a Dill & Vodka Sauce 150
Pappardelle with Smoked Haddock & Blue Cheese Sauce 152
Special Seafood Lasagna 154
Tuna & Macaroni Timbales 156
Saucy Cod & Pasta Bake 158
Pasta Provençale 160
Seared Salmon & Lemon Linguine 162
Tagliatelle with Tuna & Anchovy Tapenade 164
Hot Shrimp Noodles with Sesame Dressing 166
Pan-fried Scallops & Pasta 168
Smoked Mackerel & Pasta Frittata 170
Crispy Cod Cannelloni 172
Spaghetti alle Vongole 174
Seafood Pockets with Pappardelle & Cilantro Pesto 176
Pasta & Mussels in Tomato & Wine Sauce 178
Salmon & Spaghetti in a Creamy Egg Sauce 180
Creamy Coconut Seafood Pasta 182
Fettuccine with Sardines & Spinach 184
Sweet-and-Sour Fish with Crispy Noodles 186
Warm Swordfish Niçoise 188

MEATS

Oven-Roasted Vegetables with Sausages 190
Hot Salami & Vegetable Gratin 192
Antipasto Penne 194
Italian Risotto 196
Pan-Fried Beef with Creamy Mushrooms ...198
Oven-Baked Pork Balls with Bell Peppers ...200
Pork Chop Hotpot 202
Veal Italian 204
Roasted Lamb with Rosemary & Garlic 206
Braised Lamb with Fava Beans 208
Spaghetti Bolognese 210
Meatballs with Olives 212
Lasagna 214
Fillet Steaks with Tomato & Garlic Sauce 216
Veal Cutlets with Marsala Sauce 218
Cannelloni 220
Vitello Tonnato (Veal in Tuna Sauce) 222
Italian Pot Roast 224
Italian Meatballs in Tomato Sauce 226
Italian Calf's Liver 228
Spaghetti Bolognese 230
Lasagna 232
Cannelloni with Spicy Bolognese Filling 234
Spaghetti & Meatballs 236
Chorizo with Pasta in a Tomato Sauce 238
Moroccan Penne 240
Spicy Chili Beef 242
Pasta & Pork Ragù 244
Sausage & Red Currant Pasta Bake 246
Pappardelle Pork with Brandy Sauce 248
Tagliatelle with Spicy Sausage Ragù 250
Pasta with Beef, Capers, & Olives 252
Gnocchi & Prosciutto Bake 254
Chinese Beef with Angel Hair Pasta 256
Lamb Arrabbiata 258
Creamed Lamb & Wild Mushroom Pasta ...260
Tagliatelle with Creamy Liver & Basil 262
Ham Steak with Red Wine Sauce & Pasta 264
Prosciutto & Gruyère Carbonara 266
Gnocchi with Tuscan Beef Ragù 268

POULTRY & GAME

Saffron Roast Chicken with Crispy Onions 270
Game Hen with Mushrooms & Red Wine Gravy 272
Game Hen with Sage & Blueberries 274
Game Hens with Garlic Sage Butter 276
Chicken Cacciatore 278
Lemon Chicken with Potatoes, Rosemary, & Olives 280
Chicken with Porcini Mushrooms & Cream 282
Turkey Cutlets Marsala with Wilted Watercress 284
Lemon Chicken with Basil & Linguine 286
Chicken Liver & Tomato Sauce with Tagliolini 288
Creamy Chicken Cannelloni 290
Duck Lasagna with Porcini & Basil 292
Turkey Tetrazzini 294
Poached Chicken with Salsa Verde Herb Sauce 296
Chicken en Papillote with Zucchini & Pasta . .298
Chicken Under a Brick 300
Chicken & Asparagus with Tagliatelle 302
Marinated Game Hen Breasts with Broiled Polenta 304
Braised Chicken with Red Bell Peppers 306
Chicken & Pasta Salad 308
Hot Duck Pasta Salad 310
Chicken Tagliatelle 312
Mixed Vegetable & Chicken Pasta 314
Herb-Baked Chicken with Tagliatelle 316
Creamy Chicken & Sausage Penne 318
Creamy Turkey & Tomato Pasta 320
Prosciutto-Wrapped Chicken with Ribbon Pasta 322
Baked Eggplant with Tomato & Mozzarella 324
Mini Chicken Balls with Tagliatelle 326
Pasta & Bell Pepper Salad 328

Chicken Marengo 330
Turkey & Oven-Roasted Vegetable Salad 332
Spicy Chicken & Pasta Salad 334
Chicken, Gorgonzola, & Mushroom Macaroni 336
Spaghetti with Turkey & Bacon Sauce 338
Cheesy Baked Chicken Macaroni 340
Spicy Mexican Chicken 342
Pesto Chicken Tagliatelle 344
Chicken & Shrimp-Stacked Ravioli 346
Penne with Pan-fried Chicken & Capers . . .348

VEGETABLES & SALADS

Risi e Bisi 350
Rice & Vegetable Timbale 352
Vegetables Braised in Olive Oil & Lemon . . .354
Melanzane Parmigiana 356
Stuffed Tomatoes with Broiled Polenta 358
Rigatoni with Roasted Beets
& Arugula 360
Mixed Salad with Anchovy Dressing
& Ciabatta Croutons 362
Rice-Filled Bell Peppers 364
Pasta with Spicy Red Bell Pepper Sauce 366
Rigatoni with Oven-Dried Cherry
Tomatoes & Mascarpone 368
Red Bell Pepper & Basil Tart 370
Spinach Dumplings with Rich
Tomato Sauce 372
Venetian-Style Vegetables & Beans 374
Roast Butternut Squash Risotto 376
Hot Broiled Chicory & Pears 378
Eggplant Cannelloni with Watercress Sauce . . .380
Panzanella 382
Vegetable Frittata 384
Panzerotti 386
Pasta Primavera 388
Spaghetti with Pesto 390
Pasta Shells with Broccoli & Capers 392
Venetian Herb Orzo 394
Cheesy Pasta with Tomatoes & Cream 396
Pasta-stuffed Bell Peppers 398
Fusilli with Zucchini &
Sun-Dried Tomatoes 400
Linguine with Walnut Pesto 402
Four-Cheese Tagliatelle 404
Spaghetti alla Puttanesca 406
Tagliatelle Primavera 408
Eggplant & Ravioli Parmigiana 410
Zucchini Lasagna 412
Baked Macaroni and Cheese 414
Penne with Vodka & Caviar 416
Rigatoni with Gorgonzola & Walnuts 418
Pumpkin-Filled Pasta with Butter & Sage . . .420
Cold Sesame Noodles 422
Singapore Noodles 424
Tortellini, Cherry Tomato, &
Mozzarella Skewers 426
Tortellini & Summer Vegetable Salad 428

ENTERTAINING & DESERTS

Fettuccine with Calf's Liver & Calvados 430
Tagliatelle with Stuffed Pork Escalopes 432
Spicy Chicken with Open Ravioli
& Tomato Sauce 434
Farfalle & Chicken in White Wine Sauce . . .436
Polenta Roulade with Mozzarella
& Spinach 438
Penne with Mixed Bell Peppers & Garlic . . .440
Angel-Hair Pasta with Smoked Salmon
& Jumbo Shrimp 442
Pasta Ring with Chicken
& Sun-Dried Tomatoes 444
Salmon & Mushroom Linguine 446
Spaghetti with Hot Chili Mussels 448
Conchiglioni with Crab au Gratin 450
Pappardelle with Spicy Lamb & Bell Peppers .452
Farfalle with Zucchini & Mushrooms 454
Cannelloni with Tomato
& Red Wine Sauce 456
Pasta Triangles with Pesto & Walnut Dressing . .458
Eggplant & Tomato Layer 460
Cannelloni with Gorgonzola Sauce 462
Ratatouille & Pasta Bake 464
Lamb & Pasta Pie 466
Baked Macaroni with Mushrooms & Leeks . .468
Vanilla & Lemon Panna Cotta
with Raspberry Sauce 470
Ricotta Cheesecake with
Strawberry Coulis 472
Cantuccini 474
Almond & Pistachio Biscotti 476
Hazelnut, Chocolate, & Chestnut
Meringue Torte 478
Bomba Siciliana 480
Summer Fruit Semifreddo 482
Cassatta 484
Marzipan Cake 486
Chestnut Cake 488
Sauternes & Olive Oil Cake 490
Frozen Amaretto Soufflé
with Strawberries 492
Baked Stuffed Amaretto Peaches 494
Almond & Pine Nut Pie 496
Coffee Ricotta 498
Zabaglione with Rum-Soaked
Raisin Compote 500
Raspberry & Almond Pie 502
Goat Cheese & Lemon Pie 504
Tiramisu 506
Cannoli with Ricotta Cheese 508

Cleanliness in the Kitchen

It is well worth remembering that many foods can carry some form of bacteria. In most cases, the worst it will lead to is a bout of food poisoning or gastroenteritis, although for certain groups this can be more serious—the risk can be reduced or eliminated by good food hygiene and proper cooking.

Do not buy food that is past its sell-by date and do not consume any food that is past its use-by date. When buying food, use the eyes and nose. If the food looks a bad color or has a rank, acrid, or simply bad smell, do not buy or eat it under any circumstances.

Take special care when preparing raw meat and fish. A separate chopping board should be used for each; wash the knife, board, and the hands thoroughly before handling or preparing any other food.

Regularly clean, defrost, and clear out the refrigerator or freezer—it is worth checking the packaging to see exactly how long each product is safe to freeze.

Avoid handling food if suffering from an upset stomach, as bacteria can be passed through food preparation.

Dish towels must be washed and changed regularly. Ideally use paper towels that can be discarded after use. More durable cloths should be left to soak in bleach, then washed in the washing machine in hot water.

Keep your hands, cooking utensils, and food preparation surfaces clean, and do not allow pets to climb onto any work surfaces.

BUYING

Avoid bulk buying where possible, especially of meat, poultry, fish, fruit, and vegetables, unless buying to store in the freezer. Fresh foods lose their nutritional value rapidly so buying a little at a time minimizes the loss of nutrients. It also eliminates a packed refrigerator which can reduce the effectiveness of the refrigeration process.

When buying prepackaged goods, such as cream and yogurt, check that the packaging is intact and not damaged or pierced at all. Cans should not be dented, pierced or rusty. Check the sell-by dates for cans and packages of dry ingredients, such as flour and rice as well. Store fresh foods in the refrigerator as soon as possible—don't leave them in your car.

When buying frozen foods, ensure that they are not heavily iced on the outside and the contents feel completely frozen. Ensure that the frozen foods have been stored at the correct storage level and that the temperature is below 0° F. Bring home and place in the freezer as soon as possible after purchase.

PREPARATION

Make sure that all work surfaces and utensils are clean and dry. Hygiene should be given priority at all times. Separate chopping boards should be used for raw and cooked meats, fish, and vegetables. Currently, a variety of good-quality plastic boards come in various designs and colors. This makes differentiating easier, and the plastic has the added hygienic advantage

of being washable at high temperatures in the dishwasher. If using the board for fish, first wash in cold water, then in hot to prevent odor. Also, remember that knives and utensils should always be thoroughly cleaned after use.

When cooking, be particularly careful to keep cooked and raw food separate to avoid any contamination. It is worthwhile to wash all fruits and vegetables, regardless of whether they are going to be eaten raw or lightly cooked. This rule should apply even to prewashed herbs and salads.

Do not reheat food more than once. If using a microwave, always check that the food is piping hot all the way through. In theory, the food should reach 168° F and needs to be cooked at that temperature for at least three minutes to ensure that all bacteria are killed.

All frozen poultry must be thoroughly thawed before using, including chicken and game hen. Remove the food to be thawed from the freezer and place in a shallow dish to contain the juices. Leave the food in the refrigerator until it is completely thawed. A 3 lb. whole chicken will take about 26 to 30 hours to thaw. To speed up the process, immerse the chicken in cold water. However, make sure that the water is changed regularly. When the joints can move freely and no ice crystals remain in the cavity, the bird is completely thawed.

Once the chicken is thawed, remove the wrapper from the bird and pat the chicken dry. Place the chicken in a shallow dish, cover lightly, and store as close to the bottom of the refrigerator as possible. The chicken should be cooked as soon as possible.

Some foods can be cooked from frozen, including many prepackaged foods such as soups, sauces, casseroles, and breads. Where applicable follow the manufacturer's instructions.

Vegetables and fruits can also be cooked from frozen, but meats and fish should be thawed first. The only time food can be refrozen is when the food has been thoroughly thawed, then cooked. Once the food has cooled, it can be frozen again. On such occasions the food can only be stored for one month.

All poultry and game (except for duck) must be cooked thoroughly. When cooked, the juices will run clear from the thickest part of the bird— the best area to try is usually the thigh. Other meats, like ground meat and pork, should be cooked all the way through. Fish should turn opaque, be firm in texture, and break easily into large flakes.

When cooking leftovers, make sure they are reheated until piping hot and that any sauce or soup reaches boiling point first.

STORING, REFRIGERATING AND FREEZING

Meat, poultry, fish, seafood, and dairy products should all be refrigerated. The temperature of the refrigerator should be between 34–41° F while the freezer should not rise above - 0° F.

To ensure the optimum refrigerator and freezer temperature, avoid leaving the door open for a long time. Try not to overstock the refrigerator as this reduces the airflow inside and reduces the effectiveness of the cooling system.

When refrigerating cooked food, let it cool down completely before refrigerating. Hot food will raise the temperature of the refrigerator and possibly affect, or spoil, other food stored.

Food within the refrigerator and freezer should always be covered. Raw and cooked food should be stored in separate parts of the refrigerator. Cooked food should be kept on the top shelves of the refrigerator, while raw meat, poultry, and fish should be placed on bottom shelves to avoid drips and cross-contamination. It is recommended that eggs should be refrigerated in order to maintain their freshness and shelf life.

Take care that frozen foods are not stored in the freezer for too long. Blanched vegetables can be stored for one month; beef, lamb, poultry, and pork for six months, and unblanched vegetables and fruits in syrup for a year. Oily fish and sausages can be stored for three months. Dairy products can last four to six months, while cakes and pastries can be kept in the freezer for three to six months.

HIGH-RISK FOODS

Certain foods may carry risks to people who are considered vulnerable, such as the elderly, the ill, pregnant women, babies, young infants, and those suffering from a recurring illness.

It is advisable to avoid those foods listed below which belong to a higher-risk category.

There is a slight chance that some eggs carry the bacteria salmonella. Cook the eggs until both the yolk and the white are firm to eliminate this risk. Pay particular attention to dishes and products in-corporating lightly cooked or raw eggs which should be eliminated from the diet. Sauces such as hollandaise and mayonnaise, mousses, soufflés, and meringues all use raw or lightly cooked eggs, as do custard-based dishes, ice creams, and sorbets. These are all considered high-risk foods to the vulnerable groups mentioned above.

Certain meats and poultry also carry the potential risk of salmonella and so should be cooked thoroughly until the juices run clear and there is no pinkness left. Unpasteurized products such as milk, cheese (especially soft cheese), pâté and meat (both raw and cooked) all have the potential risk of listeria and should be avoided.

When buying seafood, buy from a reputable source that has a high turnover to ensure freshness. Fish should have bright, clear eyes, shiny skin, and bright pink or red gills. The fish should feel stiff to the touch, with a slight smell of sea air and iodine. The flesh of fish steaks and fillets should be translucent with no signs of discoloration.

Mollusks such as scallops, clams, and mussels, are sold fresh and are still alive. Avoid any that are open or do not close when tapped lightly. In the same way, univalves should withdraw back into their shells when prodded lightly. When choosing cephalopods, such as squid and octopus, they should have a firm flesh and pleasant sea smell.

As with all fish, whether it is shellfish or seafish, care is required when freezing it. It is imperative to check whether the fish has been frozen before. If it has been frozen, then it should not be frozen again under any circumstances.

Essential Ingredients

Italian cuisine is popular all over the world and basic Italian pantry ingredients are commonplace items on supermarket shelves. Even fresh ingredients that used to be difficult to find are available all year round, often in parts of the world where previously they were unheard of. For those who enjoy Italian food and cooking this is good news—delicious, authentic Italian cuisine can now be enjoyed anywhere and at any time.

CHEESES

Dolcelatte This cheese, which translates as "sweet milk," comes from the Lombardy region. Dolcelatte is a creamy, blue cheese and has a luscious, sweet taste. It is very soft and melts in the mouth, often appealing to those who find more traditional blue cheeses, like Roquefort and Gorgonzola, too strongly flavored.

Fontina This is a dense, smooth and slightly elastic cheese with a straw-colored interior. Fontina is made in the Valle d'Aosta region and has a delicate nutty flavor with a hint of mild honey. It is often served melted in which case the flavor becomes very earthy.

Gorgonzola This is a traditional blue cheese from the Lombardy region. Made from cow's milk, the cheese has a sharp, spicy flavor as well as being rich and creamy.

Mascarpone Technically, mascarpone is not a cheese but a by-product obtained from making Parmesan. A culture is added to the cream that has been skimmed off the milk, which was used to make the cheese. This is gently heated and matured and thickened. Mascarpone is most famous as the main ingredient in Tiramisu, but it is a very versatile ingredient, and is used in all sorts of sweet and savory recipes.

Mozzarella di Bufala Mozzarella is a fresh cheese, prized more for its texture than its flavor, which is really quite bland. Mozzarella cheese melts beautifully, however, on pizzas and in pasta dishes, and is also good served cold in salads. It is usually sold in cartons along with its whey and should have a floppy rather than a rubbery texture. The fresher it is when eaten, the better.

Parmigiano-Reggiano One of the world's finest cheeses, Parmigiano-Reggiano is also one of the most versatile cooking cheeses. Its production is very carefully regulated to guarantee a consistent high-quality result. The trademark is branded all over the peel, so even a small piece is easily identified. Buy it in pieces, rather than ready-grated.

Pecorino This is the generic term for cheeses made purely from sheep's milk. All pecorino cheeses are excellent for grating or shaving onto both hot and cold dishes. Each type of pecorino is characteristic of a particular region and a particular breed of sheep. Pecorino Romano is made in the countryside around Rome between November and late June. Pecorino Sardo is made in Sardinia and Pecorino Toscano comes from Tuscany, and tends to mature younger than other pecorino cheeses.

Ricotta When cheese is made, the solids in the milk are separated from the liquid by coagulation, however, some solids are always lost to the whey. To retrieve these solids, the milk is heated until they come to the surface. They are skimmed off and drained in woven baskets until the curd is solid enough to stick together. The resulting cheese is ricotta (literally meaning "recooked"). Good-quality ricotta should be firm, but not solid and consist of fine, delicate grains. Ricotta is used in both savory and sweet dishes.

CURED MEATS

Coppa This boned shoulder of pork is rolled and cured with salt, pepper, and nutmeg, then aged for about three months. It has a flavor not unlike prosciutto, but contains equal amounts of fat and lean. It is excellent for larding the breasts of game birds, adding both fat and flavor, or for wrapping leaner types of meats.

Pancetta Essentially, pancetta is Italian bacon, but its depth of flavor is unrivalled by ordinary bacon. It is often flavored with herbs, cloves, nutmeg, garlic, salt and pepper, and sometimes fennel seeds—it is often air-dried. It is also available smoked. Use it in slices or cut into lardons.

Prosciutto There are many types of cured ham available, but the two best types are *prosciutto di San Daniele* and *prosciutto di Parma*. The first comes from the Friuli region where the pigs feed in the fields and oak woods, accounting for the leanness of the meat. The second type, also known as Parma ham or *prosciutto crudo*, is made from pigs that have been fed on local grain as well as the whey left over from the making of Parmigiano-Reggiano. This meat is usually fattier.

Salami Italy produces a huge range of salamis, each with its own local character. The one most commonly available is probably Milano salami, which comes sliced in packages or in one piece from major supermarkets.

VEGETABLES AND HERBS

Artichokes Very popular in Italian cooking, artichokes are available in many different varieties and forms: from tiny, young artichokes cooked and eaten whole to enormous globe artichokes, prized for their meaty hearts, which can be sliced, stuffed or broiled. Artichokes are often cooked and preserved, and served as an antipasto, on pizzas or in pasta dishes.

Arugula This peppery salad leaf has become popular in recent years and is now very easy to find. It is known by many other names including rucola, rughetta, rocket and roquette. It does not keep well.

Cavallo Nero A member of the cabbage family, cavallo nero has long, slender, very ridged leaves, which are dark black-green in color. It has a strong but rather sweet cabbage flavor. Large supermarkets stock it in season, but if it is unavailable, use Savoy cabbage instead.

Eggplants These vegetables are popular all over the Mediterranean, probably because of their affinity with olive oil and garlic. In Britain and U.S, eggplants tend to be fatter and somewhat juicier than the Mediterranean varieties, which are often elongated and marked with bright purple streaks.

Fava Beans Fresh fava beans are a prized early-summer speciality, and in Italy are eaten raw with romano cheese. As the season pro-gresses, they are best cooked and peeled as they tend to become coarse and grainy.

Garlic Garlic is one of the most important flavors in Italian cooking. When buying garlic, check it carefully—the heads should be firm without soft spots. Look for fresh, green garlic in spring.

Herbs A number of fresh herbs are used in Italian cooking, but the most important ones are basil, parsley, rosemary, sage, marjoram, and oregano. These are all widely used herbs and are available from most supermarkets, but are also very easy to grow, even on a windowsill.

Lemons Italian lemons tend to be a little sweeter than the ones available in the U.S. They are an essential flavor in many Italian dishes, especially seafood and sweet dishes.

Exotic Mushrooms Mushroom hunting is a very popular and lucrative business in Italy, so much so that there are strict regulations regarding the minimum size for picking mushrooms. It is vital to seek expert advice before picking exotic mushrooms on your own, as some varieties are poisonous. Many large supermarkets now sell varieties of exotic mushrooms in season, but they tend to be expensive.

Pumpkins and Squashes Pumpkins and the many varieties of squash are widely used in Italian cooking. They are excellent for enriching casseroles—some varieties have flesh that breaks down during cooking. They are also used for risottos and pasta fillings. Pumpkins and squashes have an affinity with prosciutto, sage, pine nuts, Parmesan cheese, and mostardo di Cremona (see the Dry Ingredients section).

Tomatoes Tomatoes are another essential flavor in Italian recipes. Unfortunately, US tomatoes tend not to be as good as their Italian counter-parts. It is best to use tomatoes only in season and, at other times, to use good-quality, canned Italian tomatoes.

BREAD

Italian breads tend to be coarser and more open-textured than breads available in the US. Theyare made with unbleached flours and are left to prove for longer, so the flavor develops fully. Italian breads also tend to have a crustier exterior. Look out for puglise and ciabatta breads. Focaccia, a soft-crusted bread, is also popular and can be flavored with herbs, sun dried tomatoes, or garlic.

SEAFOOD

Italy has a large coastline relative to its size and, as a result, seafood is a very popular choice. A huge variety of fish and shellfish are available, and large meals, such as those served at weddings or other special celebrations will always include a fish course.

MEAT, POULTRY, AND GAME

Italians are among the world's greatest meat eaters. Most meals will be based on meat of some kind. Popular choices include beef, chicken, pork, and lamb, but duck, game hen, pheasant, squab, rabbit, veal, and many kinds of offal are also used.

Dry Ingredients

As with fresh ingredients, many items previously unavailable have, in recent years, appeared on supermarket and Italian delicatessen shelves. Many dry ingredients keep well and are worth stocking up on.

Amaretti Cookies These delicious, little crisp cookies are made from almonds and most closely resemble macaroons. They come individually wrapped in beautiful paper and are good to eat on their own or with a sweet dessert wine. They are also useful as ingredients in desserts as they add crunch and flavor.

Anchovies These come in several forms and are an essential Italian ingredient. Anchovies can be treated almost as a seasoning in many recipes. Salted anchovies are sold in bottles and must be rinsed thoroughly to remove the excess salt. If the anchovies are whole, remove the heads and bones before using. If they are preserved in oil, remove them from the oil and drain them on absorbent paper towels. Some recipes require that anchovies are soaked in milk for 10–15 minutes (this makes the fillets less salty and less oily). By doing so the anchovies will simply melt on cooking. Do not soak the anchovies in milk if the fillets are to be used uncooked as in salads, for example.

Bottarga This is the salted and sun-dried roe of either red snapper or tuna. It is available from Italian delicatessens or Italian grocery stores (tuna bottarga is less delicately flavored). Spaghetti with mullet bottarga, olive oil, and chili flakes is listed on every restaurant menu in Sardinia. Bottarga can also be finely shaved into a salad of raw fennel, lemon juice, and olive oil.

Candied Peel Citrus fruit plays an important part in Italian cooking. Candied peel is found in all sorts of desserts. Buy it whole and chop it finely for the best flavor.

Canned Tomatoes If there is not an abundance of outdoor-grown, sun-ripened tomatoes, then good-quality, canned Italian plum tomatoes are the next best thing for making sauces. The fruit should be deep red, and the liquid should be thick and not watery. Buy them whole or chopped.

Cannellini Beans These beans are long and slender with a creamy texture. Cannellini beans take up other flavors very well, especially garlic, herbs, and olive oil.

Capers The flower buds of a bush native to the Mediterranean, capers are available both salted and

preserved in vinegar. Small capers generally have a better flavor than larger ones. When using salted capers, it is important to soak and rinse them to remove the excess salt. Those preserved in vinegar should be drained and rinsed before use.

Chickpeas *Ceci* in Italian, chickpeas were introduced from the Middle East. Look out for big ones when buying them dry. They are excellent in soups and also in vegetable dishes. Chickpeas need a long cooking time.

Coffee Italians prefer dark, roasted coffee and they pioneered the drinking of cappuccino and espresso. It is best to buy whole beans, as freshly roasted as possible, and grind them yourself as needed.

Cranberry Beans These are large, rounded beans, which cook to a uniform brown color. They also have a creamy texture and are very good in soups and stews.

Dried Beans Beans are an excellent source of carbohydrate, and also contain protein, making them particularly useful to vegetarians. Dried beans should all be treated in the same way–soak them overnight in plenty of water (2 to 3 times their volume), then drain and cover with fresh water. Bring to a boil and boil them for 10 minutes, reduce the temperature and simmer gently, until tender (check package instructions for full cooking times). Do not add salt to dried beans until they are cooked as salt will make the skins tough.

Italians make use of a large number of different types of beans and lentils.

Dried Herbs These days, most recipes call for fresh herbs, but dried herbs still have their place. Oregano

dries particularly well and has a much less astringent flavor when dried; it is essential in tomato sauces. Other herbs that dry well are rosemary, sage, and thyme. Dried basil, however, is no substitute for fresh.

Dried Mushrooms The most commonly available – and most affordable–type of dried mushroom is porcini. They are usually sold in small packages which is generally plenty for one or two recipes they should be soaked in almost boiling water or stock for 20–30 minutes, until tender. Carefully squeeze out any excess liquid—it will still be hot—then chop as needed. Set aside the liquor as it contains a great deal of flavor. It is wise, however, to strain it before use as it can contain grit.

Fava Beans These are available dried; either whole, with skins or split. The whole ones are excellent in soups. The split beans are popular in Eastern European countries, as well as Greece and Turkey where they are used in dishes such as falafel.

Flour In most Italian recipes where flour is required, all-purpose flour can be easily substituted. However, when making pizza or pasta dough, look for Tipo "00" flour, which is very fine and very strong, making it ideal for these two dishes. If you cannot find it, use strong bread flour instead.

Lentils Look for *Lentilles de Puy*. Although not Italian, these lentils are possibly the best flavored of the lentil family. They are small and beautifully colored from green-brown to blue. They also hold their shape well when cooked, making them easy to serve as a side dish—simply dress with olive oil. Similar lentils named *Castelluccio* are also grown in Umbria. They are also small, but paler green in color. Lentils are traditionally served with *BollitoMisto*, a famous New Year's Eve dish consisting of various meats, lentils, and mostarda di Cremona (see below).

Mostarda di Cremona Also known as mostarda di frutta, it is made of candied fruits such as peaches, apricots, pears, figs, and cherries, which are preserved in a honey, white wine, and mustard syrup. It is available from large supermarkets and Italian grocery stores.

Nuts Almonds, hazelnuts, walnuts, and pistachios are all popular in Italian cooking, particularly in dessert recipes. Buy from a supplier with a quick turnover to guarantee that the nuts are fresh.

Olives Olives grow all over Italy and are synonymous with Italian cooking. Olives are available in most supermarkets, although it is worth looking for them in Italian grocery stores that might preserve them with more interesting flavors. If you are lucky enough to find fresh olives, soak them in a very strong brine for a couple of weeks, then rinse them and preserve in oil, and flavorings of your choice.

Panettone Generally available around Christmas, panettone is a sweet bread enriched with egg and butter, similar to French brioche. It is usually flavored with candied citrus fruits although it can be plain. It keeps very well and is delicious toasted and spread with butter, or used in bread and butter pudding.

Pine Nuts An essential ingredient in pesto sauce, pine nuts are found in all sorts of Italian recipes, both savory and sweet. They are widely available and are delicious toasted, and tossed in with pasta. They burn very easily, however, and are relatively expensive, so take care when toasting.

Raisins Italy is a large grape-producing nation so, not surprisingly, raisins feature alongside citrus fruits in many recipes. Look for plump, juicy looking fruit, and try to buy only what you need as raisins can become sugary if kept for too long.

Semolina Not to be confused with the semolina used in desserts, *semola di grano duro* is flour from Italian durum wheat. This produces a granular-textured flour as opposed to finer-textured flour used in breadmaking. Large supermarkets and Italian delicatessens sell *semola di grano duro*, but if it is unavailable, use strong bread flour instead.

Sun-dried Tomatoes Although they seem ubiquitous now, sun-dried tomatoes were unavailable outside Italy until the end of the 1980s. Sun-dried tomatoes are ripe plum tomatoes, which have been dried in the sun. Often they have been rehydrated by being soaked in water, then preserved in oil. To use them, simply drain them on absorbent paper towels and chop as necessary. Also available now are semi-dried tomatoes, which have a sweeter, fresher flavor and a softer, less leathery texture. If you find sun-dried tomatoes, which are not in oil, put them into a bowl and cover with boiling water. Let stand for about 30 minutes, or until softened, before using.

Sun-dried Tomato Paste As the name suggests, this a paste made from sun-dried tomatoes. Use it in the same way as you would tomato paste. Sometimes it has other flavors added, such as garlic or herbs, in which case it can be used in salad dressings or mixed with pesto to dress pasta.

How to make pasta

Homemade pasta has a light, almost silky texture and is very different from the fresh pasta that you can buy vacuum packed in supermarkets. It is also surprisingly easy to make and little equipment is needed; just a rolling pin and a sharp knife, although if you make pasta regularly it is worth investing in a pasta machine.

MAKING BASIC EGG PASTA DOUGH

Ingredients

2 cups type 001 pasta flour, plus extra for dusting
1 tsp salt
2 eggs, plus 1 egg yolk
1 tbsp olive oil
1–3 tsp cold water

1 Sift the flour and salt into a mound on a clean work surface and make a well in the center, keeping the sides quite high, so that the egg mixture will not trickle out when added.
2 Beat together the eggs, yolk, oil, and 1 teaspoon of water. Add to the well, then gradually work in the flour, adding extra water if needed, to make a soft but not sticky dough.
3 Knead on a lightly floured surface for 5 minutes, or until the dough is smooth and elastic. Wrap in plastic wrap and let rest for 20 minutes at room temperature.

USING A FOOD PROCESSOR

Sift the flour and salt into the bowl of a food processor fitted with a metal blade. Add the eggs, yolk, oil, and water and pulse-blend until the ingredients are mixed and the dough begins to come together, adding the extra water, if needed. Knead for 1–2 minutes, then wrap and rest as before.

ROLLING PASTA BY HAND

1 Unwrap the pasta dough and cut in half. Work with just half at a time and keep the other half wrapped in plastic wrap.
2 Place the dough on a large, clean work surface lightly dusted with flour, then flatten with your hand and start to roll out. Always roll away from you, starting from the center and giving the dough a quarter turn after each rolling. Sprinkle a little more flour over the dough if it starts to get sticky.
3 Continue rolling and turning until the dough is as thin as possible; ideally about 1/8 inch. Make sure you roll it evenly, or some shapes will cook faster than others.

ROLLING PASTA BY MACHINE

A machine makes smoother, thinner, more-even pasta than that made by hand rolling. Most pasta machines work in the same way, but you should refer to the manufacturer's instructions before using.

1 Clamp the machine securely and attach the handle. Set the rollers at their widest setting and sprinkle lightly with flour. Cut the pasta into 4 pieces. Wrap 3 of them in plastic wrap and set aside.
2 Flatten the unwrapped pasta dough slightly, then feed it through the rollers. Fold the strip of dough in 3, rotate, and feed through the rollers a second time. Continue to roll the pasta this way, narrowing the roller setting by one notch every second time and flouring the rollers if the pasta starts to get sticky. Only fold the dough the first time it goes through each roller width. The dough will get longer and thinner with every rolling—if it gets too difficult to handle, cut the strip in half and work with 1 piece at a time.

3 If making spaghetti or noodles, such as tagliatelle, the second last setting is generally used. For pasta shapes and filled pastas, the dough should be rolled to the finest setting.
4 Fresh pasta should be dried slightly before cutting. Either drape over a narrow wooden pole for 5 minutes or place on a clean dish towel sprinkled with a little flour for 10 minutes.

You can also buy electric pasta machines that carry out the whole pasta-making process, from dough mixing and kneading, to extruding it through cutters into the required shapes—all you have to do is weigh out and add the individual ingredients. They can make over 2 lb. of pasta at a time, but are expensive to buy and take up a lot of space.

SHAPING UP

When cutting and shaping freshly made pasta, have two or three lightly floured dish towels ready. Arrange the pasta in a single layer, spaced slightly apart, or you may find that they stick together. When they are dry, you can freeze them successfully for up to 6 weeks, by layering in suitable freezer containers between sheets of baking parchment. Spread them out on baking parchment for about 20 minutes, or slightly longer if filles, before cooking. When making pasta, do not throw away the trimmings. They can be cut into tiny shapes or thin slivers, and used in soups.

Farfalle Use a fluted pasta wheel to cut the pasta sheets into rectangles about 1 x 12 inches. Pinch the long sides of each rectangle in the center to make a bow. Spread out on a floured dish towel and let dry for at least 15 minutes.

Lasagna This is one of the easiest to make. Simply trim the pasta sheets until neat, and cut into lengths the same size as your lasagna dish. Spread the cut sheets on dish towels sprinkled with flour.

Macaroni This is the generic name for hollow pasta. Cut the rolled-out pasta dough into squares, then wrap each around a chopstick, thick skewer or similar, starting from one of the corners. Slip the pasta off, curve slightly, if liked and let dry for at least 15 minutes.

Noodles If using a pasta machine, use the cutter attachment to produce tagliatelle or fettuccine, or use a narrower one for tagliarini or spaghetti. To make by hand, sprinkle the rolled-out pasta with flour, then roll up like a Swiss roll and cut into thin slices. The thickness of these depends on the noodles required. For linguine, cut into ¼ inch slices and for tagliatelle cut into ⅓ inch slices. Unravel them immediately after cutting. To make thicker ribbon pasta, such as pappardelle, use a serrated pastry wheel to cut into wide strips.

Leave over a wooden pole for up to 5 minutes to dry out.

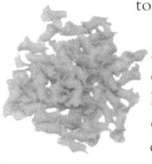

Ravioli Cut the rolled-out sheet of dough in half widthwise. Cover one half with plastic wrap to stop it drying out too quickly. Brush the other sheet of dough with beaten egg. Pipe or spoon small mounds—using about 1 teaspoon of filling in even rows, spacing them at 1½ inch intervals. Remove the plastic wrap from the reserved pasta sheet, and using a rolling pin, carefully lift over the dough with the filling. Press down firmly between the pockets of filling to push out any air. Finally, cut into squares with a pastry cutter or sharp knife. Let stand on a floured dish towel for 45 minutes before cooking.

You can also use a ravioli tray (*raviolatore*) to produce perfect even-sized ravioli. A sheet of rolled-out dough is laid over the tray, then pressed into the individual compartments. The filling can be spooned or piped into the indentations and the second sheet of dough placed on top. To create the individual ravioli squares, a rolling pin is gently rolled over the serrated top. These tins are excellent for making small ravioli containing a little filling.

Three or four simple ingredients combined together make the best fillings. Always season generously with salt and freshly ground black pepper and where the filling is soft, stir in a little beaten egg. Why not try chopped, cooked spinach, ricotta, and freshly grated nutmeg; finely ground turkey, curd cheese, tarragon, and Parmesan cheese; white crabmeat with mascarpone, finely grated lemon rind and dill; or ricotta, roasted garlic, and fresh herbs.

Silhouette Pasta If rolled out very thinly, fresh herb leaves can be sandwiched between two layers of pasta for a stunning silhouette effect. Put the pasta through a machine set on the very last setting, so it is paper-thin. Cut in half and lightly brush one piece with water. Arrange individual fresh herb leaves at regular intervals over the moistened pasta (you will need soft herbs for this—Italian parsley, basil and sage are all ideal). Place the second sheet of dry pasta on top and gently press with a rolling pin to seal them together. Sprinkle the pasta with a little flour, then put it through the machine on the second to finest setting. Use a pastry wheel, dipped in flour, to cut around the herb leaves to make squares, or use a round or oval cutter to stamp out the pasta, if preferred. Let dry on a floured dish towel for 20 minutes before cooking.

Tortellini Use a plain cutter to stamp out circles of pasta about 2 inches in diameter. Lightly brush each with beaten egg, then spoon or pipe about 1 teaspoon of filling into the center of each circle. Fold in half to make a half-moon shape, gently pressing the edges together to seal. Bend the two corners round and press together to seal. Let dry on a floured dish towel for 30 minutes before cooking. To make tortelloni, use a slightly larger cutter; about 2½ inches.

VARIATIONS

Flavored pastas are simple and there are dozens of delicious ways that you can change the flavor and color of pasta. You will find that you get an even color when using a machine, but the speckled appearance of flavored hand-rolled pasta can be equally attractive.

Chili Add 2 teaspoons of crushed, dried red chilies to the egg mixture before you mix with the flour.

Herb Stir 3 tablespoons of chopped fresh herbs such as basil, parsley, marjoram, or sage, or 2 tablespoons of finely chopped, strongly-flavored herbs like thyme or rosemary into the flour.

Olive Blend 2 tablespoons of black olive paste with the egg mixture, leaving out the water.

Porcini Soak two tablespoons dried porcini mush-rooms in almost boiling water for 20 minutes. Drain and squeeze out as much water as possible, then chop very finely. Add to the egg mixture. (Set aside the soaking liquor, strain, and use to flavor the pasta sauce.)

Saffron Sift 1 teaspoon of powdered saffron with the flour.

Spinach Cook two cups prepared spinach in a covered saucepan with just the water clinging to the leaves, until wilted. Drain and squeeze dry, then chop finely. Add to the egg mixture.

Sun-dried Tomato Blend 2 tablespoons of sun-dried tomato paste into the egg mixture, leaving out the water.

Whole-wheat Pasta Substitute half the whole-wheat flour for half of the white flour and add an extra 1–2 teaspoons water to the mixture.

Pasta Varieties

Pasta has been twisted and curled into an unimaginable number of shapes. There is a vast range of both fresh and dried pasta; short and long, tiny varieties for soup, larger ones for filling and more unusual designer shapes and flavors.

DRIED PASTAS

Buckwheat Pasta Darker in color than whole-wheat pasta, this is made from buckwheat flour. It is gluten-free buckwheat so is suitable for people who are intolerant to wheat products. Pizzoccheri are thin, flat noodles twisted into nests and are the most common type of buckwheat pasta.

Corn Pasta Now found on most supermarket shelves, corn pasta is made with corn flour and the plain variety is a bright yellow color. Like buck-wheat pasta, it is gluten-free. When cooking, make sure you use a large saucepan as it tends to cause the water to foam more than ordinary wheat pasta.

Colored and Flavored Pasta The varieties of these types of pasta are endless. The most popular and easily obtainable are spinach and tomato. Often three colors (white, red, and green) are packaged together and labeled "tricolore". Others available in larger food stores and delicatessens include beet, saffron, herb, poppy seed, garlic, chili,

mushroom, smoked saffron, and black ink. More unusual types, such as blue curaco liqueur pasta, which has a bright turquoise color, have also been created.

Durum Wheat Pasta This is the most readily available and may be made with or without eggs. Generally plain wheat pasta is used for long, straight shapes such as spaghetti, whereas pasta containing eggs is slightly more fragile, so is packed into nests or waves. Look for the words "Durum wheat" or *pasta di semola di grano duro* on the package when buying, as pastas made from soft wheat tend to become soggy when cooked.

Whole-wheat Pasta Made with whole-wheat flour, this has a higher fiber content than ordinary pasta, which gives it a slightly chewy texture, nutty flavor and rich brown color. Whole-wheat pasta takes longer to cook, however, than the refined version. We tend to think of it as a modern product associated with the growth in interest of health foods, but it has been made in north-eastern Italy for hundreds of years, where it is known as *bigoli,* and is like a thick spaghetti.

PASTA SHAPES

long pasta

Spaghetti Probably the best known type of pasta, spaghetti derives its name from the word *spago* meaning string, which describes its round, thin shape perfectly. Spaghettini is a thinner variety and spaghettoni is thicker. Vermicelli is a very fine type of spaghetti.

Tagliatelle Tagliatelle is the most common type of ribbon-noodle pasta and each ribbon of pasta is usually slightly less than ½ inch wide. It is traditionally from Bologna where it always accompanies Bolognese sauce (rather than spaghetti). It is sold coiled into nests that unravel when cooked. Thinner varieties of tagliarini or tagliolini are also available. A mixture of white and spinach-flavored tagliatelle is known as *paglia e fieno,* which translates as straw and hay. Fettuccine is the Roman version of tagliatelle and is cut slightly thinner.

Ziti Long, thick, and hollow, ziti may be ridged, but is usually smooth. It takes its name from *zita,* meaning fiancee, as it was once traditional to serve it at weddings in southern Italy. Zitoni is a similar larger pasta; mezza zita is thinner.

Short pasta

There are basically two types of short pasta: *secca* is factory-made from durum wheat and water, which is pressed into assorted shapes and sizes, and *pasta all'uovo* is made with eggs, which is particularly popular in northern Italy, where it is served with meat or creamy sauces. *Pasta all'uovo* is slightly more expensive than plain pasta, but cooks in less time and is less likely to go soggy if overcooked. It is also much more nutritious and has an attractive golden color. There are hundreds of different shapes and some of the most popular ones are listed below.

Conchiglie As the name implies, these pasta shapes resemble conch shells and are ideal for serving with thinner sauces, which will get trapped in the shells. Sizes vary from very tiny ones to large ones, which are suitable for filling. They may be smooth or ridged conchiglie rigate.

Eliche and Fusilli These are twisted into the shape of a screw, which is where their name comes from. Eliche is often wrongly labeled as fusilli as the two are similar, but fusilli is more tightly coiled and opens out slightly during cooking.

Farfalle A popular pasta shape, these are bow or butterfly shaped, often with crinkled edges.

Gnocchi Sardi These come from Sardinia and are named after the little gnocchi potato dumplings. Often served with rich meat sauces, they have a somewhat chewy texture.

Macaroni This is known as *maccheroni* in Italy. You may find it labeled as "elbow macaroni", which describes its shape (although it is sometimes almost straight). This was once the most popular imported pasta and is particularly good in baked dishes, notably macaroni cheese. A thin, quick-cook variety is also available.

Penne Slightly larger, hollow tubes than macaroni, the ends are cut diagonally and are pointed like quills. There are also less well known varieties, including the thinner pennette and even thinner pennini. They are often made with egg or flavored with tomato or spinach.

Pipe This is curved, hollow pasta and is often sold ridged as pipe rigate. The smaller type is known as pipette.

Rigatoni This is substantial, chunky, tubular pasta and is often used for baking. Because the pasta is thick, it tends to be slightly chewier than other short pastas. Rigatoni goes well with meat and strongly flavored sauces.

Rotelle This is thin, wheel-shaped pasta, also known as ruote and trulli and often sold in packages of two or three colors.

FLAT PASTA

There are many types of long, flat ribbon pastas, but there is only one flat pasta—lasagna—which is usually used for baking in the oven (*al forno*). These thin sheets are layered up with a sauce or may be curled into large tubes about 4 inches long to make cannelloni. In Italy, they are usually made from fresh sheets of lasagna rolled around the filling, however, dried tubes are easily available and simple to use. Three flavors of lasagna are available: plain, spinach, or whole-wheat. Most sheets are flat, but some have curled edges, which help trap the sauce during cooking and stop it running to the bottom of the dish. Lasagnette are long, narrow strips of flat pasta and are crimped on one or both long edges. Like lasagna, they are designed to be layered up with a sauce and baked.

STUFFED PASTA

Tortellini are the most common of dried pasta shapes and consist of tiny, filled pieces of pasta, which are folded, then the ends are joined to make a ring. A speciality of Bologna, larger ones are made from rounds or squares and are joined without leaving a hole in the center. They are called tortelloni and generally are made with a meat (*alla carne*) or cheese (*ai formaggi*) filling, and will keep for up to a year (but always check the sell-by date). Cappelletti, ravioli, and agnalotti are sometimes sold dried, but more often fresh.

SOUP PASTA

Tiny pasta shapes known as *pastina* in Italy come in hundreds of different shapes and are often added to soups. Risi is the smallest type of pasta and looks like grains of rice, whereas orzi, another soup pasta, resembles barley. Slightly larger ones include, stellette (stars), and rotelli (wheels). Many are miniature shapes of larger pasta; farfallette (little bows) and conchigliette (little shells).

FRESH PASTA

Fresh pasta has become increasingly popular over the past decade and can be found in the chilled sections of supermarkets, as well as being sold loose in Italian grocery stores. Ideally, you should buy fresh pasta on the day you are going to cook it, or use within a day or two. It must be stored in the refrigerator until you are ready to use it, as it contains eggs, which

shorten its keeping time. It is generally available in the same shapes as dried pasta, but has a much greater range of fillings. Ravioli is one of the most common. It is shaped into large squares with fluted edges and is made with many different pasta doughs, including saffron and fresh herbs. The fillings may be anything, for example, spinach and ricotta, mushroom, fish and shellfish, and meat, but especially chicken. They may also be shaped into long rectangles, circles or ovals.

NOODLES

Pasta originated in China and not in Italy, so it is hardly surprising that there is a vast range of noodles.

Buckwheat Noodles Soba are the most common and are a dark, greyish-brown color. They feature in Japanese cooking in soups and stir-fries.

Cellophane Noodles Made from mung beans, these are translucent, flavorless noodles and are only available dried. They are never boiled and simply need soaking in very hot water.

Egg Noodles Commonly used in Chinese cooking, they come in several thicknesses; thin and medium being the most popular.

Rice Noodles These are fine, delicate, opaque noodles, which are made from rice and are often used in Thai and Malaysian cooking.

Urdon Noodles These are thick Japanese noodles, which can be round or flat and are available both fresh, dried, or precooked.

White Bean Soup with Parmesan Croutons

1 Preheat the oven to 400° F. Place the cubes of bread in a bowl and pour over the peanut oil. Stir to coat the bread, then sprinkle over the Parmesan cheese. Place on a lightly greased baking sheet, and cook in the preheated oven for 10 minutes or until crisp and golden brown.

2 Heat the olive oil in a large saucepan and cook the onion for 4–5 minutes until softened. Add the bacon and thyme, and cook for an additional 3 minutes. Stir in the beans, stock, and black pepper, then simmer gently for 5 minutes.

3 Place half the bean mixture and liquid into a food processor, and blend until smooth.

4 Return the purée to the saucepan. Stir in the pesto sauce, pepperoni sausage, and lemon juice. Season to taste with salt and pepper.

5 Return the soup to the heat, and cook for an additional 2–3 minutes until piping hot. Place some of the beans in each serving bowl and add a ladleful of soup. Garnish with torn basil, and sprinkle croutons over the top.

INGREDIENTS
Serves 4

3 thick slices of white bread, cut into ½-in. cubes
3 tbsp. peanut oil
2 tbsp. Parmesan cheese, finely shredded
1 tbsp. light olive oil
1 large onion, peeled and finely chopped
½ cup diced bacon
1 tbsp. fresh thyme leaves
2 14-oz. cans canellini beans, drained
3 cups chicken stock
salt and freshly ground black pepper
1 tbsp. prepared pesto sauce
½ cup diced pepperoni sausage
1 tbsp. fresh lemon juice
1 tbsp. fresh basil, roughly torn

Tasty Tip

To make pesto, finely chop a large handful of fresh basil leaves, 2 peeled garlic cloves, 1 tablespoon pine nuts, and seasoning in a food processor. Gradually add 6–8 tablespoons good-quality olive oil. Scrape into a bowl and stir in 2–3 tablespoons freshly shredded Parmesan cheese. Add a little more olive oil if necessary and adjust the seasoning.

Rice Soup with Potato Sticks

1 Preheat the oven to 375° F. Heat ¼ stick of the butter and the olive oil in a large, heavy saucepan and cook the onion for 4–5 minutes until softened, then add the prosciutto and cook for about 1 minute. Stir in the rice, the stock, and the peas. Season to taste with salt and pepper, and simmer for 10–15 minutes or until the rice is tender.

2 Beat the egg and 1 stick of the butter together until smooth, then beat in the flour, a pinch of salt, and the mashed potatoes. Form a soft, pliable dough, adding a little flour if necessary.

3 Roll the dough out on a lightly floured surface into a rectangle about ½ inch thick, and cut into 12 thin, long sticks. Brush with milk and sprinkle with the poppy seeds. Place the sticks on a lightly greased baking sheet and cook in the preheated oven for 15 minutes or until golden.

4 When the rice is cooked, stir the remaining butter and Parmesan cheese into the soup and sprinkle with the chopped parsley. Serve immediately with the warm potato sticks.

INGREDIENTS
Serves 4

1½ sticks butter
1 tsp. olive oil
1 large onion, peeled and finely chopped
4 slices prosciutto, chopped
½ cup risotto rice
5 cups chicken stock
3 cups frozen peas
salt and freshly ground black pepper
1 medium egg
1 cup self-rising flour
¼ cup mashed potato
1 tbsp. milk
1 tbsp. poppy seeds
1 tbsp. Parmesan cheese, finely shredded
1 tbsp. freshly chopped parsley

Food Fact

The prosciutto used in this recipe is a luxury Italian ham, which originates from the northern Italian province of Parma—the same area famous for Parmesan cheese. Parma pigs enjoy a special diet of chestnuts and whey, which produces an excellent quality of meat. Prosciutto is not smoked, but seasoned, salt cured, and air dried.

Tasty Tip

These potato sticks also make a delicious snack with drinks. Try sprinkling them with sesame seeds or shredded cheese, and let cool before serving.

1

2

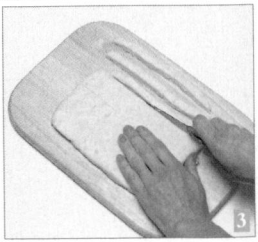
3

Rich Tomato Soup with Roasted Red Bell Peppers

1 Preheat the oven to 400° F. Lightly grease a large roasting pan with 1 teaspoon of the olive oil. Place the bell peppers and tomatoes cut-side down in the roasting pan with the onions and the garlic. Spoon over the remaining oil.

2 Cook in the preheated oven for 30 minutes or until the skins on the bell peppers have started to blacken and blister. Let the vegetables cool for about 10 minutes, then remove the skins, stalks, and seeds from the bell peppers. Peel away the skins from the tomatoes and onions, and squeeze out the garlic.

3 Place the cooked vegetables into a blender or food processor, and blend until smooth. Add the stock and blend again to form a smooth purée. Pour the puréed soup through a strainer, if a smooth soup is desired, then pour into a saucepan. Bring to a boil, simmer gently for 2–3 minutes, and season to taste with salt and pepper. Serve hot with a swirl of sour cream and a sprinkling of torn basil.

INGREDIENTS
Serves 4

2 tsp. light olive oil
1½ lbs. red bell peppers, halved and seeded
3 medium, ripe plum tomatoes, halved
2 onions, unpeeled and quartered
4 garlic cloves, unpeeled
2½ cups chicken stock
salt and freshly ground black pepper
4 tbsp. sour cream
1 tbsp. fresh basil, torn

Helpful Hint

To remove the skins of the bell peppers more easily, remove them from the oven and put immediately into a bowl covered with plastic wrap. Leave until cool enough to handle, then peel carefully.

1

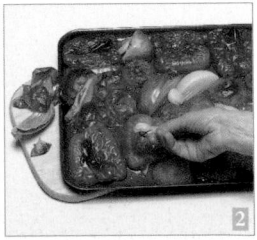
2

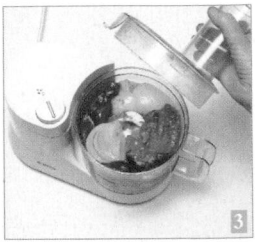
3

Bread & Tomato Soup

1 Make a small cross in the base of each tomato, then place in a bowl and cover with boiling water. Allow to stand for 2 minutes or until the skins have started to peel away, then drain, remove the skins and seeds, and chop into large pieces.

2 Heat 3 tablespoons of the olive oil in a saucepan and gently cook the onion until softened. Add the peeled tomatoes, chopped basil, garlic, and chili powder. Season to taste with salt and pepper. Pour in the stock, cover the saucepan, bring to a boil, and simmer gently for 15–20 minutes.

3 Remove the crusts from the bread and break into small pieces. Remove the tomato mixture from the heat and stir in the bread. Cover and allow to stand for 10 minutes or until the bread has blended with the tomatoes. Season to taste. Serve the soup warm or cold with a swirl of olive oil on the top, garnished with a spoonful of diced cucumber and basil leaves.

INGREDIENTS
Serves 4

6 medium, very ripe tomatoes
¼ cup olive oil
1 onion, peeled and finely chopped
1 tbsp. freshly chopped basil
3 garlic cloves, peeled and crushed
¼ tsp. hot chili powder
salt and freshly ground black pepper
2½ cups chicken stock
6 slices stale white bread
¼ small cucumber, cut into small dice
4 whole basil leaves

Tasty Tip

This soup is best made when fresh tomatoes are in season. If you want to make it at other times of the year, replace the fresh tomatoes with two 14-oz. cans of peeled plum tomatoes—Italian, if possible. You may need to cook the soup for 5–10 minutes longer.

Arugula & Potato Soup with Garlic Croutons

1 Place the potatoes in a large saucepan, cover with the stock, and simmer gently for 10 minutes. Add the arugula and simmer for an additional 5–10 minutes or until the potatoes are soft and the arugula has wilted.

2 Meanwhile, make the croutons. Cut the bread slices into small cubes and set aside. Heat the butter and peanut oil in a small skillet and cook the garlic for 1 minute, stirring well. Remove the garlic, then add the bread cubes to the butter and oil mixture in the skillet and sauté, stirring continuously, until they are golden brown. Drain the croutons on absorbent paper towels and set aside.

3 Cut the slices of ciabatta bread into small pieces and stir into the soup. Cover the saucepan and allow to stand for 10 minutes or until the bread has absorbed a lot of the liquid.

4 Stir in the olive oil, season to taste with salt and pepper, and serve at once with a few of the garlic croutons sprinkled over the top and a little shredded Parmesan cheese.

INGREDIENTS
Serves 4

1½ lbs. baby new potatoes
5 cups chicken or vegetable stock
1¼ cups arugula
4 slices thick white bread
½ stick unsalted butter
1 tsp. peanut oil
2–4 garlic cloves, peeled and chopped
4 slices stale ciabatta bread, with the crusts removed
¼ cup olive oil
salt and freshly ground black pepper
2 tbsp. Parmesan cheese, finely shredded

Helpful Hint

Arugula is now widely available in bags from most large supermarkets. If, however, you cannot get ahold of it, replace it with an equal quantity of watercress or baby spinach leaves.

Classic Minestrone

1 Heat the butter and olive oil together in a large saucepan. Chop the bacon and add to the saucepan. Cook for 3–4 minutes, then remove with a slotted spoon and set aside.

2 Finely chop the onion, garlic, celery, and carrots, and add to the saucepan, one ingredient at a time, stirring well after each addition. Cover and cook gently for 8–10 minutes until the vegetables are softened.

3 Add the chopped tomatoes, with their juice and the stock, bring to a boil, then cover the saucepan with a lid, reduce the heat, and simmer gently for about 20 minutes.

4 Stir in the cabbage, beans, peas, and spaghetti. Cover and simmer for an additional 20 minutes or until all the ingredients are tender. Season to taste with salt and pepper.

5 Return the cooked bacon to the saucepan and bring the soup to a boil. Serve the soup immediately with Parmesan cheese shavings sprinkled on the top and plenty of crusty bread.

INGREDIENTS
Serves 6–8

¼ stick butter
3 tbsp. olive oil
3 slices bacon
1 large onion, peeled
1 garlic clove, peeled
1 celery stalk, trimmed
2 carrots, peeled
14-oz. can chopped tomatoes
5 cups chicken stock
1½ cups green cabbage, finely shredded
½ cup fine green beans, trimmed and halved
3 tbsp. frozen peas
¼ cup spaghetti, broken into short pieces
salt and freshly ground black pepper
Parmesan cheese, to garnish
crusty bread, to serve

Tasty Tip

There are many different variations of minestrone. You can add drained canned canellini beans either in place of or as well as the spaghetti, or use small pasta shells. For a vegetarian version, omit the bacon and use vegetable stock and a soy cheese.

Cream of Pumpkin Soup

1 Cut the peeled and seeded pumpkin flesh into 1-inch cubes. Heat the olive oil in a large saucepan and cook the pumpkin for 2–3 minutes, coating it completely with oil. Chop the onion and leek finely, and dice the carrot and celery stalks.

2 Add the vegetables to the saucepan with the garlic and cook, stirring, for 5 minutes or until they have begun to soften. Cover the vegetables with the water and bring to a boil. Season with plenty of salt, pepper, and the grated nutmeg, then cover and simmer for 15–20 minutes or until all of the vegetables are tender.

3 When the vegetables are tender, remove from the heat, cool slightly, then pour into a food processor or blender. Blend to form a smooth paste, then pass through a strainer into a clean saucepan.

4 Adjust the seasoning to taste and add all but 2 tablespoons of the cream and enough water to obtain the correct consistency. Bring the soup to boiling point, add the cayenne pepper, and serve immediately swirled with cream and warm herb bread.

INGREDIENTS
Serves 4

2 lbs. pumpkin flesh (after peeling and discarding the seeds)
¼ cup olive oil
1 large onion, peeled
1 leek, trimmed
1 carrot, peeled
2 celery stalks
4 garlic cloves, peeled and crushed
6 cups water
salt and freshly ground black pepper
¼ tsp. freshly grated nutmeg
⅔ cup light cream
¼ tsp. cayenne pepper
warm herb bread, to serve

Tasty Tip

If you cannot find pumpkin, try replacing it with squash. Butternut or acorn squash would both make suitable substitutes. Avoid spaghetti squash, which gets too soft when cooked.

Lettuce Soup

1 Bring a large saucepan of water to a boil and blanch the lettuce leaves for 3 minutes. Drain and dry thoroughly on absorbent paper towels. Then shred with a sharp knife.

2 Heat the oil and butter in a clean saucepan, add the lettuce, scallions, and parsley, and cook together for 3–4 minutes or until very soft.

3 Stir in the flour and cook for 1 minute, then gradually pour in the stock, stirring throughout. Bring to a boil and season to taste with salt and pepper. Reduce the heat, cover, and simmer gently for 10–15 minutes or until soft.

4 Allow the soup to cool slightly, then either strain or purée in a blender. Alternatively, leave the soup chunky. Stir in the cream, add more seasoning, if desired, then add the cayenne pepper.

5 Arrange the slices of ciabatta bread in a large soup dish or in individual bowls, and pour the soup over the bread. Garnish with sprigs of parsley and serve immediately.

INGREDIENTS
Serves 4

2 heads of iceberg lettuce, quartered, with hard core removed
1 tbsp. olive oil
½ stick butter
½ cup scallions, trimmed and chopped
1 tbsp. freshly chopped parsley
1 tbsp. all-purpose flour
2½ cups chicken stock
salt and freshly ground black pepper
⅓ cup light cream
¼ tsp. cayenne pepper, or to taste
thick slices of stale ciabatta bread
sprigs of parsley, to garnish

Helpful Hint

Do not prepare the lettuce too far in advance. Iceberg lettuce has a tendency to discolor when sliced, which may in turn discolor the soup.

Antipasti with Foccacia

1 Preheat the oven to 425° F. Arrange the fresh figs, green beans, radicchio, shrimp, sardines, pitted olives, mozzarella cheese, and slices of Italian salami on a large serving platter. Drizzle over 1 tablespoon of the olive oil, then cover with plastic wrap and chill in the refrigerator while making the bread.

2 To make the focaccia bread, sift the flour, sugar, semolina, and salt into a large mixing bowl, then sprinkle in the rapid-rise yeast. Make a well in the center and add the remaining 2 tablespoons of olive oil. Add the warm water, a little at a time, and mix together until a smooth, pliable dough is formed.

3 Place the dough onto a lightly floured board and knead until it is smooth and elastic. Place the dough in a lightly greased bowl, cover with a piece of plastic wrap, and leave in a warm place for 45 minutes.

4 Knead the dough again and flatten the dough into a large, flat oval shape, about ½ inch thick. Place the dough on a large, lightly greased baking sheet, and prick the surface with the end of a wooden spoon. Brush with olive oil and sprinkle with the coarse salt. Cook the bread in the preheated oven for about 25 minutes or until it is golden brown. Serve the bread warm or cold with the prepared platter of food.

INGREDIENTS
Serves 4

3 fresh figs, quartered
⅔ cup green beans, cooked and halved
1 small head of radicchio, rinsed and shredded
8–12 large shrimp, shelled and cooked
4-oz. can sardines, drained
2 tbsp. pitted ripe olives
2 tbsp. stuffed green olives
1 cup mozzarella cheese, sliced
1 cup Italian salami sausage, thinly sliced
3 tbsp. olive oil
2½ cups high-gluten bread flour
pinch of sugar
1¼ tsp. rapid-rise active yeast
1 cup fine semolina
1 tsp. salt
1¼ cups warm water
a little extra olive oil for brushing
1 tbsp. coarse salt crystals

Helpful Hint

Fresh yeast is available from health-food stores, as well as large supermarkets with bakeries. Look for yeast that is moist and crumbly, and has no dark patches. It will keep in the freezer up to six months.

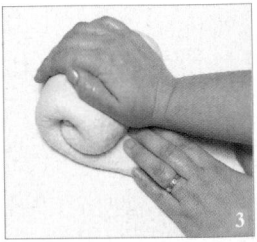

Mozzarella Frittata with Tomato & Basil Salad

1 To make the tomato and basil salad, slice the tomatoes very thinly, tear the basil leaves, and sprinkle the basil over the tomatoes. Make the dressing by beating the olive oil, lemon juice, and sugar together. Season with pepper before drizzling the dressing over the salad.

2 To make the frittata, place the eggs in a large bowl with plenty of salt and beat. Shred the mozzarella and stir into the egg with the finely chopped scallions.

3 Heat the oil in a nonstick skillet and pour in the egg mixture, stirring with a wooden spoon to spread the ingredients evenly over the skillet.

4 Broil for 5–8 minutes until the frittata is golden brown and firm on the underside. Place the whole skillet under the broiler, and cook for about 4–5 minutes or until the top is golden brown. Slide the frittata onto a serving plate, cut into 6 large wedges, and serve immediately with the tomato and basil salad and plenty of warm, crusty bread.

INGREDIENTS
Serves 6

FOR THE SALAD:
6 ripe but firm tomatoes
2 tbsp. fresh basil leaves
2 tbsp. olive oil
1 tbsp. fresh lemon juice
1 tsp. sugar
freshly ground black pepper

FOR THE FRITTATA:
7 medium eggs, beaten
salt
2¼ cups mozzarella cheese
2 scallions, trimmed and finely chopped
2 tbsp. olive oil
warm, crusty bread, to serve

Helpful Hint

Fresh mozzarella is sold in packages and is sometimes surrounded by a light brine. After shredding the cheese, firmly press between layers of absorbent paper towels to remove any excess water that might leak out during cooking.

Fried Herring with Arugula Salad

1 If the herring are frozen, thaw completely, then wipe dry with absorbent paper towels.

2 Start to heat the oil in a deep-fat fryer. Arrange the fish in a large, shallow dish and toss well in the flour, cayenne pepper, salt, and pepper.

3 Deep-fry the fish in batches for 2–3 minutes or until crisp and golden. Keep the cooked fish warm while deep-frying the remaining fish.

4 Meanwhile, to make the salad, arrange the arugula, cherry tomatoes, and cucumber on individual serving dishes. Beat the olive oil and the remaining ingredients together and season lightly. Drizzle the dressing over the salad and serve with the herring.

INGREDIENTS
Serves 4

1 lb. herring, fresh or frozen
oil for deep-frying
¼ cup all-purpose flour
½ tsp. cayenne pepper
salt and freshly ground black pepper

FOR THE SALAD:
2½ cups arugula
1 cup cherry tomatoes, halved
¼ cup cucumber, cut into dice
3 tbsp. olive oil
1 tbsp. fresh lemon juice
½ tsp. mustard
½ tsp. sugar

Tasty Tip

Why not try a different salad? Mix together some baby spinach, cooked peas, and chopped scallions, then pour 2 tablespoons of garlic olive oil over the top. If serving with a chicken dish, top the salad with some feta or cheddar cheese.

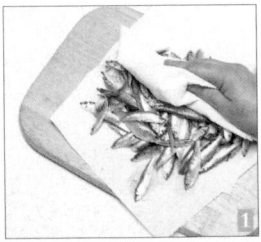

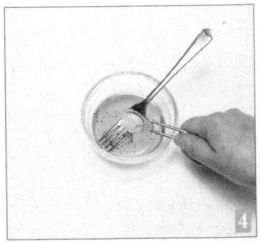

Bruschetta with Pecorino, Garlic, & Tomatoes

1 Preheat the broiler and line the broiler rack with foil just before cooking. Make a small cross in the top of the tomatoes, then place in a small bowl and cover with boiling water. Allow to stand for 2 minutes, then drain and remove the skins. Cut into quarters, remove the seeds, and dice the flesh.

2 Mix the tomato flesh with the pecorino cheese and 2 teaspoons of the fresh oregano. Season to taste with salt and pepper. Add 1 tablespoon of the olive oil and mix thoroughly.

3 Crush the garlic and spread evenly over the slices of bread. Heat 2 tablespoons of the olive oil in a large skillet, and sauté the bread slices until they are crisp and golden.

4 Place the fried bread on a greased baking sheet and spoon on the tomato and cheese topping. Place some mozzarella on the top and place under the preheated broiler for 3–4 minutes until golden and bubbling. Garnish with the remaining oregano, then arrange the bruschettas on a serving plate and serve with the olives.

INGREDIENTS
Serves 4

6 ripe but firm tomatoes
1 cup pecorino cheese, finely shredded
1 tbsp. oregano leaves
salt and freshly ground black pepper
3 tbsp. olive oil
3 garlic cloves, peeled
8 slices flat Italian bread, such as focaccia
8 thin slices mozzarella cheese
marinated ripe olives, to serve

Tasty Tip

Bitter lettuce is excellent with these bruschettas because they help to offset the richness of the cheese and tomato topping. Try a mixture of Italian red lettuce, radicchio, and arugula. If these are unavailable, use a bag of mixed lettuce.

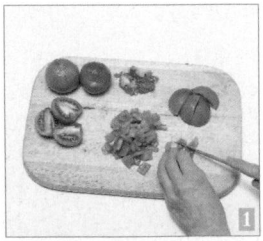
1

2

3

Crostini with Chicken Livers

1 Heat 1 tablespoon of the olive oil and 1 tablespoon of the butter in a skillet, add the shallot and garlic, and cook gently for 2–3 minutes.

2 Trim and wash the chicken livers thoroughly and pat dry on absorbent paper towels as much as possible. Cut into slices, then toss in the flour. Add the livers to the skillet with the shallot and garlic, and continue to cook for an additional 2 minutes, stirring continuously.

3 Pour in the white wine and brandy, and bring to a boil. Boil rapidly for 1–2 minutes to allow the alcohol to evaporate, then stir in the sliced mushrooms and cook gently for about 5 minutes or until the chicken livers are cooked but just a little pink inside. Season to taste with salt and pepper.

4 Cook the slices of ciabatta in the remaining oil and butter, then place on individual serving dishes. Spoon over the liver mixture and garnish with a few sage leaves and lemon wedges. Serve immediately.

INGREDIENTS
Serves 4

2 tbsp. olive oil
2 tbsp. butter
1 shallot, peeled and finely chopped
1 garlic clove, peeled and crushed
1½ cups chicken liver
1 tbsp. all-purpose flour
2 tbsp. dry white wine
1 tbsp. brandy
¼ cup mushrooms, sliced
salt and freshly ground black pepper
4 slices ciabatta or similar bread

TO GARNISH:
fresh sage leaves
lemon wedges

Tasty Tip

If you prefer a lower-fat alternative to the fried bread in this recipe, omit 1 tablespoon of the butter and brush the bread slices with the remaining 1 tablespoon of oil. Cook in a 350° F oven for about 20 minutes or until golden and crisp, then serve as above.

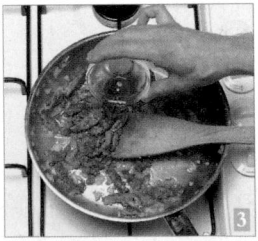

Italian Baked Tomatoes with Endive & Radicchio

1 Preheat the oven to 375° F. Lightly grease a baking sheet with the teaspoon of oil. Slice the tops off the tomatoes, remove all the tomato flesh, and strain into a large bowl. Sprinkle a little salt inside the tomato shells and then place them upside down on a plate while the filling is prepared.

2 Mix the strained tomatoes with the bread crumbs, fresh herbs, and mushrooms, and season well with salt and pepper. Place the tomato shells on the prepared baking sheet, and fill with the tomato-and-mushroom mixture. Sprinkle the cheese on the top and cook in the preheated oven for 15–20 minutes until golden brown.

3 Meanwhile, prepare the salad. Arrange the endive and radicchio on individual serving plates and mix the remaining ingredients together in a small bowl to make the dressing. Season to taste.

4 When the tomatoes are cooked, allow to rest for 5 minutes, then place on the prepared plates and drizzle over a little dressing. Serve warm.

INGREDIENTS
Serves 4

1 tsp. olive oil
4 large tomatoes
salt
½ cup fresh white bread crumbs
1 tbsp. freshly cut chives
1 tbsp. freshly chopped parsley
1 cup button mushrooms, finely chopped
salt and freshly ground black pepper
¼ cup fresh Parmesan cheese, shredded

FOR THE SALAD:
½ head endive
½ small piece of radicchio
2 tbsp. olive oil
1 tsp. balsamic vinegar
salt and freshly ground black pepper

Tasty Tip

As an alternative, try stirring in either 2 tablespoons of tapenade or pesto into the stuffing mixture. Alternatively, replace the chives with freshly chopped basil.

1

2

2

Spaghettini with Lemon Pesto and Cheese & Herb Bread

1 Preheat the oven to 400° F. Mix together the onion, oregano, parsley, butter, and cheese. Spread the bread with the cheese mixture, place on a lightly greased baking sheet, and cover with foil. Cook in the preheated oven for 10–15 minutes, then keep warm.

2 Add the spaghettini and 1 tablespoon of olive oil to a large saucepan of fast-boiling, lightly salted water, and cook for 3–4 minutes or until al dente. Drain and set aside 2 tablespoons of the cooking liquid aside.

3 Blend the basil, pine nuts, garlic, Parmesan cheese, lemon rind, lemon juice, and remaining olive oil in a food processor or blender until a purée is formed. Season to taste with salt and pepper, then place in a saucepan.

4 Heat the lemon pesto very gently until piping hot, then stir in the pasta and the cooking liquid. Add the butter and mix well together.

5 Add plenty of black pepper to the pasta and serve immediately with the warm cheese and herb bread.

INGREDIENTS
Serves 4

1 small onion, peeled and grated
2 tsp. freshly chopped oregano
1 tbsp. freshly chopped parsley
¼ stick butter
1 cup pecorino cheese, shredded
8 slices Italian bread
3¼ cups dried spaghettini
¼ cup olive oil
1 large bunch basil
¼ cup pine nuts
1 garlic clove, peeled and crushed
1 cup Parmesan cheese, shredded
2 tbsp. finely grated lemon rind
4 tbsp. lemon juice
salt and freshly ground black pepper
4 tsp. butter

Tasty Tip

It is important to use a good-quality, full-flavored olive oil for this recipe. Look for an extra-virgin or cold-pressed oil, and buy the best you can afford.

1

3

4

Mussels with Creamy Garlic & Saffron Sauce

1 Clean the mussels thoroughly in plenty of cold water and remove any beards and barnacles from the shells. Discard any mussels that are open or damaged. Place in a large bowl, cover with cold water, and leave in the refrigerator until needed.

2 Pour the wine into a large saucepan and bring to a boil. Tip the mussels into the saucepan, cover, and cook, shaking the pan periodically, for 6–8 minutes or until the mussels have opened completely.

3 Discard any mussels with closed shells, then using a slotted spoon, carefully remove the remaining open mussels from the saucepan and keep them warm. Set the cooking liquid aside.

4 Heat the olive oil in a small skillet, and cook the shallot and garlic gently for 2–3 minutes until softened. Add the cooking liquid and chopped oregano, and cook for an additional 3–4 minutes. Stir in the saffron and the cream, and heat through gently. Season to taste with salt and pepper. Place a few mussels in individual serving bowls and spoon over the saffron sauce. Serve immediately with plenty of crusty bread.

INGREDIENTS
Serves 4

1½ lbs. fresh live mussels
1¼ cups good-quality dry white wine
1 tbsp. olive oil
1 shallot, peeled and finely chopped
2 garlic cloves, peeled and crushed
1 tbsp. freshly chopped oregano
2 saffron strands
⅔ cup light cream
salt and freshly ground black pepper
crusty bread, to serve

Helpful Hint

Mussels are now farmed and are available most of the year. However, always try to buy mussels the day you intend to eat them. Place them in a bowl of cold water in the refrigerator as soon as possible, changing the water at least every 2 hours. If live mussels are unavailable, use prepacked, cooked mussels.

Peperonata (Braised Mixed Bell Peppers)

1 Remove the seeds from the bell peppers and cut into thin strips. Slice the onion into rings and chop the garlic cloves finely.

2 Heat the oil in a skillet and cook the peppers, onions, and garlic for 5–10 minutes or until soft and lightly browned. Stir continuously.

3 Make a cross on the top of the tomatoes, then place in a bowl and cover with boiling water. Allow to stand for about 2 minutes. Drain, then remove the skins and seeds, and chop the tomato flesh into cubes.

4 Add the tomatoes and oregano to the bell peppers and onion, and season to taste with salt and pepper. Cover the skillet and bring to a boil. Simmer gently for about 30 minutes or until tender, adding the chicken or vegetable stock halfway through the cooking time.

5 Garnish with sprigs of oregano and serve hot with plenty of freshly cooked focaccia bread.

INGREDIENTS
Serves 4

2 green bell peppers
1 red bell pepper
1 yellow bell pepper
1 orange bell pepper
1 onion, peeled
2 garlic cloves, peeled
2 tbsp. olive oil
4 very ripe tomatoes
1 tbsp. freshly chopped oregano
salt and freshly ground black pepper
⅔ cup light chicken or vegetable stock
sprigs of fresh oregano, to garnish
focaccia (see p. 46), to serve

Tasty Tip

Serve the peperonata cold as part of an antipasti platter. Some good accompaniments would be marinated olives, sun-dried or semidried marinated tomatoes, sliced salamis and other cold meats, and plenty of Italian bread.

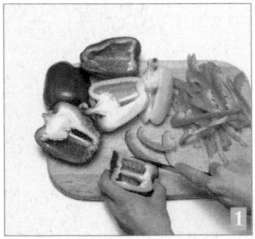

Wild Garlic Mushrooms with Pizza Grissini

1 Preheat the oven to 475° F. Place the flour in a large bowl and stir in the dry yeast, then gradually blend in the olive oil, salt, and enough warm water to make a smooth, pliable dough.

2 Knead on a lightly floured surface to form a smooth and pliable dough, then roll out again and cut the dough into sticks of equal length. Cover with plastic wrap and let rise in a warm place for 10 minutes. Brush the dough with a little more olive oil, sprinkle with salt, and then cook in the preheated oven for 10 minutes.

3 Pour 3 tablespoons of the olive oil into a skillet and add the crushed garlic. Cook over a very low heat, stirring well for 3–4 minutes to flavor the oil.

4 Cut the wild mushrooms into bite-sized slices if very large, then add to the skillet. Season well with salt and pepper and cook very gently for 6–8 minutes or until tender.

5 Beat the fresh herbs, the remaining olive oil, and lemon juice together. Pour over the mushrooms and heat through. Season to taste and place on individual serving dishes. Serve with the pizza grissini.

Helpful Hint

Never clean mushrooms under running water. Mushrooms absorb liquid very easily and then release it again during cooking, making the dish watery. When using wild mushrooms, wipe with a damp cloth or use a soft brush to remove any grit. Cut off the bases of stems to remove dirt.

INGREDIENTS
Serves 6

FOR THE PIZZA:

1 package rapid-rise active dry yeast
1 cup warm water
2⅔ cups high-gluten flour
2 tbsp. olive oil, plus extra for brushing
1 tsp. salt

FOR THE MUSHROOMS:

½ cup olive oil
4 garlic cloves, peeled and crushed
1 lb. mixed wild mushrooms
salt and freshly ground black pepper
1 tbsp. freshly chopped parsley
1 tbsp. freshly chopped basil
1 tsp. fresh oregano leaves
2 tbsp. lemon juice

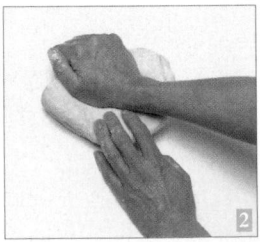

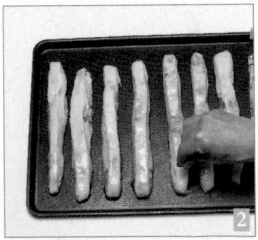

Hot Jumbo Shrimp with Prosciutto

1 Preheat the oven to 350° F. Slice the cucumber and tomatoes thinly, then arrange on four large plates and set aside. Shell the shrimp, leaving the tail shell intact, and remove the thin black vein running down the back.

2 Beat together 4 tablespoons of the olive oil, garlic, and chopped parsley in a small bowl, and season to taste with plenty of salt and pepper. Add the shrimp to the mixture, and stir until they are well coated. Remove the shrimp, then wrap each one in a piece of prosciutto and secure with a toothpick.

3 Place the prepared shrimp on a lightly greased baking sheet or dish with the slices of bread, and cook in the preheated oven for 5 minutes.

4 Remove the shrimp from the oven and spoon the wine over the shrimp and bread. Return to the oven and cook for an additional 10 minutes until piping hot.

5 Carefully remove the toothpicks and arrange 3 shrimp rolls on each slice of bread. Place on top of the sliced cucumber and tomatoes, and serve immediately.

INGREDIENTS
Serves 4

½ cucumber, peeled
4 ripe tomatoes
12 raw jumbo shrimp
6 tbsp. olive oil
4 garlic cloves, peeled and crushed
4 tbsp. freshly chopped parsley
salt and freshly ground black pepper
6 slices prosciutto, cut in half
4 slices Italian bread
¼ cup dry white wine

Helpful Hint

The black intestinal vein needs to be removed from raw shrimp because it can cause a bitter flavor. Remove the shell, then using a small, sharp knife, make a cut along the center back of the shrimp and open out the flesh. Using the tip of the knife, remove the thread that lies along the length of the shrimp, and discard.

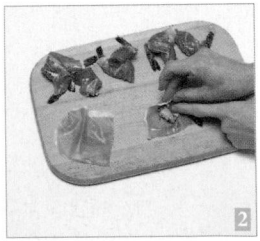

Mozzarella Pockets with Cranberry Relish

1 Slice the mozzarella thinly, remove the crusts from the bread, and make sandwiches with the bread and cheese. Cut into 2-inch squares and press them flat. Season the eggs with salt and pepper, then soak the bread in the seasoned egg for 1 minute on each side until well coated.

2 Heat the oil to 375° F and deep-fry the bread squares for 1–2 minutes or until they are crisp and golden brown. Drain on absorbent paper towels and keep warm.

3 Place the cranberries, orange juice, rind, sugar, and port into a small saucepan, and add 5 tablespoons of water. Bring to a boil, then simmer for 10 minutes or until the cranberries have "popped." Sweeten with a little more sugar, if necessary.

4 Arrange the mozzarella pockets on individual serving plates. Serve with some of the cranberry relish.

INGREDIENTS
Serves 6

FOR THE MOZZARELLA POCKETS:

1 cup mozzarella cheese
8 slices white bread
2 medium eggs, beaten
salt and freshly ground black pepper
1 cup olive oil

FOR THE RELISH:

1 cup cranberries
2 tbsp. fresh orange juice
2 tsp. grated orange rind
¼ cup brown sugar
1 tbsp. port or fortified wine

Helpful Hint

Frying in oil that is not hot enough causes food to absorb more oil than it would if fried at the correct temperature. To test the temperature of the oil without a thermometer, drop a cube of bread into the skillet. If the bread browns in 30 seconds, the oil is at the right temperature. If it does not, try again in a couple of minutes or increase the heat. If the bread gets very dark, reduce the temperature under the skillet, add about ½ cup of cold oil, and test again.

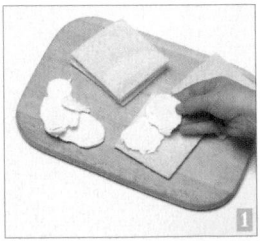

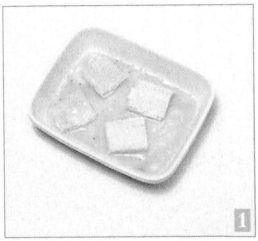

Fresh Tagliatelle with Zucchini

1 Sift the flour and salt into a large bowl. Make a well in the center and add the eggs and yolk, 1 tablespoon of oil, and 1 teaspoon of water. Gradually mix to form a soft (but not sticky) dough, adding a little more flour or water as necessary. Transfer to a lightly floured surface and knead for 5 minutes or until smooth and elastic. Cover with plastic wrap and let rest at room temperature for about 30 minutes.

2 Divide the dough into 8 pieces. Feed a piece of dough through a pasta machine. Gradually decrease the settings on the rollers, feeding the pasta through each time, until the sheet is very long and thin. If the pasta seems sticky, dust the work surface and both sides of the pasta generously with flour. Cut in half crosswise and hang over a clean pole. Repeat with the remaining dough. Leave to dry for about 5 minutes. Feed each sheet through the tagliatelle cutter, hanging the cut pasta over the pole. Leave to dry for an additional 5 minutes. Wind a handful of pasta strands into nests and leave on a floured dishtowel. Repeat with the remaining dough and leave to dry for 5 minutes.

3 Cook the pasta in plenty of salted boiling water for 2–3 minutes or until al dente.

4 Meanwhile, heat the remaining oil in a large skillet and add the zucchini, garlic, chili, and lemon zest. Cook over a medium heat for 3–4 minutes or until the zucchini is light golden and tender.

5 Drain the pasta, setting aside 2 tablespoons of the cooking water. Add the pasta to the zucchini with the basil and seasoning. Mix well, adding the reserved cooking water. Serve with Parmesan cheese.

INGREDIENTS
Serves 4–6

2 cups bread flour or type 00 pasta flour, plus extra for rolling
1 tsp. salt
2 medium eggs
1 medium egg yolk
3 tbsp. extra virgin olive oil
2 small zucchini, halved lengthwise and thinly sliced
2 garlic cloves, peeled and thinly sliced
large pinch of chili flakes
zest of ½ lemon
1 tbsp. freshly shredded basil
salt and freshly ground black pepper
freshly grated Parmesan cheese, to serve

Helpful Hint

Once made and shaped into nests, the pasta can be stored in an airtight container for 1–2 weeks.

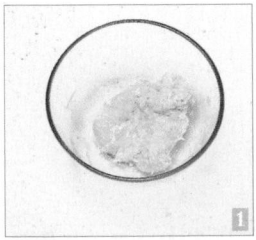
1

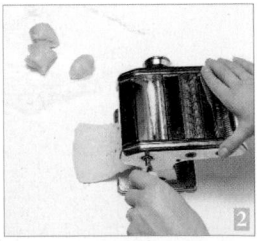
2

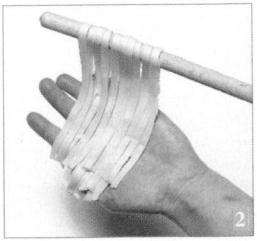
2

Beet Ravioli with Dill Cream Sauce

1 Make the pasta dough according to the recipe on page 70. Cover with plastic wrap and let rest for 30 minutes.

2 Heat the olive oil in a large skillet. Add the onion and caraway seeds, and cook over a medium heat for 5 minutes or until the onion is softened and lightly golden. Stir in the beets and cook for 5 minutes.

3 Blend the beet mixture in a food processor until smooth, then let cool. Stir in the ricotta, bread crumbs, egg yolk, and Parmesan cheese. Season the filling to taste with salt and pepper and set aside.

4 Divide the pasta dough into 8 pieces. Roll out as for tagliatelle, but do not cut the sheets in half. Lay 1 sheet on a floured surface and place 5 heaping teaspoons of the filling 1 inch apart.

5 Dampen the dough around the heaps of filling and lay a second sheet of pasta over the top. Press around the heaps to seal.

6 Cut into squares using a pastry wheel or sharp knife. Put the filled pasta shapes onto a floured dishtowel.

7 Bring a large pan of lightly salted water to a rolling boil. Drop the ravioli into the boiling water, return to a boil, and cook for 3–4 minutes, until al dente.

8 Meanwhile, heat the walnut oil in a small pan, then add the chopped dill and green peppercorns. Remove from the heat, stir in the crème fraîche, and season well. Drain the cooked pasta thoroughly and toss with the sauce. Spoon onto warmed serving dishes and serve immediately.

INGREDIENTS
Serves 4–6

fresh pasta (see Fresh Tagliatelle with Zucchini, page 70)
1 tbsp. olive oil
1 small onion, peeled and finely chopped
½ tsp. caraway seeds
1 cup chopped cooked beets
6 oz. ricotta cheese
½ cup fresh white bread crumbs
1 medium egg yolk
2 tbsp. grated Parmesan cheese
salt and freshly ground black pepper
4 tbsp. walnut oil
4 tbsp. freshly chopped dill
1 tbsp. green peppercorns, drained and coarsely chopped
6 tbsp. crème fraîche

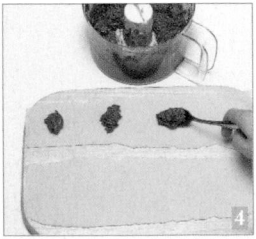
4

5

6

Gnocchi with Broiled Cherry Tomato Sauce

1 Preheat the broiler just before cooking. Bring a large pan of salted water to a boil. Add the potatoes and cook for 20–25 minutes until tender. Drain. Leave until cool enough to handle but still hot, then peel them and place in a large bowl. Mash until smooth, then work in the egg, salt, and enough of the flour to form a soft dough.

2 With floured hands, roll a spoonful of the dough into a small ball. Flatten the ball slightly onto the back of a large fork, then roll it off the fork to make a little ridged dumpling. Place each gnocchi on a floured dishtowel as you work.

3 Place the tomatoes in a flameproof shallow dish. Add the garlic, lemon zest, herbs, and olive oil. Season to taste with salt and pepper, and sprinkle over the sugar. Cook under the preheated broiler for 10 minutes or until the tomatoes are charred and tender, stirring once or twice.

4 Meanwhile, bring a large pan of lightly salted water to a boil, then reduce to a steady simmer. Dropping in 6–8 gnocchi at a time, cook in batches for 3–4 minutes or until they begin bobbing up to the surface. Remove with a slotted spoon and drain well on paper towels before transferring to a warmed serving dish; cover with foil. Toss the cooked gnocchi with the tomato sauce. Serve immediately with a little grated Parmesan cheese.

INGREDIENTS
Serves 4

1 lb. floury potatoes, unpeeled
1 medium egg
1 tsp. salt
about ¼ cup all-purpose flour
1 lb. mixed red and orange cherry tomatoes, halved lengthwise
2 garlic cloves, peeled and finely sliced
zest of ½ lemon, finely grated
1 tbsp. freshly chopped thyme
1 tbsp. freshly chopped basil
2 tbsp. extra virgin olive oil, plus extra for drizzling
salt and freshly ground black pepper
pinch of sugar
freshly grated Parmesan cheese, to serve

Helpful Hint

When cooking the gnocchi, use a very large pan with at least 8 cups of water to give them plenty of room so that they do not stick together.

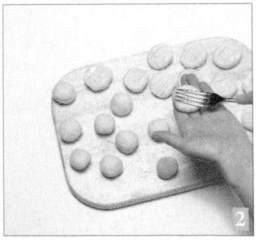

Spinach & Ricotta Gnocchi with Butter & Parmesan

1 Squeeze the excess moisture from the spinach and chop finely. Blend in a food processor with the ricotta cheese, eggs, Parmesan cheese, seasoning, and 1 tablespoon of the basil until smooth. Scrape into a bowl, then add sufficient flour to form a soft, slightly sticky dough.

2 Bring a large pan of salted water to a rolling boil. Transfer the spinach mixture to a pastry bag fitted with a large plain tip. As soon as the water is boiling, pipe 10–12 short lengths of the mixture into the water, using a sharp knife to cut the gnocchi as you go.

3 Bring the water back to a boil and cook the gnocchi for 3–4 minutes or until they begin to rise to the surface. Remove with a slotted spoon, drain on paper towels, and transfer to a warmed serving dish. Cook the gnocchi in batches if necessary.

4 Melt the butter in a small skillet, and when it begins to foam, add the garlic and remaining basil. Remove from the heat and immediately pour over the cooked gnocchi. Season well with salt and pepper and serve immediately with Parmesan cheese shavings.

INGREDIENTS
Serves 2–4

1 cup thawed frozen leaf spinach
8 oz. ricotta cheese
2 small eggs, lightly beaten
½ cup freshly grated Parmesan cheese
salt and freshly ground black pepper
2 tbsp. freshly chopped basil
about ½ cup all-purpose flour
¼ cup unsalted butter
2 garlic cloves, peeled and crushed
Parmesan cheese shavings, to serve

Food Fact

Ricotta is a crumbly, soft white cheese made from whey, a by-product from the manufacture of Pecorino Romano cheese. The curd is compacted so that the cheese can be cut with a knife. It can be eaten by itself, but normally it is used in dishes such as cheesecake.

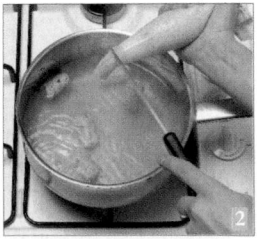

Tagliatelle with Brown Butter, Asparagus, & Parmesan

1 If using fresh pasta, prepare the dough according to the recipe on page 70. Cut into tagliatelle, wind into nests, and set aside on a floured dishtowel until ready to cook.

2 Bring a pan of lightly salted water to a boil. Add the asparagus and cook for 1 minute. Drain immediately, rinse under cold running water, and drain again. Pat dry and set aside.

3 Melt the butter in a large skillet, then add the garlic and hazelnuts, and cook over a medium heat until the butter turns golden. Immediately remove from the heat and add the parsley, chives, and asparagus. Leave for 2–3 minutes, until the asparagus is heated through.

4 Meanwhile, bring a large pan of lightly salted water to a rolling boil, then add the pasta nests. Cook until al dente: 2–3 minutes for fresh pasta and according to the package directions for dried pasta. Drain the pasta thoroughly and return to the pan. Add the asparagus mixture and toss together. Season to taste with salt and pepper and spoon into a warmed serving dish. Serve immediately with grated Parmesan cheese.

INGREDIENTS
Serves 6

fresh pasta (see Fresh Tagliatelle with Zucchini, page 70) or 1 lb. dried tagliatelle, such as the white and green variety
12 oz. asparagus, trimmed and cut into short lengths
¼ stick unsalted butter
1 garlic clove, peeled and sliced
¼ cup coarsely chopped, slivered or whole hazelnuts
1 tbsp. freshly chopped parsley
1 tbsp. freshly snipped chives
salt and freshly ground black pepper
½ cup freshly grated Parmesan cheese, to serve

Food Fact

Asparagus is available year-round, but is at its best during May and June. If you buy loose asparagus, rather than prepacked, choose stalks of similar thickness so they will all cook in the same time. It is best to buy asparagus no more than a day before using, but if necessary, you can keep stalks fresh by standing them in a little water.

Pasta with Raw Fennel, Tomato, & Red Onions

1 Trim the fennel and slice thinly. Stack the slices and cut into sticks, then cut crosswise again into fine dice. Deseed the tomatoes and chop them finely. Peel and finely chop or crush the garlic. Peel and finely chop or grate the onion.

2 Stack the basil leaves, then roll up tightly. Slice crosswise into fine shreds. Finely chop the mint.

3 Place the chopped vegetables and herbs in a medium bowl. Add the olive oil and lemon juice, and mix together. Season well with salt and pepper, then leave for 30 minutes to let the flavors develop.

4 Bring a large pan of salted water to a rolling boil. Add the pasta and cook according to the package directions or until al dente.

5 Drain the cooked pasta thoroughly. Transfer to a warmed serving dish, pour over the vegetable mixture, and toss. Serve with the grated Parmesan cheese and extra olive oil to drizzle over.

INGREDIENTS
Serves 6

1 fennel bulb
1½ lbs. tomatoes
1 garlic clove
¼ small red onion
small handful of fresh basil
small handful of fresh mint
7 tbsp. extra virgin olive oil, plus extra to serve
juice of 1 lemon
salt and freshly ground black pepper
4 cups penne or pennette
freshly grated Parmesan cheese, to serve

Food Fact

Fennel is a greenish-white bulbous vegetable that has a distinctive aniseed flavor. It is also known as "Florence fennel" to distinguish it from the herb. When buying fennel, choose a bulb that is well-rounded and as white as possible; the darker green ones may be bitter. Trim off the feathery leaves, chop them finely, and use as a garnish.

Helpful Hint

The vegetables used in this dish are not cooked, but are tossed with the hot pasta. It is important, therefore, that they are chopped finely.

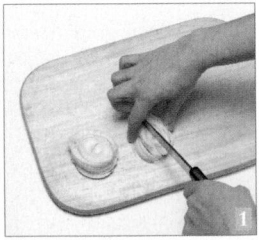

Spaghetti with Fresh Tomatoes, Chili, & Potatoes

1 Preheat the broiler to high 5 minutes before using. Cook the potatoes in plenty of boiling water until tender but firm. Let cool, then peel and cut into cubes.

2 Blend the garlic, basil, and 4 tablespoons of the olive oil in a blender or food processor until the basil is finely chopped, then set aside.

3 Place the tomatoes, basil, and oil mixture in a bowl. Add the chili and season with salt and pepper to taste. Mix together and set the sauce aside.

4 Bring a large pan of salted water to a rolling boil. Add the spaghetti and cook according to the package directions or until al dente.

5 Meanwhile, toss the potato cubes with the remaining olive oil and transfer to a baking tray. Place the potatoes under the preheated broiler until they are crisp and golden, turning once or twice, then drain on paper towels.

6 Drain the pasta thoroughly and transfer to a warmed shallow serving bowl. Add the tomato sauce and the hot potatoes. Toss well and adjust the seasoning to taste. Serve immediately with the grated Parmesan cheese, if desired.

INGREDIENTS
Serves 6

2 medium potatoes, unpeeled
3 garlic cloves, peeled and crushed
small bunch of basil, coarsely chopped
6 tbsp. olive oil
4 large ripe plum tomatoes, skinned, deseeded, and chopped
1 small red chili, deseeded and finely chopped
salt and freshly ground black pepper
1 lb. spaghetti
4 tbsp. freshly grated Parmesan cheese, to serve (optional)

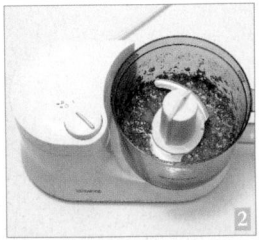
2

3

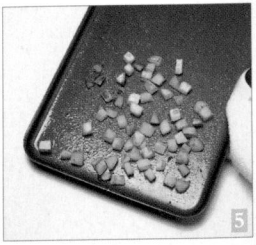
5

Pasta Genovese with Pesto, Green Beans, & Potatoes

1 Put the basil leaves, garlic, pine nuts, and Parmesan cheese into a food processor and blend until finely chopped. Transfer the mixture to a bowl and stir in the extra virgin olive oil. Season the pesto with salt and pepper and set aside.

2 Bring a pan of salted water to a boil and cook the potatoes for 12–14 minutes or until tender. About 4 minutes before the end of the cooking time, add the beans. Drain and rinse under cold water. Set aside the beans and slice the potatoes thickly or halve them if small.

3 Heat the olive oil in a skillet and add the potatoes. Fry over a medium heat for 5 minutes or until golden. Add the beans and pesto and cook for an additional 2 minutes.

4 Meanwhile, bring a large pan of lightly salted water to a boil. Cook the pasta according to the package directions or until al dente. Drain thoroughly, return to the pan, and add the pesto mixture. Toss well and heat through for 1–2 minutes. Spoon into a warmed serving bowl and serve immediately with Parmesan cheese.

INGREDIENTS
Serves 6

½ cup basil leaves
2 garlic cloves, peeled and crushed
2 tbsp. pine nuts, lightly toasted
¼ cup freshly grated Parmesan cheese
5 tbsp. extra virgin olive oil
salt and freshly ground black pepper
6 oz. new potatoes, scrubbed
4 oz. fine green beans, trimmed
2 tbsp. olive oil
4 cups pasta shapes
extra freshly grated Parmesan cheese, to serve

Tasty Tip

Classic pesto, as used in this recipe, is always made with fresh basil and pine nuts, but other herb variations work equally well. For a change try a cilantro and chili pesto, replacing the basil with fresh cilantro leaves and adding a deseeded and finely chopped red chili; or try an almond and mint pesto, replacing the pine nuts with blanched almonds and the basil with equal amounts of fresh mint and fresh parsley leaves.

Tiny Pasta with Fresh Herb Sauce

1 Bring a large pan of lightly salted water to a rolling boil. Add the pasta and cook according to the package directions or until al dente.

2 Meanwhile, place all the herbs, lemon zest, olive oil, garlic, and chili flakes in a heavy-based pan. Heat gently for 2–3 minutes or until the herbs turn bright green and become very fragrant. Remove from the heat and season to taste with salt and pepper.

3 Drain the pasta thoroughly, setting aside 2–3 tablespoons of the cooking water. Transfer the pasta to a large serving bowl.

4 Pour the heated herb mixture over the pasta and toss together until thoroughly mixed. Check and adjust the seasoning, adding a little of the pasta cooking water if the pasta mixture seems a bit dry. Transfer to warmed serving dishes and serve immediately with grated Parmesan cheese.

INGREDIENTS
Serves 6

3¼ cups tripolini (small bows with rounded ends) or small farfalle
2 tbsp. freshly chopped Italian parsley
2 tbsp. freshly chopped basil
1 tbsp. freshly snipped chives
1 tbsp. freshly chopped chervil
1 tbsp. freshly chopped tarragon
1 tbsp. freshly chopped sage
1 tbsp. freshly chopped oregano
1 tbsp. freshly chopped marjoram
1 tbsp. freshly chopped thyme
1 tbsp. freshly chopped rosemary
finely grated zest of 1 lemon
5 tbsp. extra virgin olive oil
2 garlic cloves, peeled and finely chopped
½ tsp. dried chili flakes
salt and freshly ground black pepper
freshly grated Parmesan cheese, to serve

Helpful Hint

Look for packages of mixed fresh herbs in the supermarket if you do not want to buy individual packages or bunches of all the herbs used in this fresh and vibrant sauce. If you cannot find all the herbs listed, you can increase the quantity of some of them as a substitute for others not being used. Do not add more than 1 tablespoon each of thyme or rosemary though, or their flavor may overpower the sauce.

Louisiana Shrimp & Fettuccine

1 Heat 2 tablespoons of the olive oil in a large pan and add the shrimp shells and heads. Fry over a high heat for 2–3 minutes, until the shells turn pink and are lightly browned. Add half the shallots, half the garlic, half the basil, and the carrot, onion, celery, parsley, and thyme. Season lightly with salt, pepper, and cayenne, and fry for 2–3 minutes, stirring often.

2 Pour in the wine and stir, scraping the pan well. Bring to a boil and simmer for 1 minute, then add the tomatoes. Cook for an additional 3–4 minutes, then pour in ¾ cup of water. Bring to a boil, lower the heat, and simmer for about 30 minutes, stirring often and using a wooden spoon to mash the shrimp shells in order to release as much flavor as possible into the sauce. Lower the heat if the sauce is reducing very quickly.

3 Strain through a sieve, pressing well to extract as much liquid as possible; there should be about 1½ cups. Pour the liquid into a clean pan and bring to a boil, then lower the heat and simmer gently until the liquid is reduced by about half.

4 Heat the remaining olive oil over a high heat in a clean skillet and add the shelled shrimp. Season lightly and add the lemon juice. Cook for 1 minute, lower the heat, and add the remaining shallots and garlic. Cook for 1 minute. Add the sauce and adjust the seasoning.

5 Meanwhile, bring a large pan of lightly salted water to a rolling boil and add the fettuccine. Cook according to the package directions or until al dente, and drain thoroughly. Transfer to a warmed serving dish. Add the sauce and toss well. Garnish with the remaining basil and serve immediately.

INGREDIENTS
Serves 4

4 tbsp. olive oil
1 lb. raw jumbo shrimp, washed and shelled, shells and heads set aside
2 shallots, peeled and finely chopped
4 garlic cloves, peeled and finely chopped
large handful of fresh basil leaves
1 carrot, peeled and finely chopped
1 onion, peeled and finely chopped
1 celery stalk, trimmed and finely chopped
2–3 sprigs fresh parsley
2–3 sprigs fresh thyme
salt and freshly ground black pepper
pinch of cayenne pepper
¾ cup dry white wine
2 cups coarsely chopped, ripe tomatoes
juice of ½ lemon, or to taste
12 oz. fettuccine

1

2

3

Salmon & Roasted Red Bell Pepper Pasta

1 Preheat the broiler to high. Place the salmon in a bowl. Add the shallots, parsley, 3 tablespoons of the olive oil, and the lemon juice. Set aside.

2 Brush the bell pepper quarters with a little olive oil. Cook them under the broiler for 8–10 minutes or until the skins have blackened and the flesh is tender. Place the peppers in a plastic bag until cool enough to handle. When cooled, peel the peppers and cut into strips. Put the strips into a bowl with the basil and the remaining olive oil and set aside.

3 Toast the bread crumbs until dry and lightly browned, then toss with the extra virgin olive oil and set aside.

4 Bring a large pan of salted water to a rolling boil and add the pasta. Cook according to the package directions or until al dente.

5 Meanwhile, transfer the peppers and their marinade to a hot skillet. Add the scallions and cook for 1–2 minutes or until they have just softened. Add the salmon and its marinade and cook for an additional 1–2 minutes or until the salmon is just cooked. Season with salt and pepper.

6 Drain the pasta thoroughly and transfer to a warmed serving bowl. Add the salmon mixture and toss gently. Garnish with the bread crumbs and serve immediately.

INGREDIENTS
Serves 6

8 oz. skinless and boneless salmon fillet, thinly sliced
3 shallots, peeled and finely chopped
1 tbsp. freshly chopped parsley
6 tbsp. olive oil
juice of ½ lemon
2 red bell peppers, deseeded and quartered
handful of fresh basil leaves, shredded
1 cup fresh bread crumbs
4 tbsp. extra virgin olive oil
1 lb. fettuccine or linguine
6 scallions, trimmed and shredded
salt and freshly ground black pepper

Food Fact

Olive oil is graded according to aroma, flavor, color, and acidity—virgin olive oil has less than 2 percent acidity, extra virgin olive oil less than 1 percent.

Spaghettini with Peas, Scallions, & Mint

1 Soak the saffron in 2 tablespoons hot water while you prepare the sauce. Shell the peas if using fresh ones.

2 Melt ½ stick of the butter in a medium skillet. Add the scallions and a little salt, and cook over a low heat for 2–3 minutes or until the scallions are softened. Add the garlic, then the peas and 7 tablespoons water. Bring to a boil and cook for 5–6 minutes or until the peas are just tender. Stir in the mint and keep warm.

3 Blend the remaining butter and the saffron water in a large, warmed serving bowl and set aside.

4 Meanwhile, bring a large pan of lightly salted water to a rolling boil and add the spaghettini. Cook according to the package directions or until al dente.

5 Drain thoroughly, reserving 2–3 tablespoons of the pasta cooking water. Spoon into a warmed serving bowl. Add the pea sauce and toss together gently. Season to taste with salt and pepper. Serve immediately with extra black pepper and grated Parmesan cheese.

INGREDIENTS
Serves 6

pinch of saffron strands
1½ lb. fresh peas or 3 cups frozen petit pois, thawed
¼ stick unsalted butter, softened
6 scallions, trimmed and finely sliced
salt and freshly ground black pepper
1 garlic clove, peeled and finely chopped
2 tbsp. freshly chopped mint
1 tbsp. freshly cut chives
1 lb. spaghettini
freshly grated Parmesan cheese, to serve

Helpful Hint

To develop the full flavor and deep golden color of the saffron, it should be soaked for at least 20 minutes, so do this well before you start cooking. Saffron is one of the few spices that can be kept for several years, but you must store it in an airtight container, away from light.

Fusilli with Tomato & Chorizo Sauce with Roasted Bell Peppers

1 Preheat the broiler to high. Brush the bell pepper quarters with 1 tablespoon of the olive oil, then cook under the preheated broiler, turning once, for 8–10 minutes or until the skins have blackened and the flesh is tender. Place the peppers in a plastic bag until cool enough to handle. When cooled, peel the peppers, slice very thinly, and set aside.

2 Heat the remaining oil in a skillet and add the chorizo. Cook over a medium heat for 3–4 minutes or until starting to brown. Add the garlic and chili flakes, and cook for an additional 2–3 minutes.

3 Add the tomatoes and season lightly with salt and pepper, then cook gently for about 5 minutes or until the tomatoes have broken down. Lower the heat and cook for an additional 10–15 minutes or until the sauce has thickened. Add the peppers and heat gently for 1–2 minutes.

4 Meanwhile, bring a large pan of lightly salted water to a rolling boil. Add the fusilli and cook according to the package directions or until al dente. Drain thoroughly and transfer to a warmed dish. Pour over the sauce, sprinkle with basil, and serve with Parmesan cheese.

Food Fact

There are two types of chorizo sausage: the dried, salami-type, usually about 2 inches in diameter, and the slightly softer, semidried chorizo, which looks like short fat sausages. The latter type is preferable for this recipe. Both types of chorizo are pork sausages containing chili and paprika, which gives them a vibrant orange-red color.

INGREDIENTS
Serves 6

1 red bell pepper, deseeded and quartered
1 yellow bell pepper, deseeded and quartered
4 tbsp. olive oil
¼ cup chorizo, coarsely chopped (outer skin removed)
2 garlic cloves, peeled and finely chopped
large pinch of chili flakes
3 cups ripe tomatoes, skinned and coarsely chopped
salt and freshly ground black pepper
4 cups fusilli
basil leaves, to garnish
freshly grated Parmesan cheese, to serve

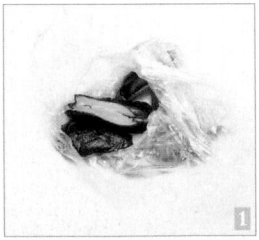

Pasta with Walnut Sauce

1 Place the toasted walnuts in a blender or food processor with the chopped scallions, one of the garlic cloves, and parsley or basil. Blend to a fairly smooth paste, then gradually add 3 tablespoons of the olive oil until it is well mixed into the paste. Season the walnut paste to taste with salt and pepper, and set aside.

2 Bring a large pan of lightly salted water to a rolling boil. Add the broccoli, return to a boil, and cook for 2 minutes. Remove the broccoli using a slotted spoon, and rinse under cold running water. Drain again and pat dry on paper towels.

3 Bring the water back to a rolling boil. Add the pasta and cook according to the package directions or until al dente.

4 Meanwhile, heat the remaining oil in a skillet. Add the remaining garlic and the chili. Cook gently for 2 minutes or until softened. Add the broccoli and walnut paste. Cook for an additional 3–4 minutes or until heated through.

5 Drain the pasta thoroughly and transfer to a large warmed serving bowl. Pour over the walnut and broccoli sauce. Toss together, adjust the seasoning, and serve immediately.

INGREDIENTS
Serves 4

½ cup walnuts, toasted
3 scallions, trimmed and chopped
2 garlic cloves, peeled and sliced
1 tbsp. freshly chopped parsley or basil
5 tbsp. extra virgin olive oil
salt and freshly ground black pepper
1 lb. broccoli, cut into florets
3 cups pasta shapes
1 red chili, deseeded and finely chopped

Helpful Hint

There is no hard-and-fast rule about which shape of pasta to use with this recipe; it is really a matter of personal preference. Spirali have been used here, but rigatoni, farfalle, garganelle, or pipe rigate would all work well, or you could choose flavored pasta, such as tomato, or a whole-wheat variety for a change.

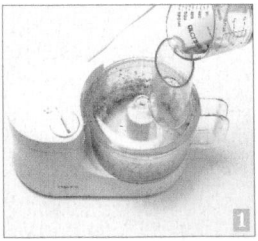

Pasta & Bean Soup

1 Heat the olive oil in a heavy-based pan. Add the celery and prosciutto, and cook gently for 6–8 minutes or until softened. Add the chopped chili and potato cubes and cook for an additional 10 minutes.

2 Add the garlic to the chili and potato mixture, and cook for 1 minute. Add the chopped tomatoes and simmer for 5 minutes. Stir in two thirds of the beans, then pour in the chicken or vegetable stock and bring to a boil.

3 Add the pasta shapes to the soup stock and return it to simmering point. Cook the pasta for about 10 minutes or until al dente.

4 Meanwhile, place the remaining beans in a food processor or blender and blend with enough of the soup stock to make a smooth, thin purée.

5 When the pasta is cooked, stir in the puréed beans with the torn basil. Season the soup to taste with salt and pepper. Ladle into serving bowls. Garnish with shredded basil and serve immediately with plenty of crusty bread.

INGREDIENTS
Serves 4–6

3 tbsp. olive oil
2 celery stalks, trimmed and finely chopped
¼ cup prosciutto or speck, cut in pieces
1 red chili, deseeded and finely chopped
2 large potatoes, peeled and cut into 1 in. cubes
2 garlic cloves, peeled and finely chopped
3 ripe plum tomatoes, skinned and chopped
14-oz. can cranberry beans, drained and rinsed
4 cups chicken or vegetable stock
1 cup pasta shapes
large handful of basil leaves, torn
salt and freshly ground black pepper
shredded basil leaves, to garnish
crusty bread, to serve

Food Fact

Oval cranberry beans have red-streaked, pinkish-brown skin. They have a moist texture and a bittersweet flavor, which makes them excellent in soups. Other canned beans may be used if preferred. Try pinto beans, a smaller, paler version of the cranberry bean, or cannellini beans, which have a soft creamy texture.

Gnocchetti with Broccoli & Bacon Sauce

1 Bring a large pan of salted water to a boil. Add the broccoli florets and cook for about 8–10 minutes or until very soft. Drain thoroughly and leave to cool slightly; then chop finely and set aside.

2 Heat the olive oil in a heavy-based pan. Add the pancetta or bacon and cook over a medium heat for 5 minutes or until golden and crisp. Add the onion and cook for an additional 5 minutes or until soft and lightly golden. Add the garlic and cook for 1 minute.

3 Transfer the chopped broccoli to the bacon or pancetta mixture and pour in the milk. Bring slowly to a boil and simmer rapidly for about 15 minutes or until reduced to a creamy texture.

4 Meanwhile, bring a large pan of lightly salted water to a rolling boil. Add the pasta and cook according to the package directions or until al dente.

5 Drain the pasta thoroughly, setting aside a little of the cooking water. Add the pasta and the Parmesan cheese to the broccoli mixture. Toss, adding enough of the cooking water to make a creamy sauce. Season to taste with salt and pepper. Serve immediately with extra Parmesan cheese.

INGREDIENTS
Serves 6

1 lb. broccoli florets
4 tbsp. olive oil
½ cup finely chopped pancetta or smoked bacon
1 small onion, peeled and finely chopped
3 garlic cloves, peeled and sliced
¼ cup milk
4 cups gnocchetti (little elongated ribbed shells)
½ cup freshly grated Parmesan cheese, plus extra to serve
salt and freshly ground black pepper

Food Fact

Pancetta is an Italian bacon that may be either smoked or unsmoked. You can buy it sliced or in a piece, but it is often sold prepacked, cut into tiny cubes ready for cooking. Thickly cut, smoked bacon makes a good alternative.

Penne with Artichokes, Bacon, & Mushrooms

1 Heat the olive oil in a skillet and add the pancetta or bacon and the onion. Cook over a medium heat for 8–10 minutes or until the bacon is crisp and the onion is just golden. Add the mushrooms and garlic and cook for an additional 5 minutes or until softened.

2 Add the artichoke hearts to the mushroom mixture and cook for 3–4 minutes. Pour in the wine and bring to a boil, then simmer rapidly until the liquid is reduced and syrupy.

3 Pour in the chicken stock and bring to a boil, then simmer rapidly for about 5 minutes or until slightly reduced. Reduce the heat slightly, then slowly stir in the heavy cream and Parmesan cheese. Season the sauce to taste with salt and pepper.

4 Meanwhile, bring a large pan of lightly salted water to a rolling boil. Add the pasta and cook according to the package directions or until al dente.

5 Drain the pasta thoroughly and transfer to a large warmed serving dish. Pour over the sauce and toss together. Garnish with shredded basil and serve with extra Parmesan cheese.

INGREDIENTS
Serves 6

2 tbsp. olive oil
¾ cup chopped smoked bacon or pancetta
1 small onion, peeled and finely sliced
1½ cups sliced chestnut mushrooms
2 garlic cloves, peeled and finely chopped
14-oz. can artichoke hearts, drained and halved, or quartered if large
7 tbsp. dry white wine
7 tbsp. chicken stock
3 tbsp. heavy cream
½ cup freshly grated Parmesan cheese, plus extra to serve
salt and freshly ground black pepper
4 cups penne
shredded basil leaves, to garnish

Tasty Tip

Brown-capped chestnut mushrooms are similar in appearance to cultivated button mushrooms, but they have a rich orange-brown color and a slightly stronger, nutty flavor. Tiny, baby chestnut mushrooms are sometimes available and could be used whole or halved in this recipe.

Fettuccine with Wild Mushrooms & Prosciutto

1 Place the dried mushrooms in a small bowl and pour over the hot chicken stock. Leave to soak for 15–20 minutes or until the mushrooms have softened.

2 Meanwhile, heat the olive oil in a large skillet. Add the onion and cook for 5 minutes over a medium heat or until softened. Add the garlic and cook for 1 minute; then add the prosciutto and cook for an additional minute.

3 Drain the dried mushrooms, setting aside the soaking liquid. Coarsely chop and add to the skillet along with the fresh mushrooms. Cook over a high heat for 5 minutes, stirring often or until softened. Strain the mushroom soaking liquid into the pan.

4 Meanwhile, bring a large pan of lightly salted water to a rolling boil. Add the pasta and cook according to the package directions or until al dente.

5 Stir the crème fraîche and parsley seasoning into the mushroom mixture, and heat through gently. Drain the pasta well, transfer to a large warmed serving dish, and pour over the sauce. Serve immediately with grated Parmesan cheese.

INGREDIENTS
Serves 6

½ oz. dried porcini mushrooms
⅔ cup hot chicken stock
2 tbsp. olive oil
1 small onion, peeled and finely chopped
2 garlic cloves, peeled and finely chopped
4 slices prosciutto, chopped or torn
8 oz. mixed wild or cultivated mushrooms, sliced if necessary
1 lb. fettuccine
3 tbsp. crème fraîche
2 tbsp. freshly chopped parsley
salt and freshly ground black pepper
freshly grated Parmesan cheese, to serve (optional)

Food Fact

Prosciutto is produced from pigs fed on whey, a by-product of the local Parmesan cheese industry. The ham is dry-cured, then weighted to flatten it and give it a dense texture. The delicious flavor develops during the year it is left to mature. It is always served in paper-thin slices, either raw or lightly fried.

Tagliarini with Fava Beans, Saffron, & Crème Fraîche

1 If using fresh fava beans, bring a pan of lightly salted water to the boil. Pod the beans and drop them into the boiling water for 1 minute. Drain and rinse under cold water. Drain again. Remove the outer skin of the beans and discard. If using thawed frozen fava beans, remove and discard the skins. Set aside the peeled beans.

2 Heat the olive oil in a saucepan. Add the peeled fava beans and the garlic, and cook gently for 2–3 minutes. Stir in the basil, the crème fraîche, and the pinch of saffron strands, and simmer for 1 minute.

3 Meanwhile, bring a large pan of lightly salted water to a rolling boil. Add the pasta and cook according to the package directions or until al dente. Drain the pasta well and add to the sauce. Toss together and season to taste with salt and pepper.

4 Transfer the pasta and sauce to a warmed serving dish. Sprinkle with chives and serve immediately with Parmesan cheese.

INGREDIENTS
Serves 2–3

8 oz. fresh young fava beans in pods or 1 cup thawed frozen fava beans
1 tbsp. olive oil
1 garlic clove, peeled and chopped
small handful of basil leaves, shredded
about ¼ cup crème fraîche
large pinch of saffron strands
12 oz. tagliarini
salt and freshly ground black pepper
1 tbsp. freshly cut chives
freshly grated Parmesan cheese, to serve

Helpful Hint

If you buy fresh fava beans in their pods (they are available from May to July), look for smooth, plump, bright green pods and use within two days of purchase; they should be cooked the same day as shelling. The skins on the beans become tougher as they age, so if the beans are very young and fresh, there is no need to peel them.

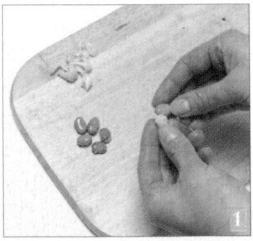

Linguine with Fennel, Crab, & Chervil

1 Bring a large pan of lightly salted water to a rolling boil. Add the pasta and cook according to the package directions or until al dente.

2 Meanwhile, melt the butter in a large pan. Add the carrots, shallots, celery, fennel, and three quarters of the chopped scallions. Cook the vegetables gently for 8–10 minutes or until tender, stirring frequently and taking care that they do not brown.

3 Add the heavy cream and chopped chervil to the vegetable mixture. Scrape the crab meat over the sauce, then stir to mix the sauce ingredients.

4 Season the sauce to taste with salt and pepper and stir in the lemon juice. Drain the pasta thoroughly and transfer to a large warmed serving dish. Pour over the sauce and toss. Garnish with extra chervil, the remaining scallions, and a sprig of dill. Serve immediately.

Helpful Hint

If you prefer to prepare a cooked crab yourself, start by twisting off the legs and claws, then cracking them open and removing the meat. Next, turn the crab onto its back and twist off the bony, pointed flap. Put the tip of a knife between the main shell and where the legs and claws were attached, twist the blade to lift up and remove, then scrape out the brown meat in the main shell. Pull away and discard the gray, soft gills. Split the body in half and, using a skewer, remove all the white meat from the cavities. An average-sized crab should produce about 8 oz. of white and brown meat.

INGREDIENTS
Serves 6

1 lb. linguine
2 tbsp. butter
2 carrots, peeled and finely diced
2 shallots, peeled and finely diced
2 celery stalks, trimmed and finely diced
1 fennel bulb, trimmed and finely diced
6 scallions, trimmed and finely chopped
1¼ cups heavy cream
3 tbsp. freshly chopped chervil, plus extra for garnish
1 large cooked crab
salt and freshly ground pepper
juice of ½ lemon
sprig of dill, to garnish

Pea & Shrimp Risotto

1 Peel the shrimp and set aside the heads and shells. Remove the black vein from the back of each shrimp, then wash and dry on absorbent paper towels. Melt half the butter in a large skillet, add the shrimp heads and shells, and cook, stirring occasionally, for 3–4 minutes or until golden. Strain the butter, discard the heads and shells, and return the butter to the skillet.

2 Add an additional ¼ stick of butter to the skillet, and cook the onion and garlic for 5 minutes until softened but not browned. Add the rice and stir the grains in the butter for 1 minute until they are coated thoroughly. Add the white wine and boil rapidly until the wine is reduced by half.

3 Bring the stock to a gentle simmer, and add to the rice, a ladleful at a time. Stir constantly, adding the stock as it is absorbed until the rice is creamy but still has a bite in the center.

4 Melt the remaining butter and stir-fry the shrimp for 3–4 minutes. Stir into the rice, along with the pan juices and the peas. Add the chopped mint and season to taste with salt and pepper. Cover the skillet and let the shrimp infuse for 5 minutes before serving.

INGREDIENTS
Serves 6

1 lb. whole raw shrimp
1 stick butter
1 red onion, peeled and chopped
4 garlic cloves, peeled and finely chopped
1 cup risotto rice
⅔ cup dry white wine
5 cups vegetable or fish stock
3 cups frozen peas
4 tbsp. freshly chopped mint
salt and freshly ground black pepper

Tasty Tip

Cooking the shrimp shells and heads before cooking the dish adds a great deal of flavor to the rice. Alternatively, the shells and heads could be added to the stock and simmered for 10 minutes. Strain the stock, pressing the shells and heads well to extract the maximum flavor.

Stuffed Calamari with Romesco Sauce

1 Preheat the oven to 450° F. Clean the calamari, rinse lightly, pat dry with absorbent paper towels, and finely chop the tentacles.

2 Heat 2 tablespoons of the olive oil in a large nonstick skillet, and cook the pancetta for 5 minutes or until crisp. Remove the pancetta and set aside. Add the tentacles, onion, 2 garlic cloves, thyme, and sun-dried tomatoes to the oil remaining in the skillet, and cook gently for 5 minutes or until softened.

3 Remove the skillet from the heat and stir in the diced pancetta. Blend in a food processor if a smoother stuffing is preferred, then stir in the bread crumbs, basil, and lime juice. Season to taste with salt and pepper, and set aside. Spoon the stuffing into the cavity of the calamari, and secure the tops with toothpicks.

4 Place the calamari in a large roasting pan, and sprinkle over 2 tablespoons each of oil and water. Place in the preheated oven and cook for 20 minutes.

5 Heat the remaining oil in a saucepan and cook the remaining garlic for 3 minutes. Add the tomatoes, chili flakes, and oregano, and simmer gently for 15 minutes before stirring in the red bell pepper. Cook gently for an additional 5 minutes. Blend the mixture in a food processor to make a smooth sauce, and season to taste. Pour the sauce over the calamari and serve immediately with mixed salad.

INGREDIENTS
Serves 4

8 small calamari
¼ cup olive oil
½ cup pancetta, diced
1 onion, peeled and chopped
3 garlic cloves, peeled and finely chopped
2 tsp. freshly chopped thyme
¼ cup sun-dried tomatoes in oil, drained and chopped
¼ cup fresh white bread crumbs
2 tbsp. freshly chopped basil
3 tsp. lime juice
salt and freshly ground black pepper
2 vine-ripened tomatoes, peeled and finely chopped
pinch of dried chili flakes
1 tsp. dried oregano
1 large red bell pepper, peeled and chopped
mixed salad, to serve

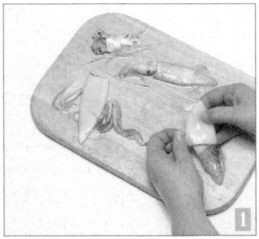

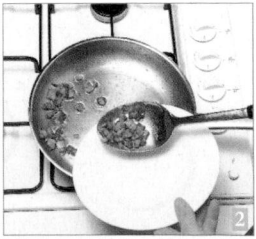

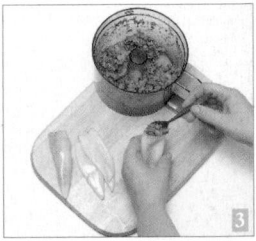

Scallops & Monkfish Kabobs with Fennel Sauce

1 Place the monkfish on a chopping board, and remove and discard the skin and the bone that runs down the center of the tail. Lightly rinse and pat dry. Cut the 2 fillets into 12 equal-size pieces and then place in a shallow bowl.

2 Remove the scallops from their shells if necessary, and clean thoroughly, discarding the black vein. Rinse lightly and pat dry with absorbent paper towels. Put in the bowl with the fish.

3 Blend the 2 tablespoons of olive oil, the crushed garlic, and a pinch of black pepper in a small bowl, then pour the mixture over the monkfish and scallops, making sure they are well coated. Cover lightly and let them marinate in the refrigerator for at least 30 minutes, or longer if time permits. Spoon over the marinade occasionally.

4 Lightly crush the fennel seeds and chili flakes. Stir in the 4 tablespoons of olive oil and lemon juice, then season to taste with salt and pepper. Cover and let it infuse for 20 minutes.

5 Drain the monkfish and scallops, and set the marinade aside. Thread the fish and scallops onto four skewers.

6 Spray a griddle pan with a fine spray of oil, then heat until almost smoking, and cook the kabobs for 5–6 minutes, turning halfway through and brushing with the marinade throughout.

7 Brush the fennel slices with the fennel sauce, and cook on the griddle for 1 minute on each side. Serve the fennel slices topped with the kabobs and drizzled with the fennel sauce. Serve with mixed salad.

INGREDIENTS
Serves 4

1½ lbs. monkfish tail
8 large, fresh scallops
2 tbsp. olive oil
1 garlic clove, peeled and crushed
freshly ground black pepper
1 fennel bulb, trimmed and thinly sliced
mixed salad, to serve

FOR THE SAUCE:
2 tbsp. fennel seeds
pinch of chili flakes
¼ cup olive oil
2 tsp. lemon juice
salt and freshly ground black pepper

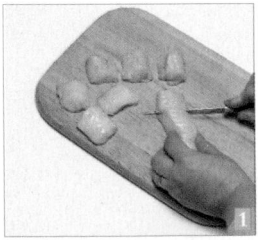

Red Pesto & Clam Spaghetti

1 To make the red pesto, place the garlic, pine nuts, basil leaves, sun-dried tomatoes, and olive oil in a food processor, and blend in short, sharp bursts until smooth. Scrape into a bowl, stir in the Parmesan cheese, and season to taste with salt and pepper. Cover and leave in the refrigerator until required.

2 Scrub the clams with a soft brush, remove any beards from the shells, and discard any shells that are open or damaged. Wash in plenty of cold water, then leave in a bowl covered with cold water in the refrigerator until needed. Change the water frequently.

3 Heat the oil in a saucepan, and gently cook the garlic and onion for 5 minutes until softened but not browned. Add the wine and stock, and bring to a boil. Add the clams, cover, and cook for 3–4 minutes or until the clams have opened.

4 Discard any clams that have not opened, and stir in the red pesto sauce. Bring a large saucepan of lightly salted water to a boil, and cook the spaghetti for 5–7 minutes or until al dente. Drain and return to the saucepan. Add the sauce to the spaghetti, mix well, spoon into a serving dish, and serve immediately.

INGREDIENTS
Serves 4

FOR THE RED PESTO:
2 garlic cloves, peeled and finely chopped
½ cup pine nuts
6 tbsp. fresh basil leaves
4 sun-dried tomatoes in oil, drained
¼ cup olive oil
¼ cup Parmesan cheese, shredded
salt and freshly ground black pepper

FOR THE CLAM SAUCE:
1 lb. live clams, in their shells
1 tbsp. olive oil
2 garlic cloves, peeled and crushed
1 small onion, peeled and chopped
½ cup medium-dry white wine
⅔ cup fish or chicken stock
3¼ cups spaghetti

Tasty Tip

This dish looks particularly attractive with the clams left in their shells. If you prefer, you could remove the meat from the shells at the end of step 3, leaving just a few in for garnishing and stir back into the saucepan with the pasta.

Sardines in Grape Leaves

1 Preheat the broiler and line the broiler rack with foil just before cooking. Cut 8 pieces of kitchen string about 10 inches long, and let soak in cold water for about 10 minutes. Cover the vine leaves in almost-boiling water. Leave for 20 minutes, then drain and rinse thoroughly. Pat the vine leaves dry with absorbent paper towels.

2 Trim the scallions, chop finely, and then place into a small bowl. With a whisk, beat in the olive oil, lime juice, oregano, mustard powder, and season to taste with salt and pepper. Cover with plastic wrap and leave in the refrigerator until needed. Stir the mixture before using.

3 Prepare the sardines by making 2 slashes on both sides of each fish, and brush with a little of the lime juice mixture. Place a bay leaf and a dill sprig inside each sardine cavity, and wrap with 1–2 vine leaves, depending on size. Brush with the lime mixture and tie the vine leaves in place with string.

4 Broil the fish for 4–5 minutes on each side under a medium heat, brushing with a little more of the lime mixture if necessary. Let the fish rest, unwrap, and discard the vine leaves. Garnish with lime wedges and sprigs of fresh dill, and serve immediately with the remaining lime mixture, olive salad, and crusty bread.

INGREDIENTS
Serves 4

8–16 grape leaves in brine, drained
2 scallions
½ cup olive oil
2 tbsp. lime juice
2 tbsp. freshly chopped oregano
1 tsp. mustard powder
salt and freshly ground black pepper
8 sardines, cleaned
8 bay leaves
8 sprigs of fresh dill

TO GARNISH:
lime wedges
sprigs of fresh dill

TO SERVE:
olive salad
crusty bread

Helpful Hint

To clean sardines, first gut the fish. Insert a knife or point of a pair of kitchen scissors and make a cut along the belly. Remove the insides and discard. Wash the fish well. Remove the scales by gently rubbing your thumb along the fish from tail to head. Sardines have very delicate skin, so rub gently.

1

3

3

Parmesan & Garlic Lobster

1 Preheat the oven to 350° F. Halve the lobster and crack the claws. Remove the gills, the green sac behind the head, and the black vein running down the body. Place the 2 lobster halves in a shallow ovenproof dish.

2 Melt the butter in a small saucepan and gently cook the garlic for 3 minutes until softened. Add the flour and stir over a medium heat for 1 minute. Draw the saucepan off the heat, then gradually stir in the milk, stirring until the sauce thickens. Return to the heat and cook for 2 minutes, stirring throughout until smooth and thickened. Stir in half the Parmesan cheese, continue to cook for 1 minute, and season to taste with salt and pepper.

3 Pour the cheese sauce over the lobster halves, and sprinkle with the remaining Parmesan cheese. Cook in the preheated oven for 20 minutes or until heated through and the cheese sauce is golden brown. Serve with mixed salad.

INGREDIENTS
Serves 2

1 large cooked lobster
¼ stick unsalted butter
4 garlic cloves, peeled and crushed
1 tbsp. all-purpose flour
1 cup milk
1¼ cups Parmesan cheese, shredded
sea salt and freshly ground black pepper
mixed salad, to serve

Food Fact

Today we consider lobster to be a luxury. However, up until the end of nineteenth century, lobster was so plentiful that it was used as fish bait.

Helpful Hint

This impressive-looking dish makes a wonderful appetizer for two. Make the sauce in advance and cover the surface with a layer of plastic wrap. Refrigerate until ready to use.

Roasted Cod with Saffron Aioli

1 Preheat the oven to 350° F. Crush the garlic, saffron, and a pinch of salt to form a paste. Place in a blender with the egg yolk, and blend for 30 seconds. With the motor running, slowly add the olive oil in a thin, steady stream until the mayonnaise is smooth and thick. Spoon into a small bowl and stir in the lemon juice. Cover and leave in the refrigerator until needed.

2 Combine the olive oil, garlic, red onion, rosemary, and thyme for the marinade, and let infuse for about 10 minutes.

3 Place the sprigs of rosemary and slices of lemon in the bottom of a lightly greased roasting pan. Add the cod, skinned-side up. Pour over the prepared marinade and let it marinate in the refrigerator for 15–20 minutes. Cook in the preheated oven for 15–20 minutes or until the cod is cooked and the flesh flakes easily with a fork. Let the cod rest for 1 minute before serving with the saffron aioli and vegetables.

INGREDIENTS
Serves 4

FOR THE SAFFRON AIOLI:
2 garlic cloves, peeled
¼ tsp. saffron strands
sea salt, to taste
1 medium egg yolk
¾ cup extra-virgin olive oil
2 tbsp. lemon juice

FOR THE MARINADE:
2 tbsp. olive oil
4 garlic cloves, peeled and finely chopped
1 red onion, peeled and finely chopped
1 tbsp. freshly chopped rosemary
2 tbsp. freshly chopped thyme
4–6 sprigs of fresh rosemary
1 lemon, sliced
4 thick cod fillets, with skin
freshly cooked vegtables, to serve

Helpful Hint

Vulnerable groups, such as the very young, the elderly, and pregnant women, should avoid eating raw and undercooked eggs. Instead, make the garlic and saffron paste as above and use a store-bought mayonnaise.

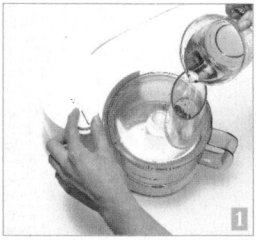
1

2

3

Foil-Baked Fish

1 Preheat the oven to 350° F. Heat the olive oil and gently cook the garlic and shallots for 2 minutes. Stir in the tomatoes and simmer for 10 minutes, breaking the tomatoes down with a wooden spoon. Add the parsley and basil, season to taste with salt and pepper, and cook for an additional 2 minutes. Set aside and keep warm.

2 Lightly rinse the fish fillets and cut into 4 pieces. Scrub the mussels thoroughly, removing the beard and any barnacles from the shells. Discard any mussels that are open. Clean the calamari and cut into rings. Shell the shrimp and remove the thin black intestinal vein that runs down the back.

3 Cut 4 large pieces of foil, then place them on a large baking sheet and brush with olive oil. Place 1 fish piece in the center of each piece of foil. Close the foil to form pockets, cook in the preheated oven for 10 minutes, then remove.

4 Carefully open up the pockets and add the mussels, calamari, and shrimp. Pour in the wine and spoon over a little of the tomato sauce. Sprinkle with the basil leaves and return to the oven and cook for 5 minutes or until cooked thoroughly. Discard any unopened mussels, then garnish with lemon wedges and serve with the extra tomato sauce.

Helpful Hint

This is an excellent basic tomato sauce. Make a large batch and serve it with pasta. Keep covered in the refrigerator until needed, or freeze for up to 2 months. Thaw completely and reheat gently before using.

INGREDIENTS
Serves 4

FOR THE TOMATO SAUCE:

8 tbsp. olive oil
4 garlic cloves, peeled and finely chopped
4 shallots, peeled and finely chopped
14-oz. can chopped Italian tomatoes
2 tbsp. freshly chopped Italian parsley
3 tbsp. basil leaves
salt and freshly ground black pepper

1½ lbs. sea bass or haddock fillets
1 lb. live mussels
4 calamari
8 large raw shrimp
2 tbsp. olive oil
3 tbsp. dry white wine
3 tbsp. freshly chopped basil leaves
lemon wedges, to garnish

Roasted Monkfish with Prosciutto

1 Preheat the oven to 400° F. Discard any skin from the monkfish tail, and cut away and discard the central bone. Cut the fish into 4 equal-size pieces and season to taste with salt and pepper. Lay a bay leaf and a slice of cheese on each fillet.

2 Wrap each fillet with 2 slices of the prosciutto, so that the fish is covered completely. Tuck the ends of the prosciutto in and secure with a toothpick.

3 Lightly grease a baking sheet and place in the preheated oven for a few minutes. Place the fish on the preheated baking sheet, put in the oven, and cook for 12–15 minutes.

4 Bring a large saucepan of lightly salted water to a boil, then slowly add the pasta and cook for 5 minutes until al dente or according to package directions. Drain, setting aside 2 tablespoons of the pasta cooking liquid. Return the pasta to the saucepan, and add the pasta liquid, butter, lemon zest, and juice. Toss until the pasta is well coated and glistening.

5 Twirl the pasta into small nests on four warmed serving plates, and top with the monkfish pockets. Garnish with sprigs of cilantro, and serve with grilled zucchini and tomatoes.

INGREDIENTS
Serves 4

1½ lbs. monkfish tail
sea salt and freshly ground black pepper
4 bay leaves
4 slices fontina cheese, rind removed
8 slices prosciutto
3 cups angel-hair pasta
½ stick butter
1 tbsp. lemon zest
2 tbsp. lemon juice
sprigs of fresh cilantro, to garnish

TO SERVE:
grilled zucchini
grilled tomatoes

Helpful Hint

Monkfish is also sold in boneless fillets, sometimes called loins. Remove the skin from the fish before cooking, and if cubes or strips are required, remove the central bone.

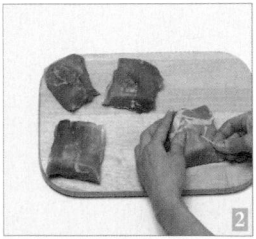

Mussels Arrabbiata

1 Clean the mussels by scrubbing with a small, soft brush, removing the beard and any barnacles from the shells. Discard any mussels that are open or have damaged shells. Place in a large bowl and cover with cold water. Change the water frequently before cooking, and leave in the refrigerator until needed.

2 Heat the olive oil in a large saucepan and fry the onion, garlic, and chili until soft but not colored. Add the tomatoes and bring to a boil, then simmer for 15 minutes.

3 Add the white wine to the tomato sauce, bring the sauce to a boil, and add the mussels. Cover and carefully shake the saucepan. Cook the mussels for 5–7 minutes or until the shells have opened.

4 Add the olives to the saucepan and cook uncovered for about 5 minutes to warm through. Season to taste with salt and pepper, and sprinkle over the chopped parsley. Discard any mussels that have not opened, and serve immediately with lots of crusty bread.

INGREDIENTS
Serves 4

4 lbs. mussels
3–4 tbsp. olive oil
1 large onion, peeled and sliced
4 garlic cloves, peeled and finely chopped
1 red chili, seeded and finely chopped
3 14-oz. cans chopped tomatoes
⅔ cup white wine
1 cup ripe olives, halved and pitted
salt and freshly ground black pepper
2 tbsp. freshly chopped parsley
crusty bread, to serve

Food Fact

Arrabbiata sauce is a classic Italian tomato-based sauce, usually containing onions, bell peppers, garlic, and fresh herbs. It needs slow simmering to bring out the flavor and is excellent with meat, poultry, and pasta, as well as seafood.

Tuna Cannelloni

1 Preheat the oven to 375° F. Heat the olive oil in a skillet, and cook the scallions and bell pepper until soft. Remove from the skillet with a slotted spoon and place in a large bowl.

2 Drain the tuna, and mix with the scallions and bell pepper. Beat the ricotta cheese with the lemon zest, lemon juice, and chives, and season to taste with salt and pepper until soft and blended. Add to the tuna and mix together. If the mixture is still a little stiff, add some extra lemon juice.

3 With a teaspoon, carefully spoon the mixture into the cannelloni tubes, then lay the filled tubes in a lightly greased, shallow, ovenproof dish. Beat the egg, cottage cheese, yogurt, and nutmeg together, and pour over the cannelloni. Sprinkle over the shredded mozzarella cheese, and cook in the preheated oven for 15–20 minutes or until the topping is golden brown and bubbling. Serve immediately with a tossed green salad.

INGREDIENTS
Serves 4

1 tbsp. olive oil
6 scallions, trimmed and finely sliced
1 red bell pepper, seeded and finely chopped
7-oz. can tuna in water
9 oz. tub ricotta cheese
1 tbsp. lemon zest
2 tbsp. lemon juice
1 tbsp. freshly cut chives
salt and freshly ground black pepper
8 dried cannelloni tubes
1 medium egg, beaten
¼ cup cottage cheese
½ cup plain yogurt
pinch of freshly grated nutmeg
¼ cup mozzarella cheese, shredded
tossed green salad, to serve

Helpful Hint

It may seem tempting to partly cook the cannelloni tubes before stuffing them, but this makes them too slippery to handle. The moisture in the sauce is sufficient to cook them thoroughly while they are cooking in the oven.

1

2

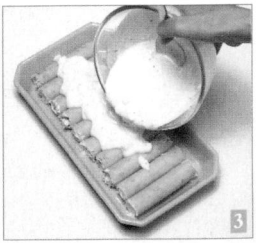
3

Seared Tuna with Italian Salsa

1 Wipe the fish and season lightly with salt and pepper, then place in a shallow dish. Mix together the Pernod, olive oil, lemon zest, lemon juice, thyme, fennel seeds, sun-dried tomatoes, and chili flakes, and pour over the fish. Cover lightly and let marinate for 1–2 hours, occasionally spooning the marinade over the fish.

2 Meanwhile, mix all the ingredients for the salsa together in a small bowl. Season to taste with salt and pepper, cover with plastic wrap, and leave for about 30 minutes to allow the flavors to develop.

3 Lightly oil a griddle pan and heat until hot. When the pan is very hot, drain the fish and set the marinade aside. Cook the fish for 3–4 minutes on each side, taking care not to overcook them—the tuna steaks should be a little pink inside. Pour any remaining marinade into a small saucepan, bring to a boil, and boil for 1 minute. Serve the steaks hot with the marinade and chilled salsa.

INGREDIENTS
Serves 4

4 tuna or swordfish steaks
salt and freshly ground black pepper
3 tbsp. Pernod
2 tbsp. olive oil
1 tbsp. lemon zest
2 tbsp. lemon juice
2 tsp. fresh thyme leaves
2 tsp. fennel seeds, lightly roasted
4 sun-dried tomatoes, chopped
1 tsp. dried chili flakes

FOR THE SALSA:
1 white onion, peeled and finely chopped
2 tomatoes, seeded and sliced
2 tbsp. freshly torn basil leaves
1 red chili, seeded and finely sliced
3 tbsp. extra-virgin olive oil
2 tsp. balsamic vinegar
1 tsp. sugar

Food Fact

The word "salsa" simply means "sauce," but is generally used to indicate a chunky sauce of uncooked vegetables or fruit. If tightly covered and stored in the refrigerator, this salsa should last for five days.

Mediterranean Fish Stew

1 Heat the olive oil in a large saucepan. Add the onion, garlic, fennel, and celery, and cook over a low heat for 15 minutes, stirring frequently, until the vegetables are soft and just beginning to turn brown.

2 Add the canned tomatoes with their juice, the oregano, bay leaf, orange zest, orange juice, and saffron strands. Bring to a boil, reduce the heat, and simmer for 5 minutes. Add the fish stock, vermouth, and season to taste with salt and pepper. Bring to a boil. Reduce the heat and simmer for 20 minutes.

3 Wipe or rinse the haddock and sea bass fillets and remove as many of the bones as possible. Place on a chopping board and cut into 2-inch cubes. Add to the saucepan and cook for 3 minutes. Add the shrimp and cook for an additional 5 minutes. Adjust the seasoning to taste and serve with crusty bread.

Food Fact

In this recipe, saffron is used for color and favor. The flower from which it is grown provides only three stigmas, which must be carefully handpicked and dried, so it is no surprise that it is the world's most expensive spice.

Helpful Hint

Use the list of fish here as a guideline—any combination of fish and shellfish that you prefer will work well in a stew such as this. Try serving with toasted French bread and some homemade mayonnaise or aioli.

INGREDIENTS
Serves 4–6

4 tbsp. olive oil
1 onion, peeled and finely sliced
5 garlic cloves, peeled and finely sliced
1 fennel bulb, trimmed and finely chopped
3 celery stalks, trimmed and finely chopped
14-oz. can chopped tomatoes
1 tbsp. freshly chopped oregano
1 bay leaf
1 tbsp. orange zest
3 tbsp. orange juice
1 tsp. saffron strands
3 cups fish stock
3 tbsp. dry vermouth
salt and freshly ground black pepper
½ lb. thick haddock fillets
½ lb. sea bass fillets
2 cups raw jumbo shrimp, shelled
crusty bread, to serve

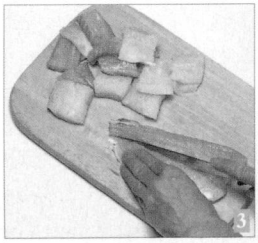

Flounder with Parmesan & Anchovies

1 Preheat the oven to 425° F. Put the flounder on a chopping board, and holding the tail, strip off the skin from both sides. With a filleting knife, fillet the fish, then wipe and set aside.

2 Place the fillets on a large chopping board, skinned-side up, and halve lengthwise along the center. Dot each one with some of the chopped anchovies, then roll up from the thickest end and set aside.

3 Pour boiling water over the spinach, leave for 2 minutes, and drain, squeezing out as much moisture as possible. Place in the base of an ovenproof dish and arrange the tomatoes on top of the spinach. Stand the rolled-up fillets in the dish and pour over the cream.

4 Place the ciabatta and arugula in a food processor, and blend until finely chopped. Stir in the shredded Parmesan cheese.

5 Sprinkle the topping over the fish and cook in the preheated oven for 8–10 minutes, or until the fish is cooked, has lost its translucency, and the topping is golden. Serve with freshly cooked pasta.

INGREDIENTS
Serves 4

4 flounder fillets
4 anchovy fillets, finely chopped
10 cups spinach leaves, rinsed
3 firm tomatoes, sliced
¾ cup heavy cream
5 slices olive ciabatta bread or similar-style bread
1¼ cups arugula
½ cup Parmesan cheese, shredded
freshly cooked pasta, to serve

Helpful Hint

Anchovies can either be preserved in oil (usually olive oil) or salt. If you buy them preserved in oil, simply lift them from the oil and drain on paper towels before using. If you buy salted anchovies, soak them in several changes of water to remove most of the salt before using. Also, season dishes containing anchovies carefully to avoid oversalting.

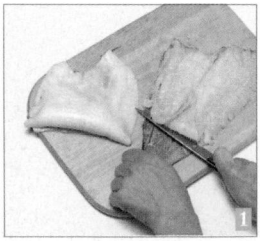
1

2

3

Broiled Red Mullet with Orange & Anchovy Sauce

1 Preheat the broiler and line the broiler rack with foil just before cooking. Peel the oranges with a sharp knife over a bowl in order to catch the juice. Cut into thin slices and set aside. If necessary, make up the juice to ⅔ cup with extra orange juice.

2 Place the fish on a chopping board and make 2 diagonal slashes across the thickest part of both sides of the fish. Season well, both inside and out, with salt and pepper. Tuck a rosemary sprig and a few lemon slices inside the cavity of each fish. Brush the fish with a little of the olive oil and then cook under the preheated broiler for 4–5 minutes on each side. The flesh should just fall away from the bone.

3 Heat the remaining oil in a saucepan, and gently cook the garlic and anchovies for 3–4 minutes. Do not allow to brown. Add the chopped rosemary and plenty of black pepper. The anchovies will be salty enough, so do not add any salt. Stir in the orange slices with their juice and the lemon juice. Simmer gently until heated through. Spoon the sauce over the fish and serve immediately.

INGREDIENTS
Serves 4

2 oranges
4 red mullet, cleaned and scaled
salt and freshly ground black pepper
4 sprigs of fresh rosemary
1 lemon, sliced
2 tbsp. olive oil
2 garlic cloves, peeled and crushed
6 anchovy fillets in oil, drained and coarsely chopped
2 tsp. freshly chopped rosemary
1 tsp. lemon juice

Helpful Hint

Red mullet is a fairly common fish, but size can vary enormously—often only very large fish are available. Substitute gray mullet or snapper, if necessary.

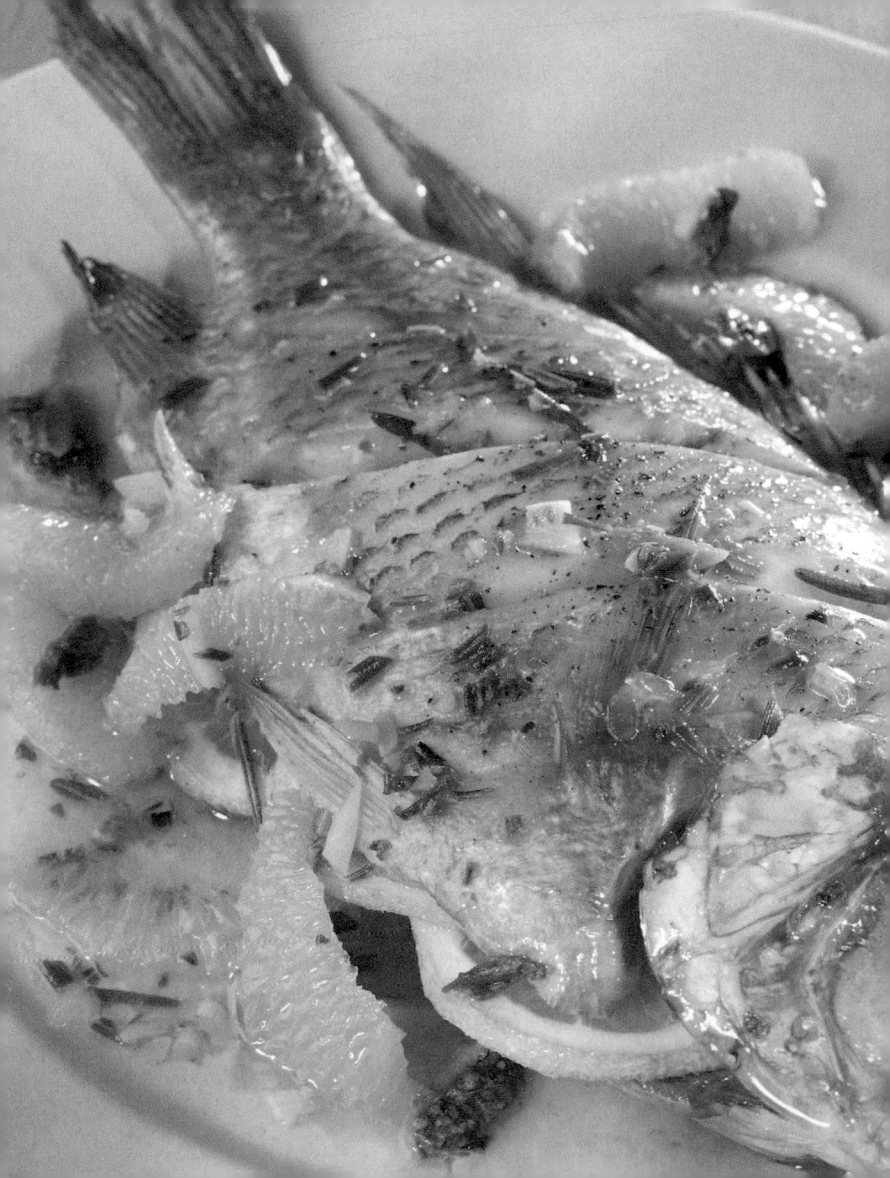

Broiled Snapper with Roasted Bell Pepper

1 Preheat the broiler to a high heat and line the broiler rack with foil. Cut the tops off the bell peppers and divide into quarters. Remove the seeds and the membrane, then place on the foil-lined broiler rack and cook for 8–10 minutes, turning frequently until the skins have become charred and blackened. Remove from the broiler rack, place in a plastic container, and allow to cool. When the bell peppers are cool, strip off the skin, slice thinly, and set aside.

2 Cover the broiler rack with another piece of foil, then place the snapper fillets skin-side up on the broiler rack. Season to taste with salt and pepper and brush with a little of the olive oil. Cook for 10-12 minutes, turning over once and brushing again with a little olive oil.

3 Pour the cream and wine into a small saucepan, bring to a boil, then simmer for about 5 minutes until the sauce has thickened slightly. Add the dill, season to taste, and stir in the sliced bell peppers. Arrange the cooked snapper fillets on warm serving plates, and pour over the cream and pepper sauce. Garnish with sprigs of dill and serve immediately with freshly cooked tagliatelle.

INGREDIENTS
Serves 4

1 medium red bell pepper
1 medium green bell pepper
4–8 snapper fillets, depending on size, about 1 lb. total
sea salt and freshly ground black pepper
1 tbsp. olive oil
⅓ cup heavy cream
½ cup white wine
1 tbsp. freshly chopped dill
sprigs of fresh dill, to garnish
freshly cooked tagliatelle, to serve

Tasty Tip

This dish would be just as tasty with a variety of broiled vegetables—try different-colored bell peppers, red onions, zucchini, and eggplants. Cut into slices or wedges and broil as above. Chop or slice when cool enough to handle.

1

2

3

Pan-Fried Salmon with Herb Risotto

1 Wipe the salmon fillets with a clean, damp cloth. Mix together the flour, mustard powder, and seasoning on a large plate, and use to coat the salmon fillets. Set aside.

2 Heat half the olive oil in a large skillet, and cook the shallots for 5 minutes until softened but not browned. Add the rice and stir for 1 minute, then slowly add the wine, bring to a boil and boil rapidly until reduced by half.

3 Bring the stock to a gentle simmer, then add to the rice, a ladleful at a time. Cook, stirring frequently, adding the stock as needed until the rice is cooked yet firm. Stir in the butter, freshly chopped herbs, and season to taste with salt and pepper.

4 Heat the remaining olive oil and the pat of butter in a large griddle pan, add the salmon fillets, and cook for 2–3 minutes on each side or until done. Arrange the herb risotto on warm serving plates and top with the salmon. Garnish with slices of lemon and sprigs of dill, and serve immediately with a tomato salad.

INGREDIENTS
Serves 4

4 salmon fillets
3–4 tbsp. all-purpose flour
1 tsp. dried mustard powder
salt and freshly ground black pepper
2 tbsp. olive oil
3 shallots, peeled and chopped
1 cup risotto rice
⅔ cup dry white wine
5¼ cups vegetable or fish stock
½ stick butter
2 tbsp. freshly cut chives
2 tbsp. freshly chopped dill
2 tbsp. freshly chopped Italian parsley
pat of butter

TO GARNISH:
lemon slices
sprigs of fresh dill
tomato salad, to serve

Helpful Hint

Stirring the butter into the risotto at the end is an important step—in Italian it is called *mantecare*, possibly from the Spanish *mantequilla*, which means "butter." This final addition of butter gives the risotto its fine texture and a beautiful shine. Serve risotto as soon as it is cooked.

Sea Bass in Creamy Watercress & Prosciutto Sauce

1 Remove the leaves from the watercress stalks and set aside. Chop the stalks coarsely and put in a large saucepan with the stock. Bring to a boil slowly, cover, and simmer for 20 minutes. Strain and discard the stalks. Make the stock up to 1¼ cups with the wine.

2 Bring a large saucepan of lightly salted water to a boil and cook the pasta for 8–10 minutes or until al dente. Drain and set aside.

3 Melt the butter in a saucepan and cook the prosciutto gently for 3 minutes. Remove with a slotted spoon. Stir the flour into the saucepan and cook on a medium heat for 2 minutes. Remove from the heat and gradually pour in the hot watercress stock, stirring continuously. Return to the heat and bring to a boil, stirring throughout. Simmer for 3 minutes or until the sauce has thickened and is smooth. Purée the watercress leaves and cream in a food processor, then add to the sauce with the prosciutto. Season to taste with salt and pepper, add the pasta, toss lightly, and keep warm.

4 Meanwhile, spray a griddle pan lightly with olive oil, then heat until hot. When hot, cook the fillets for 3–4 minutes on each side or until done. Arrange the sea bass on a bed of pasta and drizzle with a little sauce. Garnish with watercress and serve immediately.

INGREDIENTS
Serves 4

2½ cups watercress
2 cups fish or chicken stock
⅔ cup dry white wine
3 cups tagliatelle
½ stick butter
¾ cup prosciutto
2 tbsp. all-purpose flour
1 cup light cream
salt and freshly ground black pepper
olive oil, for spraying
4 sea bass fillets
fresh watercress, to garnish

Helpful Hint

Always wash watercress thoroughly before using, then either dry in a clean dishtowel or a salad spinner to remove all the excess moisture.

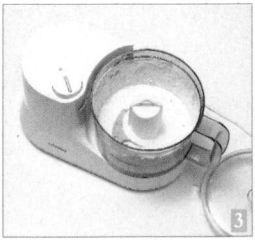

Marinated Mackerel with Tomato & Basil Salad

1 Remove as many of the fine pin bones as possible from the mackerel fillets. Lightly rinse and pat dry the fillets with absorbent paper towels. Place in a shallow dish.

2 Blend all the marinade ingredients together and pour over the mackerel fillets. Make sure the marinade has covered the fish completely. Cover with plastic wrap and leave in a cool place for at least 8 hours, but preferably overnight. As the fillets marinate, they will lose the translucency and look as if they are cooked.

3 Place the tomatoes, watercress, oranges, and mozzarella in a large bowl and toss.

4 To make the dressing, beat the lemon juice with the mustard, sugar, and seasoning in a bowl. Pour over half the dressing, toss again, and then arrange on a serving platter. Remove the mackerel from the marinade, cut into bite-sized pieces, and sprinkle with the torn basil. Arrange on top of the salad, drizzle over the remaining dressing, sprinkle with basil leaves, garnish with a basil sprig, and then serve.

Food Fact

This dish is based on ceviche—thinly sliced, raw fish marinated in lemon juice with other flavorings. Make sure that the fish is absolutely fresh for this dish—use a busy fish merchant, who will have a high turnover and therefore a fresh supply.

INGREDIENTS
Serves 3

3 mackerel, filleted
3 large tomatoes, sliced
2½ cups watercress
2 oranges, peeled and segmented
¼ cup mozzarella cheese, sliced
2 tbsp. basil leaves, torn
sprig of fresh basil, to garnish

FOR THE MARINADE:
½ cup lemon juice
¼ cup olive oil
4 tbsp. basil leaves

FOR THE DRESSING:
1 tbsp. lemon juice
1 tsp. mustard
1 tsp. sugar
salt and freshly ground black pepper
⅓ cup olive oil

Seafood Special

1 Heat the olive oil in a saucepan. Chop half of the garlic, add to the saucepan, and gently cook for 1–2 minutes. Add the calamari, ⅔ cup of the wine, and the tomatoes, and simmer for 10–15 minutes.

2 Chop the remaining garlic, and place with the remaining wine and 2 tablespoons of the parsley in another pan. Add the cleaned mussels to the saucepan, cover, and cook for 7–8 minutes. Discard any mussels that have not opened, then remove the remaining mussels and add to the calamari and tomato mixture. Set the liquid aside.

3 Cut the monkfish and tuna into chunks, and place in the saucepan with the mussels' cooking liquid. Simmer for about 5 minutes or until the fish is just tender.

4 Mix all the cooked fish nd shellfish, with the exception of the shrimp and langoustines, with the tomato mixture and cooking liquid in a large, heavy-based saucepan. Heat everything through until piping hot.

5 Toast the slices of Italian bread and place in the base of a large, shallow serving dish.

6 Pour the fish mixture over the toasted Italian bread and garnish with the shrimp, langoustines, and freshly chopped parsley. Serve immediately.

INGREDIENTS
Serves 4

2 tbsp. olive oil
4 garlic cloves, peeled
1 cup calamari, cut into rings
1¼ cups medium-dry white wine
14-oz. can chopped tomatoes
2 tbsp. fresh parsley, finely chopped
2 cups live mussels, cleaned and beards removed
1 cup monkfish fillet
1 cup fresh tuna
4 slices Italian bread

TO GARNISH:
2 cups large, unshelled shrimp, cooked
4 langoustines, cooked
3 tbsp. freshly chopped parsley

Tasty Tip

This dish requires a well-flavored bread—use a good quality ciabatta or Pugliese loaf from an Italian delicatessen.

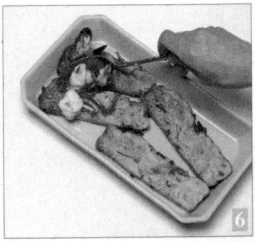

Farfalle with Smoked Trout in a Dill & Vodka Sauce

1 Bring a large pan of lightly salted water to a rolling boil. Add the pasta and cook according to the package directions or until al dente.

2 Meanwhile, cut the smoked trout into thin slivers, using scissors. Sprinkle lightly with the lemon juice and set aside.

3 Place the cream, mustard, chopped dill, and vodka in a small pan. Season lightly with salt and pepper. Bring the contents of the pan to a boil and simmer gently for 2-3 minutes or until slightly thickened.

4 Drain the cooked pasta thoroughly, then return to the pan. Add the smoked trout to the dill and vodka sauce, then pour over the pasta. Toss gently until the pasta is coated and the trout evenly mixed.

5 Spoon into a warmed serving dish or onto individual plates. Garnish with sprigs of dill and serve immediately.

INGREDIENTS
Serves 4

3½ cups farfalle
5 oz. smoked trout
2 tsp. lemon juice
about ¼ cup heavy cream
2 tsp. whole-grain mustard
2 tbsp. freshly chopped dill
4 tbsp. vodka
salt and freshly ground black pepper
sprigs of dill, to garnish

Food Fact

Two types of smoked trout are available. One resembles smoked salmon in color, texture, and flavor, and can be cut into thin slivers as shown here. Equally delicious is hot smoked rainbow trout, which is available as a whole fish or in fillets. These should be skinned and the bones removed before use. The flesh can then be broken into large flakes. Smoked salmon would also be nice in this recipe.

Pappardelle with Smoked Haddock & Blue Cheese Sauce

1 Place the smoked haddock in a pan with 1 bay leaf and pour in the milk. Bring to a boil slowly, cover and simmer for 6–7 minutes or until the fish is opaque. Remove and roughly flake the fish, discarding the skin and any bones. Strain the milk and set aside.

2 Bring a large pan of lightly salted water to a rolling boil. Add the pasta and cook according to the package directions or until al dente.

3 Meanwhile, put the butter, flour, and cream (or milk, if preferred) in a pan and stir to mix. Stir in the reserved warm milk and add the remaining bay leaf. Bring to a boil, whisking all the time until smooth and thick. Gently simmer for 3–4 minutes, stirring frequently. Discard the bay leaf.

4 Add the Dolcelatte or Gorgonzola cheese to the sauce. Heat gently, stirring until melted. Add the flaked haddock and season to taste with nutmeg and salt and pepper.

5 Drain the pasta thoroughly and return to the pan. Add the sauce and toss gently to coat, taking care not to break up the flakes of fish. Spoon into a warmed serving bowl, sprinkle with toasted walnuts and parsley, and serve immediately.

INGREDIENTS
Serves 4

12 oz. smoked haddock
2 bay leaves
1¼ cups milk
14 oz. pappardelle or tagliatelle
2 tbsp. butter
¼ cup all-purpose flour
⅔ cup light cream or extra milk
4 oz. Dolcelatte or Gorgonzola cheese, cut into small pieces
¼ tsp. freshly grated nutmeg
salt and freshly ground black pepper
⅓ cup chopped toasted walnuts
1 tbsp. freshly chopped parsley

Tasty Tip

Dolcelatte is an Italian, semisoft, blue-veined cheese made from cows' milk. It has a smooth creamy texture and a delicate taste. For a more strongly flavored blue cheese sauce, a young Gorgonzola, Roquefort, or blue Stilton can be used instead.

Special Seafood Lasagna

1 Preheat the oven to 400° F. Place the haddock in a pan with the wine, fish stock, onion, and bay leaf. Bring to a boil slowly, cover, and simmer gently for 5 minutes or until the fish is opaque. Remove and flake the fish, discarding any bones. Strain the cooking juices and set aside.

2 Melt ½ stick of the butter in a large saucepan. Add the leeks and garlic, and cook gently for 10 minutes. Remove from the pan using a slotted spoon, and set aside.

3 Melt the remaining butter in a small pan. Stir in the flour, then gradually whisk in the cream, off the heat, followed by the reserved cooking juices. Bring to a boil slowly, whisking until thickened. Stir in the dill and season to taste with salt and pepper.

4 Spoon a little of the sauce into the base of a buttered, shallow, ovenproof dish. Top with a layer of lasagna, followed by the haddock, seafood cocktail, and leeks. Spoon over enough sauce to cover. Continue layering up, finishing with sheets of lasagna topped with sauce.

5 Sprinkle over the grated Gruyère cheese and bake in the preheated oven for 40–45 minutes or until golden brown and bubbling. Serve immediately.

INGREDIENTS
Serves 4–6

1 lb. fresh haddock fillet, skinned
⅔ cup dry white wine
⅔ cup fish stock
½ onion, peeled and thickly sliced
1 bay leaf
¼ stick butter
2 cups trimmed and thickly sliced leeks
1 garlic clove, peeled and crushed
¼ cup all-purpose flour
⅔ cup light cream
2 tbsp. freshly chopped dill
salt and freshly ground black pepper
8–12 sheets dried lasagna verde, cooked
1½ cups ready-cooked seafood cocktail
½ cup grated Gruyère cheese

Helpful Hint

Cook the lasagna in a large pan of boiling salted water with 1 teaspoon olive oil for about 7 minutes, or according to the package directions. Do this even if using pasta labeled pre-cooked. Drain thoroughly and rinse briefly under cold water.

Tuna & Macaroni Timbales

1 Preheat the oven to 350° F. Oil and line the bases of 4 individual timbales or ovenproof molds with nonstick baking parchment and stand in a small roasting pan.

2 Bring a large pan of lightly salted water to a rolling boil. Add the macaroni and cook according to the package directions or until al dente. Drain the cooked pasta thoroughly.

3 Flake the tuna and mix with the macaroni. Divide between the timbales or molds.

4 Pour the light and heavy cream into a small pan. Bring to a boil slowly, remove from the heat, and stir in the Gruyère cheese until melted. Leave to cool for 1–2 minutes, then whisk into the beaten egg and season lightly with salt and pepper. Pour the mixture over the tuna and macaroni and cover each timbale with a small piece of foil.

5 Pour enough hot water into the roasting pan to come halfway up the timbales. Place in the preheated oven and cook for 25 minutes. Remove the timbales from the water and leave to stand for 5 minutes.

6 For the tomato dressing, whisk together the mustard and vinegar in a small bowl, using a fork. Gradually whisk in the sunflower and nut oils, then stir in the chopped tomatoes and the snipped chives.

7 Unmold the timbales onto warmed serving plates and spoon the tomato dressing over the top and around the bottom. Garnish with fresh chives and serve immediately.

INGREDIENTS
Serves 4

1 cup macaroni
7-oz. can tuna in water, drained
⅔ cup light cream
⅔ cup heavy cream
½ cup grated Gruyère cheese
3 medium eggs, lightly beaten
salt and freshly ground black pepper
fresh chives, to garnish

FRESH TOMATO DRESSING:

1 tsp. Dijon mustard
1 tsp. red wine vinegar
2 tbsp. sunflower oil
1 tbsp. hazelnut or walnut oil
1¼ cups firm ripe tomatoes, skinned, deseeded, and chopped
2 tbsp. freshly snipped chives

Tasty Tip

Other fish can be used to make these pasta timbales. Try a 7-oz. can of white crabmeat, rinsed and drained, or pink salmon with all the bones removed.

Saucy Cod & Pasta Bake

1 Preheat the oven to 400° F. Cut the cod into bite-sized pieces and set aside.

2 Heat the sunflower oil in a large pan. Add the onion and bacon and cook for 7–8 minutes. Add the mushrooms and celery, and cook for 5 minutes or until fairly soft.

3 Add the zucchini and tomatoes to the bacon mixture, and pour in the fish stock or wine. Bring to a boil, then simmer uncovered for 5 minutes or until the sauce has thickened slightly. Remove from the heat and stir in the cod pieces and the tarragon. Season with salt and pepper, then spoon into a large, greased baking dish.

4 Meanwhile, bring a large pan of lightly salted water to a rolling boil. Add the pasta shells and cook according to the package directions or until al dente.

5 For the topping, place the butter and flour in a pan, and pour in the milk. Bring to a boil slowly, whisking until thickened and smooth.

6 Drain the pasta thoroughly and stir into the sauce. Spoon carefully over the fish and vegetables. Place in the preheated oven and bake for 20–25 minutes or until the top is lightly browned and bubbling.

Helpful Hint

If you are short of time, you can make a simpler topping. Beat together 2 eggs, 3 tablespoons of plain yogurt, and 3 tablespoons of heavy cream; season to taste with salt and pepper. Add the drained pasta and mix well. Spoon on top of the fish and vegetables, and bake as above for 15–20 minutes or until the top is set and golden brown.

INGREDIENTS
Serves 4

1 lb. cod fillets, skinned
2 tbsp. sunflower oil
1 onion, peeled and chopped
4 slices smoked bacon, rind removed and chopped
1½ cups wiped baby button mushrooms
2 celery stalks, trimmed and thinly sliced
2 small zucchini, halved lengthwise and sliced
14-oz. can chopped tomatoes
7 tbsp. fish stock or dry white wine
1 tbsp. freshly chopped tarragon
salt and freshly ground black pepper

PASTA TOPPING:
2–2½ cups pasta shells
2 tbsp. butter
4 tbsp all-purpose flour
1½ cups milk

Pasta Provençale

1 Heat the olive oil in a large pan. Add the garlic and onion, and cook gently for 5 minutes. Add the fennel and cook for an additional 5 minutes. Stir in the chopped tomatoes and rosemary sprig. Half-cover the pan and simmer for 10 minutes.

2 Cut the monkfish into bite-sized pieces and sprinkle with the lemon juice. Add to the tomatoes, cover, and simmer gently for 5 minutes or until the fish is opaque.

3 Meanwhile, bring a large pan of lightly salted water to a rolling boil. Add the pasta and cook according to the package directions or until al dente. Drain the pasta thoroughly and return to the saucepan.

4 Remove the rosemary from the tomato sauce. Stir in the black olives, flageolet beans, and chopped oregano, then season to taste with salt and pepper. Add the sauce to the pasta and toss gently together to coat, taking care not to break up the monkfish. Spoon into a warmed serving bowl. Garnish with rosemary and oregano sprigs, and serve immediately.

INGREDIENTS
Serves 4

2 tbsp. olive oil
1 garlic clove, peeled and crushed
1 onion, peeled and finely chopped
1 small fennel bulb, trimmed, halved, and thinly sliced
14-oz. can chopped tomatoes
1 rosemary sprig, plus extra sprig to garnish
12 oz. monkfish, skinned
2 tsp. lemon juice
3½ cups gnocchi pasta
½ cup pitted black olives
7-oz. can flageolet beans, drained and rinsed
1 tbsp. freshly chopped oregano, plus sprig to garnish
salt and freshly ground black pepper

Helpful Hint

Only the tail of the monkfish is eaten and this is usually sold skinned. It has a firm, very white, meaty flesh and a delicious seafood taste, earning it the nickname "poorman's lobster." It may still have a tough transparent membrane covering it, which should be carefully removed before cooking.

Seared Salmon & Lemon Linguine

1 Brush the salmon fillets with the sunflower oil, sprinkle with crushed peppercorns, and press on firmly. Set aside.

2 Bring a large pan of lightly salted water to a rolling boil. Add the linguine and cook according to the package directions or until al dente.

3 Meanwhile, melt the butter in a pan and cook the shredded scallions gently for 2–3 minutes or until soft. Stir in the sour cream and the lemon zest, and remove from the heat.

4 Preheat a griddle or heavy-based skillet until very hot. Add the salmon and sear for 1½–2 minutes on each side. Remove from the pan and leave to cool slightly.

5 Bring the sour cream sauce to a boil, and stir in the Parmesan cheese and lemon juice. Drain the pasta thoroughly and return to the pan. Pour over the sauce and toss gently to coat.

6 Spoon the pasta onto warmed serving plates and top with the salmon fillets. Serve immediately with sprigs of dill and lemon slices.

Helpful Hint

For a less rich and lower-fat version of the sauce, use plain yogurt instead, but do not boil as in step 5. Instead, heat gently with the Parmesan cheese until the cheese melts, then pour over the pasta and toss to coat in the sauce, as above.

INGREDIENTS
Serves 4

4 small skinless salmon fillets, each about 3 oz.
2 tsp. sunflower oil
½ tsp. mixed or black peppercorns, crushed
14 oz. linguine
1 tbsp. unsalted butter
1 bunch scallions, trimmed and shredded
1¼ cups sour cream
zest of 1 lemon, finely grated
½ cup freshly grated Parmesan cheese
1 tbsp. lemon juice
pinch of salt

TO GARNISH:
dill sprigs
lemon slices

Tagliatelle with Tuna & Anchovy Tapenade

1 Bring a large pan of lightly salted water to a rolling boil. Add the tagliatelle and cook according to the package directions or until al dente.

2 Meanwhile, place the tuna, anchovy fillets, olives, and capers in a food processor with the lemon juice and 2 tablespoons of the olive oil, and blend for a few seconds until coarsely chopped.

3 With the motor running, pour in the remaining olive oil in a steady stream; the resulting mixture should be slightly chunky rather than smooth.

4 Spoon the sauce into a bowl. Stir in the chopped parsley and season to taste with black pepper. Check the taste of the sauce and add a little more lemon juice, if needed.

5 Drain the pasta thoroughly. Pour the sauce into the pan and cook over a low heat for 1–2 minutes to warm through.

6 Return the drained pasta to the pan and mix together with the sauce. Spoon into a warmed serving bowl or onto warm individual plates. Garnish with sprigs of Italian parsley and serve immediately.

INGREDIENTS
Serves 4

14 oz. tagliatelle
4-oz. can tuna in oil, drained
2-oz. can anchovy fillets, drained
1¼ cups pitted black olives
2 tbsp. capers in brine, drained
2 tsp. lemon juice
7 tbsp. olive oil
2 tbsp. freshly chopped parsley
freshly ground black pepper
sprigs of Italian parsley, to garnish

Food Fact

Capers are the flower buds of the caper bush, which grows throughout the Mediterranean region. The buds are picked before they open and preserved in vinegar and salt. The word "tapenade" (a mixture of capers, olives, and fish—usually anchovies—pounded to a paste with olive oil) comes from the Provençal word for capers—*tapeno*.

Hot Shrimp Noodles with Sesame Dressing

1 Pour the vegetable stock into a large saucepan and bring to a boil. Add the egg noodles, stir once, then cook according to the package directions, usually about 3 minutes.

2 Meanwhile, heat the sunflower oil in a small skillet. Add the chopped garlic and chili and cook gently for a few seconds. Add the sesame seeds and cook, stirring continuously, for 1 minute or until golden.

3 Add the soy sauce, sesame oil, and shrimp to the skillet. Continue cooking for a few seconds until the mixture starts to bubble, then remove immediately from the heat.

4 Drain the noodles thoroughly and return to the pan. Add the shrimp in the dressing mixture, then the chopped cilantro, and season to taste with black pepper. Toss gently to coat the noodles with the hot dressing.

5 Spoon into a warmed serving bowl or onto individual plates and serve immediately, garnished with sprigs of fresh cilantro.

INGREDIENTS
Serves 4

2½ cups vegetable stock
12 oz. Chinese egg noodles
1 tbsp. sunflower oil
1 garlic clove, peeled and very finely chopped
1 red chili, deseeded and finely chopped
3 tbsp. sesame seeds
3 tbsp. dark soy sauce
2 tbsp. sesame oil
1½ cups shelled cooked shrimp
3 tbsp. freshly chopped cilantro
freshly ground black pepper
fresh cilantro sprigs, to garnish

Food Fact

There are two types of sesame oil that are frequently featured in Asian cooking: the pale and light version, made from untoasted seeds, and the rich dark kind, made from toasted seeds. The latter has a very strong nutty flavor, which can be overpowering in large quantities. If you use the toasted variety in the dressing for this dish, use just 1 tablespoon mixed together with 1 tablespoon of peanut or sunflower oil.

Pan-fried Scallops & Pasta

1 Rinse the scallops and pat dry on paper towels. Place in a bowl and add the olive oil, crushed garlic, and thyme. Cover with plastic wrap and chill in the refrigerator until ready to cook.

2 Bring a large pan of lightly salted water to a rolling boil. Add the penne and cook according to the package directions or until al dente.

3 Meanwhile, make the dressing. Place the sun-dried tomatoes in a small bowl or glass jar and add the vinegars, tomato paste, sugar, salt, and pepper. Whisk well, then pour into a food processor.

4 With the motor running, pour in the sun-dried tomato oil and olive oil in a steady stream to make a thick, smooth dressing.

5 Preheat a large, dry cast-iron griddle pan over a high heat for about 5 minutes. Lower the heat to medium, then add the scallops to the pan. Cook for 1½ minutes on each side. Remove from the pan.

6 Drain the pasta thoroughly and return to the pan. Add the sliced sun-dried tomatoes and dressing, and toss. Divide between individual serving plates. Top each portion with 4 scallops, garnish with fresh thyme or oregano sprigs, and serve immediately.

Handy Hint

Try to buy ready-shelled fresh scallops. If you buy in shells, follow this quick and simple method of opening them. Preheat the oven to 300° F. Place the scallops on a baking sheet, rounded-side down, and put in the oven for about 10 minutes or until the shells just open. When pan-frying the scallops, take care not to overcook them, or they will toughen and lose their moist, tender texture.

INGREDIENTS
Serves 4

16 large scallops, shelled
1 tbsp. olive oil
1 garlic clove, peeled and crushed
1 tsp. freshly chopped thyme
3½ cups penne
4 sun-dried tomatoes in oil, drained and thinly sliced
thyme or oregano sprigs, to garnish

TOMATO DRESSING:
2 sun-dried tomatoes in oil, drained and chopped
1 tbsp. red wine vinegar
2 tsp. balsamic vinegar
1 tsp. sun-dried tomato paste
1 tsp. sugar
salt and freshly ground black pepper
2 tbsp. oil from a jar of sun-dried tomatoes
2 tbsp. olive oil

Smoked Mackerel & Pasta Frittata

1 Preheat the broiler to high just before cooking. Bring a pan of lightly salted water to a rolling boil. Add the pasta and cook according to the package directions or until al dente. Drain thoroughly and set aside.

2 Remove the skin from the mackerel and break the fish into large flakes, discarding any bones, and set aside.

3 Place the eggs, milk, mustard, and parsley in a bowl and whisk together. Season with salt and plenty of freshly ground black pepper, and set aside.

4 Melt the butter in a large, heavy-based skillet. Cook the scallions gently for 3–4 minutes, until soft. Pour in the egg mixture, then add the drained pasta, peas, and half of the mackerel.

5 Gently stir the mixture in the pan for 1–2 minutes or until beginning to set. Stop stirring and cook for about 1 minute until the underneath is golden brown.

6 Spread the remaining mackerel over the frittata, followed by the grated cheese. Place under the preheated broiler for about 1½ minutes or until golden brown and set. Cut into wedges and serve immediately with salad and crusty bread.

INGREDIENTS
Serves 4

¼ cup tricolor pasta spirals or shells
8 oz. smoked mackerel (or salmon)
6 medium eggs
3 tbsp. milk
2 tsp. whole-grain mustard
2 tbsp. freshly chopped parsley
salt and freshly ground black pepper
2 tbsp. unsalted butter
6 scallions, trimmed and diagonally sliced
2 oz. frozen peas, thawed
¼ cup grated sharp cheddar cheese

TO SERVE:
green salad
warm crusty bread

Food Fact

A frittata is a thick-set Italian omelette, similar to the Spanish tortilla, which may be served hot or cold, cut into wedges or fingers. To ensure even cooking, it should be cooked very slowly over a low heat and gently stirred only until the mixture starts to set.

Crispy Cod Cannelloni

1 Add 1 teaspoon of the olive oil to a large pan of lightly salted water and bring to a rolling boil. Add the cannelloni tubes and cook uncovered for 5 minutes. Drain and leave in a bowl of cold water.

2 Melt the butter with the remaining oil in a pan. Add the mushrooms and leeks, and cook gently for 5 minutes. Turn up the heat, and cook for 1–2 minutes or until the mixture is fairly dry. Add the cod and cook, stirring, for 2–3 minutes or until the fish is opaque.

3 Add the cream cheese to the pan and stir until melted. Season to taste with salt and pepper, then let the cod mixture cool.

4 Drain the cannelloni. Using a pastry bag without a tip or a spoon, fill the cannelloni with the cod mixture.

5 Mix the Parmesan cheese and bread crumbs together on a plate. Dip the filled cannelloni into the flour, then into the beaten egg, and finally into the bread crumb mixture. Dip the ends twice to ensure they are thoroughly coated. Refrigerate for 30 minutes.

6 Heat the oil for deep frying to 350° F. Fry the stuffed cannelloni in batches for 2–3 minutes or until the coating is crisp and golden brown. Drain on paper towels and serve immediately with fresh herbs or salad leaves.

INGREDIENTS
Serves 4

1 tbsp. olive oil
8 dried cannelloni tubes
2 tbsp. unsalted butter
2½ cups thinly sliced button mushrooms
1 cup trimmed and finely chopped leeks
2 cups skinned and diced cod
¼ cup cream cheese
salt and freshly ground black pepper
2 tbsp. grated Parmesan cheese
1 cup fine fresh white bread crumbs
3 tbsp. all-purpose flour
1 medium egg, lightly beaten
oil for deep-frying
fresh herbs or salad leaves, to serve

Handy Hint

Use a deep, heavy-based pan or a deep-fat fryer for deep-frying. Fill the pan to no more than one-third full with oil. If you do not have a food thermometer to check the oil's temperature, test by dropping in a cube of stale bread; if the oil is hot enough, it will turn golden brown in 40 seconds.

Spaghetti alle Vongole

1 Soak the clams in lightly salted cold water for 8 hours before needed, changing the water once or twice. Scrub the clams, discarding any that have broken shells or that remain open when tapped.

2 Place the prepared clams in a large saucepan and pour in the wine. Cover with a tight-fitting lid and cook over medium heat for 5–6 minutes, shaking the pan occasionally until the shells have opened.

3 Strain the clams and cooking juices through a sieve lined with cheesecloth and set aside. Discard any clams that remain unopened.

4 Heat the olive oil in a pan, and fry the onion and garlic gently for 10 minutes or until very soft.

5 Meanwhile, bring a large pan of lightly salted water to a boil. Add the spaghetti and cook according to the package directions or until al dente.

6 Add the cooked clams to the onions and garlic, and pour in the cooking juices. Bring to a boil, then add the parsley and basil and season to taste with salt and black pepper.

7 Drain the spaghetti thoroughly. Return to the pan and add the clams with their sauce. Toss together gently, then spoon into a large warmed serving bowl or into individual bowls. Serve immediately, sprinkled with oregano leaves.

INGREDIENTS
Serves 4

4 lbs. small fresh clams
6 tbsp. dry white wine
2 tbsp. olive oil
1 small onion, peeled and finely chopped
2 garlic cloves, peeled and crushed
14 oz. spaghetti
2 tbsp. freshly chopped parsley
2 tbsp. freshly chopped or torn basil
salt and freshly ground black pepper
oregano leaves, to garnish

Handy Hint

Cook and eat clams within 24 hours of buying them. Steam them until the shells have just opened, as overcooking will toughen them.

Seafood Pockets with Pappardelle & Cilantro Pesto

1 Preheat the oven to 350° F. To make the pesto, blend the cilantro leaves, garlic, pine nuts, and lemon juice with 1 tablespoon of the olive oil to a smooth paste in a food processor. With the motor running, slowly add the remaining oil. Stir the Parmesan cheese into the pesto, and season to taste with salt and pepper.

2 Bring a pan of lightly salted water to a rolling boil. Add the pasta and cook for 3 minutes only. Drain thoroughly, return to the pan, and spoon over two thirds of the pesto. Toss to coat.

3 Cut out 4 rounds, about 12 inches in diameter, from nonstick baking parchment. Spoon the pasta onto one half of each round. Top each pile of pasta with 2 shrimp, 3 scallops, and a few squid rings. Spoon 1 tablespoon of wine over each serving, then drizzle with the remaining cilantro pesto and top with a slice of lemon.

4 Close the pockets by folding over the other half of the paper to make a semicircle, then turn and twist the edges of the paper to secure.

5 Place the pockets on a baking sheet and bake in the preheated oven for 15 minutes. Serve immediately, letting each person open their own.

INGREDIENTS
Serves 4

11 oz. pappardelle or tagliatelle
8 raw jumbo shrimp, shelled
12 raw bay scallops
8 oz. baby squid, cleaned and cut into rings
4 tbsp. dry white wine
4 thin slices of lemon

CILANTRO PESTO:
1 cup fresh cilantro leaves
1 garlic clove, peeled
¼ cup toasted pine nuts
1 tsp. lemon juice
5 tbsp. olive oil
1 tbsp. grated Parmesan cheese
salt and freshly ground black pepper

Helpful Hint

Prepare whole squid by firmly pulling the pouch and tentacles apart. Remove the transparent quill from the pouch and discard. Rinse the pouch under cold running water, then peel off the dark skin and discard. Slice the pouch and tentacles into rings.

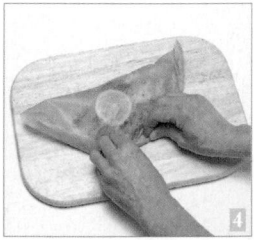

Pasta & Mussels in Tomato & Wine Sauce

1 Scrub the mussels and remove any beards. Discard any that do not close when lightly tapped. Place in a large pan with the bay leaf and pour in the wine. Cover with a tight-fitting lid and steam, shaking the pan occasionally, for 3–4 minutes or until the mussels open. Remove the mussels with a slotted spoon, discarding any that have not opened, and set aside. Strain the cooking liquid through a cheesecloth-lined sieve and set aside.

2 Melt the butter with the oil in a large pan, and gently cook the onion and garlic for 10 minutes until soft. Add the cooking liquid and the tomatoes and simmer uncovered for 6–7 minutes or until soft and the sauce has reduced slightly.

3 Meanwhile, bring a large pan of lightly salted water to a rolling boil. Add the pasta and cook acording to the package directions or until al dente.

4 Drain the pasta thoroughly and return to the pan. Add the mussels, removing the shells if you prefer, with the tomato sauce. Stir in the basil and season to taste with salt and pepper. Toss together gently. Spoon into warmed serving bowls. Garnish with basil leaves and serve with crusty bread.

INGREDIENTS
Serves 4

2 lb. fresh live mussels
1 bay leaf
⅔ cup light red wine
1 tbsp. unsalted butter
1 tbsp. olive oil
1 red onion, peeled and thinly sliced
2 garlic cloves, peeled and crushed
1¼ cups ripe tomatoes, skinned, deseeded, and chopped
3½ cups fiochetti or penne
3 tbsp. freshly chopped or torn basil
salt and freshly ground black pepper
basil leaves, to garnish
crusty bread, to serve

Helpful Hint

Some fish sellers still offer mussels by volume rather than weight: 2¼ pints is the equivalent of 2 pounds. If you are not cooking mussels within a few hours of buying them, store in a bowl of water in a cold place or in the warmest part of the refrigerator on a hot day. Do not add anything to the water.

Salmon & Spaghetti in a Creamy Egg Sauce

1 Beat the eggs in a bowl with the parsley, dill, half of the Parmesan and pecorino cheeses, and the white wine. Season to taste with freshly ground black pepper and set aside.

2 Bring a large pan of lightly salted water to a rolling boil. Add the spaghetti and cook according to the package directions or until al dente.

3 Meanwhile, cut the salmon into bite-size pieces. Melt the butter in a large skillet with the oil and cook the salmon for 3–4 minutes or until opaque.

4 Drain the spaghetti thoroughly, return to the pan, and immediately add the egg mixture. Remove from the heat and toss well; the eggs will cook in the heat of the spaghetti to make a creamy sauce.

5 Stir in the remaining cheeses and the cooked pieces of salmon, and toss again. Spoon into a warmed serving bowl or onto individual plates. Garnish with sprigs of Italian parsley and serve immediately.

INGREDIENTS
Serves 4

3 medium eggs
1 tbsp. freshly chopped parsley
1 tbsp. freshly chopped dill
½ cup freshly grated Parmesan cheese
½ cup freshly grated pecorino cheese
2 tbsp. dry white wine
freshly ground black pepper
14 oz. spaghetti
12 oz. salmon fillet, skinned
2 tbsp. butter
1 tsp. olive oil
Italian parsley sprigs, to garnish

Food Fact

This recipe is based on the classic spaghetti alla carbonara, which is made with smoked bacon or pancetta. Here, fresh salmon makes an equally delicious alternative. Make sure that you remove the spaghetti from the heat before adding the egg mixture and keep turning the spaghetti until the eggs cook to a light creamy sauce.

Helpful Hint

You will not need to add salt in this recipe, as the pecorino cheese is very salty.

Creamy Coconut Seafood Pasta

1 Bring a large pan of lightly salted water to a rolling boil. Add the pasta and cook according to the package directions or until al dente.

2 Meanwhile, heat the sunflower and sesame oils together in a saucepan. Add the scallions, garlic, chili, and ginger, and cook for 3–4 minutes or until softened.

3 Blend the coconut milk and cream together in a pitcher. Add the shrimp and crab meat to the pan, and stir over a low heat for a few seconds. Gradually pour in the coconut cream, stirring all the time.

4 Stir the chopped cilantro into the seafood sauce and season to taste with salt and pepper. Continue heating the sauce gently until piping hot, but do not let it boil.

5 Drain the pasta thoroughly and return to the pan. Add the seafood sauce and gently toss together to coat the pasta. Spoon into a warmed serving dish or onto individual plates. Serve immediately, garnished with fresh cilantro sprigs.

INGREDIENTS
Serves 4

14 oz. egg tagliatelle
1 tsp. sunflower oil
1 tsp. sesame oil
4 scallions, trimmed and sliced diagonally
1 garlic clove, peeled and crushed
1 red chili, deseeded and finely chopped
1-in. piece fresh ginger, peeled and grated
⅔ cup coconut milk
7 tbsp. heavy cream
2 cups cooked, shelled jumbo shrimp
1½ cups fresh white crab meat
2 tbsp. freshly chopped cilantro, plus sprigs to garnish
salt and freshly ground black pepper

Helpful Hint

Coconut milk can either be bought in cans or you can make it yourself if you prefer. Put 1 cup natural coconut into a food processor or blender with 1 cup boiling water, and process for 30 seconds. Leave to cool for 5 minutes, then pour into a sieve lined with cheesecloth over a bowl. Leave to drain for a few minutes, then squeeze out as much liquid as possible. Discard the coconut.

Fettuccine with Sardines & Spinach

1 Drain the sardines and cut in half lengthwise. Remove the bones, then cut the fish into 1-inch pieces.

2 Bring a large pan of lightly salted water to a rolling boil. Add the pasta and cook according to the package directions or until al dente.

3 Meanwhile, melt half the butter with the olive oil in a large pan. Add the bread crumbs and fry, stirring until they begin to turn crisp. Add the garlic and pine nuts, and continue to cook until golden brown. Remove from the pan and set aside. Wipe the pan clean.

4 Melt the remaining butter in the pan. Add the mushrooms and cook for 4–5 minutes or until soft. Add the spinach and cook, stirring for 1 minute or until they begin to wilt. Stir in the crème fraîche and lemon zest, and bring to a boil. Simmer gently until the spinach is just cooked. Season the sauce to taste with salt and pepper.

5 Drain the pasta thoroughly and return to the pan. Add the spinach sauce and sardine pieces, and gently toss together. Spoon into a warmed serving dish. Sprinkle with the toasted bread crumbs and pine nuts, and serve immediately.

INGREDIENTS
Serves 4

4-oz. can sardines in olive oil
14 oz. fettuccine or tagliarini
1½ tbsp. butter
2 tbsp. olive oil
1 cup day-old white bread crumbs
1 garlic clove, peeled and finely chopped
½ cup pine nuts
1-1¼cup chestnut mushrooms, wiped and sliced
1½ cups baby spinach leaves, rinsed
⅔ cup crème fraîche
zest of 1 lemon, finely grated
salt and freshly ground black pepper

Helpful Hint

Choose a full-fat crème fraîche for this recipe rather than half-fat, otherwise it may curdle. Alternatively, use sour cream if you prefer. Other canned fish, such as mackerel fillets, may be substituted for the sardines, but when you buy them, check that they are packed in oil.

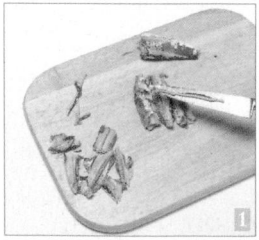

Sweet-and-Sour Fish with Crispy Noodles

1 Cut the flounder fillets into 2-inch slices. Mix the flour with the five-spice powder in a bowl. Add the fish, a few pieces at a time, and toss to coat thoroughly. Set aside.

2 Put the ginger, scallions, sherry, soy sauce, sugar, vinegar, and chili sauce in a small pan and season lightly with salt and pepper. Heat gently until the sugar has dissolved, then simmer the sauce for 2–3 minutes.

3 Break the noodles into pieces about 3 inches long. Heat the oil in a deep fryer to 350° F. Deep-fry small handfuls of noodles for about 30 seconds until puffed up and crisp. Remove and drain on paper towels.

4 Deep-fry the flounder for 1-2 minutes or until firm and cooked. Remove and drain on paper towels.

5 Place the cooked fish in a warmed serving bowl. Drizzle the sauce over the fish, and garnish with scallion tassels and slices of red chili. Pile the noodles into another bowl and serve immediately.

INGREDIENTS
Serves 4

12 oz. flounder fillets, skinned
3 tbsp. all-purpose flour
pinch of Chinese five-spice powder
1-in. piece fresh ginger, peeled and grated
4 scallions, trimmed and finely sliced
3 tbsp. dry sherry
1 tbsp. dark soy sauce
2 tsp. soft light brown sugar
1 tsp. rice or sherry vinegar
1 tsp. chili sauce
salt and freshly ground black pepper
4 oz. thin, transparent rice noodles or rice sticks
oil for deep-frying

TO GARNISH:
scallion tassels
slices of red chili

Food Fact

Chinese five-spice powder adds a taste not unlike licorice to this dish. It is made from a mixture of Szechuan pepper, cloves, cassia, fennel, and star anise, ground together to make a golden-brown powder. Add just a tiny pinch, as it has a powerful flavor.

2

3

4

Warm Swordfish Niçoise

1 Place the swordfish steaks in a shallow dish. Mix the lime juice with the oil, and season to taste with salt and pepper. Spoon over the steaks and turn them to coat them evenly. Cover and place in the refrigerator to marinate for 1 hour.

2 Bring a large pan of lightly salted water to a rolling boil. Add the farfalle and cook according to the package directions or until al dente. Add the green beans about 4 minutes before the end of cooking time.

3 Mix the mustard, vinegar, and sugar together in a small jug. Gradually whisk in the olive oil to make a thick dressing.

4 Cook the swordfish in a griddle pan or under a hot preheated broiler for 2 minutes on each side or until just cooked through; overcooking will make it tough and dry. Remove and cut into ¾-inch chunks.

5 Drain the pasta and beans thoroughly and place in a large bowl. Pour over the dressing and toss to coat. Add the cooked swordfish, tomatoes, olives, hard-boiled eggs, and anchovy fillets. Gently toss together, taking care not to break up the eggs.

6 Spoon into a warmed serving bowl or divide the pasta between individual plates. Serve immediately.

INGREDIENTS
Serves 4

4 swordfish steaks, about 1 in. thick, weighing about 6 oz. each
juice of 1 lime
2 tbsp. olive oil
salt and freshly ground black pepper
3½ cups farfalle
1½ cups green beans, trimmed and cut in half
1 tsp. Dijon mustard
2 tsp. white wine vinegar
pinch of sugar
3 tbsp. olive oil
8 oz. ripe tomatoes, quartered
½ cup pitted black olives
2 medium eggs, hard-boiled and quartered
8 anchovy fillets, drained and cut in half lengthwise

Helpful Hint

This dish can also be made with fresh tuna steaks. Prepare and cook in exactly the same way as the swordfish, although tuna can be served slightly rare, if you wish. Do not marinate the fish for more than the time suggested, or it may become overtenderized and lose its firm texture.

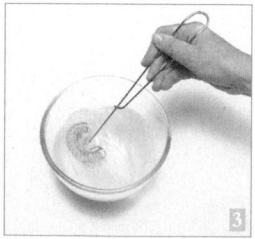
3

4

5

Oven-Roasted Vegetables with Sausages

1 Preheat the oven to 400° F. Cut the eggplants and zucchini into bite-sized chunks. Place the olive oil in a large roasting pan and heat in the preheated oven for 3 minutes or until very hot. Add the eggplants, zucchini, and garlic cloves, stir until coated in the hot oil, and cook in the oven for 10 minutes.

2 Remove the roasting pan from the oven and stir. Lightly prick the sausages, add to the roasting pan, and return to the oven. Continue to roast for an additional 20 minutes, turning once during cooking until the vegetables are tender and the sausages are golden brown.

3 Meanwhile, coarsely chop the plum tomatoes and drain the canellini beans. Remove the sausages from the oven and stir in the tomatoes and canellini beans. Season to taste with salt and pepper, then return to the oven for 5 minutes or until heated thoroughly.

4 Sprinkle with the torn basil leaves, plenty of shredded Parmesan cheese, and extra freshly ground black pepper. Serve immediately.

INGREDIENTS
Serves 4

2 medium eggplants, trimmed
3 medium zucchini, trimmed
¼ cup olive oil
6 garlic cloves
8 Italian-style sausages
4 plum tomatoes
2 11-oz. cans canellini beans
salt and freshly ground black pepper
1 bunch fresh basil, torn into coarse pieces
4 tbsp. Parmesan cheese, shredded

Helpful Hint

Although it is worth seeking out Italian-style sausages for this dish, a good alternative would be to use Toulouse or French-style sausages instead. If they are not available in the supermarket, try a specialty store.

1

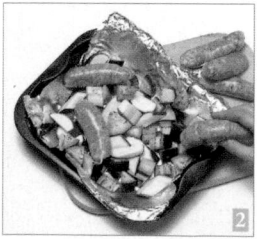
2

3

Hot Salami & Vegetable Gratin

1 Preheat the oven to 400° F. Peel and slice the carrots, trim the beans and asparagus, then set aside. Cook the carrots in a saucepan of lightly salted, boiling water for 5 minutes. Add the remaining vegetables, except for the spinach, and cook for an additional 5 minutes or until tender. Drain and place in an ovenproof dish.

2 Discard any skin from the outside of the salami if necessary, then chop coarsely. Heat the oil in a skillet and cook the salami for 4–5 minutes, stirring occasionally until golden. Using a slotted spoon, transfer the salami to the ovenproof dish and sprinkle with the mint.

3 Add the butter to the skillet and cook the spinach for 1–2 minutes or until just wilted. Stir in the heavy cream, and season well with salt and pepper. Spoon the mixture over the vegetables.

4 Finely chop the ciabatta loaf in a food processor to make bread crumbs. Stir in the Parmesan cheese and sprinkle over the vegetables. Cook in the preheated oven for 20 minutes until golden and heated through. Serve with a green salad.

INGREDIENTS
Serves 4

2 cups carrots
1½ cups fine green beans
1½ cups asparagus tips
1½ cups frozen peas
2 cups Italian salami
1 tbsp. olive oil
1 tbsp. freshly chopped mint
¼ stick butter
3 cups baby spinach leaves
½ cup heavy cream
salt and freshly ground black pepper
1 small or ½ olive ciabatta loaf
¼ cup Parmesan cheese, shredded
green salad, to serve

Tasty Tip

Prepare this dish ahead up to the end of Step 3, and refrigerate When ready to cook, top with bread crumbs and add about 5 minutes to the final cooking time.

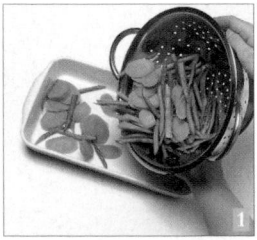

Antipasto Penne

1 Preheat the broiler just before cooking. Cut the zucchini into thick slices. Cut the tomatoes into quarters, then cut the ham into strips. Pour the oil into a baking dish, and place under the broiler for 2 minutes or until almost smoking. Remove from the broiler and stir in the zucchini. Return to the broiler and cook for 8 minutes. Remove from the broiler and add the tomatoes and cook for 3 minutes.

2 Add the ham to the baking dish and cook under the broiler for 4 minutes until all the vegetables are charred and the ham is brown. Season to taste with salt and pepper.

3 Meanwhile, plunge the pasta into a large saucepan of lightly salted, boiling water, return to a rolling boil, stir, and cook for 8 minutes or until al dente. Drain well and return to the saucepan.

4 Stir the antipasto into the vegetables and cook under the broiler for 2 minutes or until heated through. Add the cooked pasta and toss together gently with the remaining ingredients. Broil for an additional 4 minutes, then serve immediately.

INGREDIENTS
Serves 4

3 medium zucchini, trimmed
4 tomatoes
1½ cups Italian ham
2 tbsp. olive oil
salt and freshly ground black pepper
4½ cups dried penne pasta
10 oz. jar antipasto
1 cup mozzarella cheese, drained and diced
1 cup Gorgonzola cheese, crumbled
3 tbsp. freshly chopped Italian parsley

Food Fact

The term "antipasto" refers to the course served before the *pasto,* or "meal," begins and its purpose is to whet the appetite for the following courses. In Italy, these are served in small quantities, though two or three different dishes may be served at once. There are no hard and fast rules as to what constitutes a suitable dish for antipasti—there are literally thousands of regional variations.

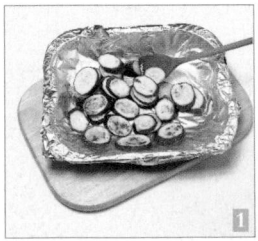
1

2

4

Italian Risotto

1 Chop the onion and garlic, and set aside. Heat the olive oil in a large skillet, and cook the salami for 3–5 minutes or until golden. Transfer to a plate and keep warm. Add the asparagus and stir-fry for 2–3 minutes until just wilted. Transfer to the plate with the salami. Add the onion and garlic, and cook for 5 minutes or until softened.

2 Add the rice to the skillet and cook for 2 minutes. Add the wine, bring to a boil, then simmer, stirring until the wine has been absorbed. Add half the stock and return to a boil. Simmer, stirring, until the liquid has been absorbed.

3 Add half of the remaining stock and the fava beans to the rice mixture. Bring to a boil, then simmer for an additional 5–10 minutes or until all of the liquid has been absorbed.

4 Add the remaining stock, bring to a boil, then simmer until all the liquid is absorbed and the rice is tender. Stir in the remaining ingredients until the cheese has just melted. Serve immediately.

INGREDIENTS
Serves 4

1 onion, peeled
2 garlic cloves, peeled
1 tbsp. olive oil
2 cups Italian salami, chopped
½ cup asparagus tips
1½ cups risotto rice
1¼ cups dry white wine
4 cups chicken stock, warmed
¼ cup frozen fava beans, thawed
1 cup dolcelatte or blue cheese, diced
3 tbsp. freshly chopped mixed herbs, such as parsley and basil
salt and freshly ground black pepper

Food Fact

Cheese is a common ingredient in the making of risotto and in fact helps to provide some of its creamy texture. Usually Parmesan cheese is added at the end of cooking, but here a good-quality dolcelatte or blue cheese is used instead.

Pan-Fried Beef with Creamy Mushrooms

1 Cut the shallots in half if large, then chop the garlic. Heat the oil in a large skillet and cook the shallots for about 8 minutes, stirring occasionally until almost softened. Add the garlic and beef, and cook for 8–10 minutes, turning once during cooking, until the meat is browned all over. Using a slotted spoon, transfer the beef to a plate and keep warm.

2 Rinse the tomatoes and cut into eighths. Wipe the mushrooms and slice. Add them to the skillet and cook for 5 minutes, stirring frequently until the mushrooms have softened.

3 Pour in the brandy and heat through. Draw the skillet off the heat and ignite. Let the flames subside. Pour in the wine, return to the heat, and bring to a boil. Boil until reduced by one third. Draw the skillet off the heat, season to taste with salt and pepper, add the cream, and stir.

4 Arrange the beef on serving plates and spoon over the sauce. Serve with baby new potatoes and green beans.

INGREDIENTS
Serves 4

1 cup shallots, peeled
2 garlic cloves, peeled
2 tbsp. olive oil
4 medallions of beef
4 plum tomatoes
1¼ cups mushrooms
3 tbsp. brandy
⅔ cup red wine
salt and freshly ground black pepper
4 tbsp. heavy cream

TO SERVE:
baby new potatoes
freshly cooked green beans

Helpful Hint

To prepare medallions of beef, buy a piece of fillet weighing approximately 1½ lbs. Cut crosswise into 4 pieces.

Oven-Baked Pork Balls with Bell Peppers

1 Preheat the oven to 400° F. Crush the garlic, then blend with the softened butter, the parsley, and enough lemon juice to give a soft consistency. Shape into a roll, wrap in baking parchment, and chill in the refrigerator for at least 30 minutes.

2 Mix together the pork, basil, 1 chopped garlic clove, sun-dried tomatoes, and seasoning until well combined. With damp hands, roll into 16 balls and set aside.

3 Spoon the olive oil into a large roasting pan, and place in the preheated oven for about 3 minutes until very hot. Remove from the heat and stir in the pork balls, the remaining chopped garlic, and bell peppers. Cook for about 15 minutes. Remove from the oven, stir in the cherry tomatoes, and season to taste with plenty of salt and pepper. Cook for an additional 20 minutes.

4 Just before the pork balls are ready, slice the bread, toast lightly, and spread with the prepared garlic butter. Remove the pork balls from the oven, stir in the vinegar, and serve immediately with garlic bread.

Helpful Hint

Prepare the garlic butter ahead to the end of Step 1. Refrigerate for up to 1 week or freeze for up to 2 months.

INGREDIENTS
Serves 4

FOR THE GARLIC BREAD:

2–4 garlic cloves, peeled
½ stick butter, softened
1 tbsp. freshly chopped parsley
2–3 tsp. lemon juice
1 focaccia loaf

FOR THE PORK BALLS:

2 cups fresh ground pork
4 tbsp. freshly chopped basil
2 garlic cloves, peeled and chopped
3 sun-dried tomatoes, chopped
salt and freshly ground black pepper
3 tbsp. olive oil
1 medium red bell pepper, seeded and cut into chunks
1 medium green bell pepper, seeded and cut into chunks
1 medium yellow bell pepper, seeded and cut into chunks
2 cups cherry tomatoes
2 tbsp. balsamic vinegar

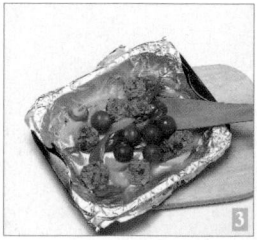

Pork Chop Hotpot

1 Preheat the oven to 375° F. Trim the pork chops, removing any excess fat, wipe with a clean, damp cloth, then dust with a little flour and set aside. Cut the shallots in half if large. Chop the garlic and slice the sun-dried tomatoes.

2 Heat the olive oil in a large casserole dish and cook the pork chops for about 5 minutes, turning occasionally during cooking until browned all over. Using a slotted spoon, carefully lift out of the dish and set aside. Add the shallots and cook for 5 minutes, stirring occasionally.

3 Return the pork chops to the casserole dish, and sprinkle with the garlic and sun-dried tomatoes, then pour over the can of tomatoes with their juice.

4 Blend the red wine, stock, and tomato paste together, and add the chopped oregano. Season to taste with salt and pepper, then pour over the pork chops and bring to a gentle boil. Cover with a close-fitting lid and cook in the preheated oven for 1 hour or until the pork chops are tender. Adjust the seasoning to taste, sprinkle with a few oregano leaves, and serve immediately with potatoes and green beans.

INGREDIENTS
Serves 4

4 pork chops
flour, for dusting
1 cup shallots, peeled
2 garlic cloves, peeled
¼ cup sun-dried tomatoes
2 tbsp. olive oil
14-oz. can tomatoes
⅔ cup red wine
⅔ cup chicken stock
3 tbsp. tomato paste
2 tbsp. freshly chopped oregano
salt and freshly ground black pepper
fresh oregano leaves, to garnish

TO SERVE:
freshly cooked new potatoes
fine green beans

Tasty Tip

Choose bone-in chops for this recipe. Remove any excess fat and rind before cooking.

1

3

4

Veal Italian

1 Trim the veal if necessary. Chop the bacon and set aside. Chop the garlic and onion, slice the carrot thinly, and trim and chop the celery.

2 Heat the butter and 1 tablespoon of the oil in a large saucepan, and brown the veal for 5 minutes, stirring frequently, until sealed all over. Transfer the veal to a plate and set aside.

3 Add the garlic, bacon, celery, carrot, and onion to the saucepan and cook for an additional 5 minutes, stirring occasionally until softened, then return the veal to the saucepan and pour over the tomatoes with their juice and the wine. Season to taste with salt and pepper. Bring to a boil, cover, reduce the heat, and simmer for 45 minutes.

4 Meanwhile, wipe the mushrooms, and if large, cut in half. Heat the remaining oil in a small skillet and sauté the mushrooms for 2 minutes. Drain, then add to the veal and cook for 15 minutes or until the veal is tender. Season to taste, and serve immediately with freshly cooked pasta and a green salad.

INGREDIENTS
Serves 4

1 lb. diced veal, thawed if frozen
6 slices bacon
1 garlic clove, peeled
1 onion, peeled
1 carrot, peeled
1 celery stalk
¼ stick butter
2 tbsp. olive oil
14-oz. can chopped tomatoes
⅔ cup red wine
salt and freshly ground black pepper
1¼ cups mushrooms

TO SERVE:
freshly cooked pasta
green salad

Helpful Hint

As an alternative, replace the veal with chicken and follow the recipe in the same way. Serve with roasted Mediterranean vegetables as a side dish.

Roasted Lamb with Rosemary & Garlic

1 Preheat the oven to 400° F. Wipe the leg of lamb with a clean damp cloth, then place the lamb in a large roasting pan. With a sharp knife, make small, deep incisions into the meat. Cut 2–3 garlic cloves into small slivers, then insert, along with a few small sprigs of rosemary, into the lamb. Season to taste with salt and pepper, and cover the lamb with the slices of pancetta.

2 Drizzle over 1 tablespoon of the olive oil and lay some additional rosemary sprigs across the lamb. Roast for 30 minutes, then pour over the vinegar.

3 Peel and dice the potatoes. Peel the onion and cut into thick wedges, then thickly slice the remaining garlic. Arrange around the lamb. Pour the remaining olive oil over the potatoes, then reduce the oven temperature to 350° F and roast for an additional 1 hour or until the lamb is tender. Garnish with fresh sprigs of rosemary and serve immediately with the roast potatoes and ratatouille.

INGREDIENTS
Serves 6

3½ lb. leg of lamb
8 garlic cloves, peeled
few sprigs of fresh rosemary
salt and freshly ground black pepper
4 slices pancetta
4 tbsp. olive oil
4 tbsp. red wine vinegar
6 medium potatoes
1 large onion
sprigs of fresh rosemary, to garnish
freshly cooked ratatouille, to serve

Helpful Hint

If you are unable to get a leg of lamb weighing exactly 3½ pounds, calculate the cooking time as follows: 20 minutes per pound, plus 30 minutes for rare; 25 minutes per pound, plus 30 minutes for medium; and 30 minutes per pound, plus 30 minutes for well done.

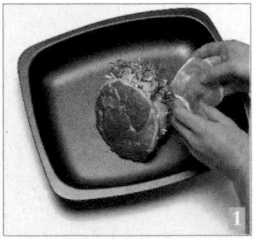
1

2

3

Braised Lamb with Fava Beans

1 Trim the lamb, discarding any fat or gristle, then place the flour in a plastic container, add the lamb, and toss until coated thoroughly. Peel and slice the onion and garlic, then set aside. Heat the olive oil in a heavy saucepan and when hot, add the lamb and cook, stirring until the meat is sealed and browned all over. Using a slotted spoon, set aside.

2 Add the onion and garlic to the saucepan, and cook for 3 minutes, stirring frequently, until softened. Return the lamb to the saucepan and add the chopped tomatoes with their juice, the stock, chopped thyme, and oregano to the saucepan. Season to taste with salt and pepper. Bring to a boil, then cover with a close-fitting lid, reduce the heat, and simmer for 1 hour.

3 Add the fava beans to the lamb and then simmer for about 20–30 minutes or until the lamb is tender. Garnish with sprigs of fresh oregano, and serve immediately with mashed potatoes.

INGREDIENTS
Serves 4

1½ lbs. lamb, cut into large chunks
1 tbsp. all-purpose flour
1 onion
2 garlic cloves
1 tbsp. olive oil
14-oz. can chopped tomatoes
1¼ cups lamb stock
2 tbsp. freshly chopped thyme
2 tbsp. freshly chopped oregano
salt and freshly ground black pepper
1 cup frozen fava beans
sprigs of fresh oregano, to garnish
mashed potatoes, to serve

Tasty Tip

If you want to use fresh fava beans when in season, you will need about 1 lb. of beans in their pods for this recipe. If you prefer to peel the beans, plunge them first into boiling, salted water for about 30 seconds, drain, and rinse under cold water. The skins will come off very easily.

Spaghetti Bolognese

1 Peel and chop the carrot, trim and chop the celery, then peel and chop the onion and garlic. Heat a large nonstick skillet and sauté the beef and bacon for 5–10 minutes, stirring occasionally until browned. Add the prepared vegetables to the skillet and cook for about 3 minutes or until softened, stirring occasionally.

2 Add the flour and cook for 1 minute. Stir in the red wine, tomatoes, tomato paste, mixed herbs, and sugar. Bring to a boil, then cover and simmer for 45 minutes, stirring occasionally.

3 Meanwhile, bring a large saucepan of lightly salted water to a boil and cook the spaghetti for 10–12 minutes or until al dente. Drain well and divide among 4 serving plates. Spoon over the sauce, garnish with a few sprigs of oregano, and serve immediately with plenty of Parmesan shavings.

INGREDIENTS
Serves 4

1 carrot
2 celery stalks
1 onion
2 garlic cloves
2 cups lean ground beef
2 cups bacon, chopped
1 tbsp. all-purpose flour
⅔ cup red wine
13-oz. can chopped tomatoes
2 tbsp. tomato paste
2 tsp. dried mixed herbs
salt and freshly ground black pepper
pinch of sugar
4 cups spaghetti
sprigs of fresh oregano, to garnish
shavings of Parmesan cheese, to serve

Tasty Tip

This is an ideal sauce to use in a baked lasagna. Preheat the oven to 375° F. Alternate layers of the sauce with sheets of fresh or precooked lasagna, and top with a béchamel sauce and Parmesan cheese. Cook for 30–40 minutes or until the top is golden.

Meatballs with Olives

1 Chop 2 of the shallots finely and place in a bowl with the garlic, beef, bread crumbs, basil, and seasoning. With damp hands, bring the mixture together and shape into small balls about the size of apricots.

2 Heat the olive oil in a skillet, and cook the meatballs for 8–10 minutes, turning occasionally until browned and the beef is tender. Remove and drain on absorbent paper towels.

3 Slice the remaining shallots, add to the skillet, and cook for 5 minutes until softened. Blend the pesto and mascarpone together, then stir into the skillet with the olives. Bring to a boil, reduce the heat and return the meatballs to the skillet. Simmer for 5–8 minutes or until the sauce has thickened and the meatballs are cooked thoroughly.

4 Meanwhile, bring a large saucepan of lightly salted water to a boil, and cook the noodles for 8–10 minutes. Drain the noodles, setting aside 2 tablespoons of the cooking liquid. Return the noodles to the saucepan with the cooking liquid and pour in the sauce. Stir the noodles, then sprinkle with chopped parsley. Garnish with parsley and serve immediately with shredded Parmesan cheese.

INGREDIENTS
Serves 4

1 cup shallots, peeled
2–3 garlic cloves, peeled
2 cups ground beef
2 tbsp. fresh white or whole-wheat bread crumbs
3 tbsp. freshly chopped basil
salt and freshly ground black pepper
2 tbsp. olive oil
5 tbsp. pesto sauce
5 tbsp. mascarpone cheese
5 tbsp. pitted ripe olives, halved
3¼ cups thick pasta noodles
freshly chopped Italian parsley
sprigs of fresh Italian parsley, to garnish
freshly shredded Parmesan cheese, to serve

Helpful Hint

To pit olives, make a cut lengthwise around the olive, then place on a chopping board with the cut facing upward. Put the side of the knife (with the blade facing away from you) on top of the olive and tap sharply with the heel of your hand. The pit should come away, leaving the olive in 2 pieces.

Lasagna

1 Preheat the oven to 400° F. Cook the beef and pancetta in a large, heavy saucepan for 10 minutes, stirring to break up any lumps. Add the onion, celery, and mushrooms, and cook for 4 minutes or until softened slightly.

2 Stir in the garlic and 1 tablespoon of the flour, then cook for 1 minute. Stir in the stock, herbs, and tomato paste. Season to taste with salt and pepper. Bring to a boil, then cover, reduce the heat, and simmer for 45 minutes.

3 Meanwhile, melt the butter in a small saucepan and stir in the remaining flour, mustard powder, and nutmeg until well blended. Cook for 2 minutes. Remove from the heat and gradually blend in the milk until smooth. Return to the heat and bring to a boil, stirring until thickened. Gradually stir in half the Parmesan and cheddar until melted. Season to taste.

4 Spoon half the meat mixture into the base of a large ovenproof dish. Top with a single layer of pasta. Spread over half the sauce and sprinkle with half the cheese. Repeat layers, finishing with cheese. Cook in the preheated oven for 30 minutes or until the pasta is cooked and the top is golden brown and bubbly. Serve immediately with crusty bread and a green salad.

Helpful Hint

This is a useful dish for entertaining. Assemble the lasagna ahead of time, then either refrigerate or even freeze until needed. Allow to come to room temperature or to thaw completely, and cook as above, adding an extra 5 minutes or so to the cooking time.

INGREDIENTS
Serves 4

2 cups lean ground beef
¾ cup pancetta or bacon, chopped
1 large onion, peeled and chopped
2 celery stalks, trimmed and chopped
1 cup button mushrooms, wiped and chopped
2 garlic cloves, peeled and chopped
1 cup all-purpose flour
1¼ cups beef stock
1 tbsp. dried mixed herbs
5 tbsp. tomato paste
salt and freshly ground black pepper
½ stick butter
1 tsp. mustard powder
pinch of freshly grated nutmeg
3 cups milk
1¼ cups Parmesan cheese, shredded
1 cup cheddar cheese, shredded
8–12 precooked lasagna sheets

TO SERVE:
crusty bread
fresh green salad leaves

2

3

4

Fillet Steaks with Tomato & Garlic Sauce

1 Make a small cross on the top of each tomato and place in a large bowl. Cover with boiling water and leave for 2 minutes. Using a slotted spoon, remove the tomatoes and peel carefully. Repeat until all the tomatoes are peeled. Place on a chopping board, cut into quarters, remove the seeds, chop coarsely, and then set aside.

2 Peel and chop the garlic. Heat half the olive oil in a saucepan and cook the garlic for 30 seconds. Add the chopped tomatoes with the basil, oregano, and red wine, and season to taste with salt and pepper. Bring to a boil, then reduce the heat, cover, and simmer for 15 minutes, stirring occasionally or until the sauce is reduced and thickened. Stir the olives into the sauce and keep warm while cooking the steaks.

3 Meanwhile, lightly oil a heavy skillet with the remaining olive oil and cook the steaks for 2 minutes on each side to seal. Continue to cook the steaks for an additional 2–4 minutes, depending on personal preference. Serve the steaks immediately with the garlic sauce and freshly cooked vegetables.

INGREDIENTS
Serves 4

1½ lbs. ripe tomatoes
2 garlic cloves
2 tbsp. olive oil
2 tbsp. freshly chopped basil
2 tbsp. freshly chopped oregano
2 tbsp. red wine
salt and freshly ground black pepper
½ cup pitted ripe olives, chopped
4 fillet steaks
freshly cooked vegetables, to serve

Helpful Hint

Fillet steak should be a deep mahogany color, with a good marbling of fat. If the meat is bright red or the fat is bright white, the meat has not been aged properly and will probably be quite tough.

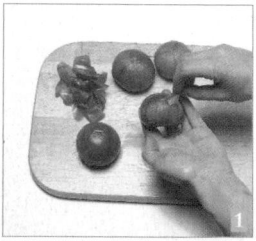
1

2

3

Veal Cutlets with Marsala Sauce

1 Place the veal cutlets between sheets of plastic wrap, and using a mallet or rolling pin, pound lightly to flatten until about ¼ inch thick. Remove the plastic wrap and sprinkle the veal cutlets with lemon juice, salt, and black pepper.

2 Place a sage leaf in the center of each cutlet. Top with a slice of prosciutto, making sure it just fits, then carefully roll up the cutlets enclosing the prosciutto and sage leaves. Secure each cutlet with a toothpick.

3 Heat the olive oil and butter in a large nonstick skillet, and cook the onions for 5 minutes or until softened. Add the garlic and rolled cutlets, and cook for about 8 minutes, turning occasionally until the cutlets are browned all over.

4 Add the Marsala wine and cream to the skillet, and bring to a boil, cover, and simmer for 10 minutes or until the veal is tender. Season to taste and then sprinkle with the parsley. Discard the toothpicks and serve immediately with freshly cooked vegetables.

INGREDIENTS
Serves 6

6 veal cutlets
lemon juice
salt and freshly ground black pepper
6 sage leaves
6 slices prosciutto
2 tbsp. olive oil
¼ stick butter
1 onion, peeled and sliced
1 garlic clove, peeled and chopped
2 tbsp. Marsala or Italian fortified wine
4 tbsp. heavy cream
2 tbsp. freshly chopped parsley
sage leaves, to garnish
selection of freshly cooked vegetables, to serve

Tasty Tip

If you prefer not to use veal, substitute thinly sliced, boneless pork loin or thin slices of turkey or chicken breast. Alternatively, you can substitute basil sprigs for the sage leaves, and add some sliced cheese, such as Gruyère or cheddar.

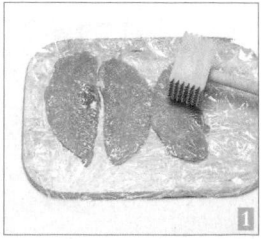
1

2

3

Cannelloni

1 Preheat the oven to 375° F. Heat the olive oil in a skillet, and cook the ground pork and chicken livers for about 5 minutes, stirring occasionally, until browned all over. Break up any lumps with a wooden spoon.

2 Add the onion and garlic, and cook for 4 minutes until softened. Add the spinach, oregano, and nutmeg, and season to taste with salt and pepper. Cook until all the liquid has evaporated, then remove the skillet from the heat and allow to cool. Stir in the ricotta cheese.

3 Meanwhile, melt the butter in a small saucepan and stir in the flour to form a roux. Cook for 2 minutes, stirring occasionally. Remove from the heat and blend in the milk until smooth. Return to the heat and bring to a boil, stirring until the sauce has thickened. Set aside.

4 Spoon a thin layer of the tomato sauce on the base of a large ovenproof dish. Divide the pork filling among the cannelloni tubes. Arrange on top of the tomato sauce. Spoon over the remaining tomato sauce.

5 Pour over the white sauce and sprinkle with the Parmesan cheese. Cook in the preheated oven for 30–35 minutes or until the cannelloni is tender and the top is golden brown. Serve immediately with a green salad.

INGREDIENTS
Serves 4

2 tbsp. olive oil
¼ cup fresh ground pork
⅓ cup chicken livers, chopped
1 small onion, peeled and chopped
1 garlic clove, peeled and chopped
1 cup frozen chopped spinach, thawed
1 tbsp. dried oregano
pinch of freshly grated nutmeg
salt and freshly ground black pepper
¼ cup ricotta cheese
¼ stick butter
¼ cup all-purpose flour
2½ cups milk
2½ cups tomato sauce
16 precooked cannelloni tubes
½ cup Parmesan cheese, shredded
green salad, to serve

Tasty Tip

To make chicken cannelloni, substitute ½ lb. boneless, skinless chicken breast that has been finely chopped in a food processor. Ground chicken is also available from large supermarkets.

1

2

4

Vitello Tonnato (Veal in Tuna Sauce)

1 Place the veal in a large bowl and pour over the wine. Add the onion, carrot, celery, bay leaf, garlic cloves, parsley, salt, and pepper. Cover tightly and chill overnight in the refrigerator. Transfer the contents of the bowl to a large saucepan, and add just enough water to cover the meat. Bring to a boil, cover, and simmer for 1–1¼ hours or until the veal is tender.

2 Remove from the heat and let the veal cool in the juices. Using a slotted spoon, transfer the veal to a plate, pat dry with absorbent paper towels, and set aside.

3 Place the tuna, capers, anchovy fillets, mayonnaise, and lemon juice in a food processor or blender, and blend until smooth, adding a few spoonfuls of the pan juices to make the sauce of a coating consistency, if necessary. Season to taste with salt and pepper.

4 Using a sharp knife, slice the veal thinly and arrange on a large serving platter.

5 Spoon the sauce over the veal. Cover with plastic wrap and chill overnight. Garnish with lemon wedges, capers, and olives. Serve with salad and tomato wedges.

Tasty Tip

Look for tuna steak that has been packed in olive oil—it has the best flavor for this dish. Drain well before using to remove any excess oil.

INGREDIENTS
Serves 6–8

2 lb. boned, rolled leg or loin of veal
1¼ cups dry white wine
1 onion, peeled and chopped
1 carrot, peeled and chopped
2 celery stalks, trimmed and chopped
1 bay leaf
2 garlic cloves
few sprigs of parsley
salt and freshly ground black pepper
7-oz. can tuna in oil
2 tbsp. capers, drained
6 anchovy fillets
1 cup mayonnaise
1 tbsp. lemon juice

TO GARNISH:
lemon wedges
capers
ripe olives

TO SERVE:
green salad
tomato wedges

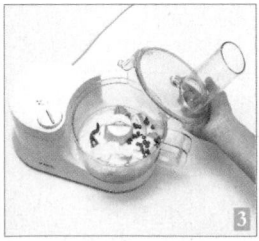

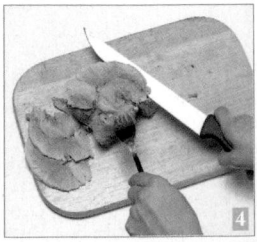

Italian Pot Roast

1 Preheat the oven to 300° F. Put the beef, onions, garlic, celery, and carrots in a bowl. Place the tomatoes in a separate bowl and cover with boiling water. Let stand for 2 minutes, then drain. Peel away the skins, discard the seeds, and chop, then add, along with the red wine, to the bowl with the beef mixture. Cover tightly and marinate in the refrigerator overnight.

2 Lift the marinated beef from the bowl and pat dry with absorbent paper towels. Heat the olive oil in a large casserole dish, cook the beef until it is browned all over, and then remove from the dish. Drain the vegetables from the marinade and set the marinade aside. Add the vegetables to the casserole dish and cook gently for 5 minutes, stirring occasionally, until all the vegetables are browned.

3 Return the beef to the casserole dish with the marinade, beef stock, tomato paste, and mixed herbs, and season with salt and pepper. Bring to a boil, then cover and cook in the preheated oven for 3 hours.

4 Using a slotted spoon, transfer the beef and any large vegetables to a plate, and leave in a warm place. Blend the butter and flour to form a paste. Bring the casserole juices to a boil and then gradually stir in small spoonfuls of the paste. Cook until thickened. Serve immediately with the sauce and a selection of vegetables.

INGREDIENTS
Serves 6

4 lb. brisket of beef
1 cup small onions, peeled
3 garlic cloves, peeled and chopped
2 celery stalks, trimmed and chopped
2 carrots, peeled and sliced
3 medium ripe tomatoes
1¼ cups Italian red wine
2 tbsp. olive oil
1¼ cups beef stock
1 tbsp. tomato paste
2 tsp. dried mixed herbs
salt and freshly ground black pepper
¼ stick butter
¼ cup all-purpose flour
freshly cooked vegetables, to serve

Helpful Hint

Many supermarkets do not sell brisket, but good butchers will be able to order it. Brisket is an excellent cut for all kinds of pot roasts, but make sure it is professionally trimmed, as it can contain a lot of gristle and fat.

Italian Meatballs in Tomato Sauce

1 To make the tomato sauce, heat half the olive oil in a saucepan and cook half the chopped onion for 5 minutes until softened.

2 Add the garlic, chopped tomatoes, tomato paste, mixed herbs, and red wine to the saucepan, and season to taste with salt and pepper. Stir well until blended. Bring to a boil, then cover and simmer for 15 minutes.

3 To make the meatballs, place the pork, bread crumbs, remaining onion, egg yolk, and half the Parmesan cheese in a large bowl. Season well and mix together with your hands. Divide the mixture into 20 balls.

4 Flatten one ball out in the palm of your hands, place an olive in the center, then squeeze the meat around the olive to enclose completely. Repeat with remaining mixture and olives.

5 Place the meatballs on a baking sheet, cover with plastic wrap, and chill in the refrigerator for 30 minutes.

6 Heat the remaining oil in a large skillet, and cook the meatballs for 8–10 minutes, turning occasionally until golden brown. Pour in the sauce and heat through. Sprinkle with chives and the remaining Parmesan. Serve immediately with the freshly cooked pasta.

Tasty Tip

There are many different kinds of stuffed olives readily available—try pimiento, almond, or even anchovy-stuffed olives in this recipe.

INGREDIENTS
Serves 4

FOR THE TOMATO SAUCE:

4 tbsp. olive oil
1 large onion, peeled and finely chopped
2 garlic cloves, peeled and chopped
14-oz. can chopped tomatoes
1 tbsp. sun-dried tomato paste
1 tbsp. dried mixed herbs
⅔ cup red wine
salt and freshly ground black pepper

FOR THE MEATBALLS:

2 cups fresh ground pork
½ cup fresh bread crumbs
1 medium egg yolk
¼ cup Parmesan cheese, shredded
20 small stuffed green olives
freshly cut chives, to garnish
freshly cooked pasta, to serve

Italian Calf's Liver

1 Cut the liver into very thin slices and place in a shallow dish. Sprinkle with the onion, bay leaves, parsley, sage, and peppercorns. Blend the red currant jelly with 1 tablespoon of the oil and the vinegar. Pour over the liver, cover, and let it marinate for at least 30 minutes. Turn the liver occasionally or spoon over the marinade.

2 Remove the liver from the marinade, strain, and set aside. Season the flour with salt and pepper, then use to coat the liver. Add the remaining oil to a heavy skillet, then sauté the garlic and bell peppers for 5 minutes. Using a slotted spoon, remove from the skillet.

3 Add the liver to the skillet, turn the heat up to high, and cook until the meat is browned on all sides. Return the garlic and bell peppers to the skillet, and add the marinade, sun-dried tomatoes, and stock. Bring to a boil, then reduce the heat and simmer for 3–4 minutes or until the liver is cooked. Add more seasoning to taste, then garnish with a few fresh sage leaves and serve immediately with potatoes.

INGREDIENTS
Serves 4

1 lb. calf's liver, trimmed
1 onion, peeled and sliced
2 fresh bay leaves, coarsely torn
sprigs of fresh parsley
fresh sage leaves
5 black peppercorns, lightly crushed
1 tbsp. red currant jelly, warmed
4 tbsp. walnut or olive oil
4 tbsp. red wine vinegar
3 tbsp. all-purpose flour
salt and freshly ground black pepper
2 garlic cloves, peeled and crushed
1 red bell pepper, seeded and sliced
1 yellow bell pepper, seeded and sliced
3 tbsp. sun-dried tomatoes, chopped
⅔ cup chicken stock
fresh sage leaves, to garnish
diced, sautéed potatoes, to serve

Tasty Tip

Be careful not to overcook the liver in this recipe, as it will become tough and dry, even though it is cooked in a sauce. Liver is best left a little pink in the center.

Spaghetti Bolognese

1 Heat the olive oil in a large heavy-based pan. Add the bacon and cook for 5 minutes or until slightly colored. Add the onion, carrot, celery, garlic, and bay leaf, and cook, stirring, for 8 minutes or until the vegetables are soft.

2 Add the ground beef to the pan and cook, stirring with a wooden spoon to break up any lumps in the meat for 5–8 minutes or until browned.

3 Stir the tomatoes and tomato paste into the meat and pour in the wine and stock. Bring to a boil, lower the heat, and simmer for a least 40 minutes, stirring occasionally. The longer you leave the sauce to cook, the more intense the flavor. Season to taste with salt and pepper, and remove the bay leaf.

4 Meanwhile, bring a large pan of lightly salted water to a rolling boil. Add the spaghetti and cook for about 8 minutes or until al dente. Drain and arrange on warmed serving plates. Top with the prepared Bolognese sauce and serve immediately, sprinkled with grated Parmesan cheese.

INGREDIENTS
Serves 4

3 tbsp. olive oil
¼ cup unsmoked bacon, chopped
1 small onion, peeled and finely chopped
1 carrot, peeled and finely chopped
1 celery stalk, trimmed and finely chopped
2 garlic cloves, peeled and crushed
1 bay leaf
5¼ cups ground beef
14-oz. can chopped tomatoes
2 tbsp. tomato paste
⅔ cup red wine
⅔ cup beef stock
salt and freshly gound black pepper
1 lb. spaghetti
freshly grated Parmesan cheese, to serve

Food Fact

Bolognese sauce, or *ragù alla Bolognese*, as it is known in Italy, is enjoyed throughout the world, especially in the United States and Britain. It originated in the city of Bologna in Emilia-Romagna, where it is always served with tagliatelle, rather than spaghetti.

Lasagna

1 Preheat the oven to 400° F. To make the white sauce, melt the butter in a small heavy-based pan. Add the flour and cook gently, stirring, for 2 minutes. Remove from the heat and gradually stir in the milk. Return to the heat and cook, stirring, for 2 minutes or until the sauce thickens. Bring to a boil, remove from the heat, and stir in the mustard. Season to taste with salt, pepper, and nutmeg.

2 Butter a rectangular ovenproof dish and spread a thin layer of the white sauce over the base. Cover completely with 3 sheets of lasagna.

3 Spoon a quarter of the prepared Bolognese sauce over the lasagna. Spoon over a quarter of the remaining white sauce, then sprinkle with a quarter of the grated Parmesan cheese. Repeat the layers, finishing with Parmesan cheese.

4 Bake in the preheated oven for 30 minutes or until golden brown. Garnish with chopped parsley and serve immediately with warm garlic bread.

INGREDIENTS
Serves 4

¼ stick butter
4 tbsp. all-purpose flour
3 cups milk
1 tsp. whole-grain mustard
salt and freshly ground black pepper
¼ tsp. freshly grated nutmeg
9 sheets lasagna
1 quantity of prepared Bolognese sauce (see page 230)
¼ cup freshly grated Parmesan cheese
freshly chopped parsley, to garnish
garlic bread, to serve

Helpful Hint

For a change, use lasagna verdi—this is green lasagna made with spinach. The shape varies according to the manufacturer, and may be flat or wavy. Some have crimped edges, which help to trap the sauce and keep it from running to the bottom of the dish. As sizes differ slightly, it is worth trying several until you find the one that fits your lasagna dish perfectly!

Cannelloni with Spicy Bolognese Filling

1 Preheat the oven to 400° F. To make the Bolognese filling, heat the oil in a large heavy-based pan, add the onion and garlic, and cook for 8 minutes or until soft. Add the ground beef and cook, stirring with a wooden spoon to break up lumps, for 5–8 minutes or until the meat is browned.

2 Stir in the chili flakes, fennel seeds, oregano, tomatoes, and tomato paste. Pour in the wine, and season well with salt and pepper. Bring to a boil, cover, and lower the heat, then simmer for at least 30 minutes, stirring occasionally. Remove the lid and simmer for an additional 10 minutes. Leave to cool slightly.

3 Using a teaspoon, fill the cannelloni tubes with the meat filling. Lay the stuffed cannelloni side-by-side in a lightly greased ovenproof dish.

4 Mix the cream with three-quarters of the Parmesan cheese and the nutmeg. Pour over the cannelloni and sprinkle with the remaining cheese. Bake in the preheated oven for 30 minutes or until golden brown and bubbling. Serve immediately with a green salad.

Helpful Hint

The Bolognese filling can be made with all ground beef, as shown here, or more traditionally with a mixture of half beef and half lean ground pork. Ground chicken or turkey also works well in this recipe, although the color is paler and the flavor less rich, but you can compensate for this by slightly increasing the quantity of herbs and spices.

INGREDIENTS
Serves 6

12 dried cannelloni tubes
1¼ cups heavy cream
¼ cup freshly grated Parmesan cheese
¼ tsp. freshly grated nutmeg
crisp green salad, to serve

SPICY BOLOGNESE FILLING:
2 tbsp. olive oil
1 small onion, peeled and finely chopped
2 garlic cloves, peeled and crushed
5¼ cups ground beef
¼ tsp. crushed chili flakes
1 tsp. fennel seeds
2 tbsp. freshly chopped oregano
14-oz. can chopped tomatoes
1 tbsp. sun-dried tomato paste
⅔ cup red wine
salt and freshly ground black pepper

Spaghetti & Meatballs

1 Preheat the oven to 400° F. Place the chopped tomatoes, tomato paste, chili sauce, and sugar in a pan. Season to taste with salt and pepper, and bring to a boil. Cover and simmer for 15 minutes, then cook uncovered for an additional 10 minutes or until the sauce has reduced and thickened.

2 Meanwhile, make the meatballs. Place the meat, bread crumbs, and onion in a food processor. Blend until all the ingredients are well mixed. Add the beaten egg, tomato paste, parsley, and oregano, and season to taste with salt and pepper. Blend again.

3 Shape the mixture into small balls, about the size of an apricot, and place on a greased baking sheet. Cook in the preheated oven for 25–30 minutes or until browned and cooked.

4 Meanwhile, bring a large pan of lightly salted water to a rolling boil. Add the pasta and cook according to the package directions or until al dente.

5 Drain the pasta and return to the pan. Pour over the tomato sauce and toss gently to coat the spaghetti. Spoon into a warmed serving dish and top with the meatballs. Garnish with chopped parsley and serve immediately with grated cheese.

INGREDIENTS
Serves 4

14-oz. can chopped tomatoes
1 tbsp. tomato paste
1 tsp. chili sauce
¼ tsp. brown sugar
salt and freshly ground black pepper
12 oz. spaghetti
¼ cup grated cheddar cheese, plus extra to serve
freshly chopped parsley, to garnish

FOR THE MEATBALLS:
5 cups ground lean pork or beef
2 cups fresh bread crumbs
1 large onion, peeled and finely chopped
1 medium egg, beaten
1 tbsp. tomato paste
2 tbsp. freshly chopped parsley
1 tbsp. freshly chopped oregano

Tasty Tip

For a crispier outside to the meatballs, you can fry them instead of baking. Heat 2 tablespoons of olive oil in a very large skillet, and cook over a medium heat for about 15 minutes, turning occasionally until well-browned.

Chorizo with Pasta in a Tomato Sauce

1 Melt the butter with the olive oil in a large heavy-based pan. Add the onions and sugar, and cook over a very low heat, stirring occasionally, for 15 minutes or until soft and starting to caramelize.

2 Add the garlic and chorizo to the pan and cook for 5 minutes. Stir in the chili, chopped tomatoes, and tomato paste, and pour in the wine. Season well with salt and pepper. Bring to a boil, cover, reduce the heat, and simmer for 30 minutes, stirring occasionally. Remove the lid and simmer for an additional 10 minutes or until the sauce starts to thicken.

3 Meanwhile, bring a large pan of lightly salted water to a rolling boil. Add the pasta and cook according to the package directions or until al dente.

4 Drain the pasta, setting aside 2 tablespoons of the water, and return to the pan. Add the chorizo sauce with the cooking water, and toss gently until the pasta is evenly covered. Spoon into a warmed serving dish, sprinkle with the parsley, and serve immediately.

INGREDIENTS
Serves 4

2 tbsp. butter
2 tbsp. olive oil
2 large onions, peeled and finely sliced
1 tsp. brown sugar
2 garlic cloves, peeled and crushed
8 oz. chorizo, sliced
1 chili, deseeded and finely sliced
14-oz. can chopped tomatoes
1 tbsp. sun-dried tomato paste
⅔ cup red wine
salt and freshly ground black pepper
4 cups rigatoni
freshly chopped parsley, to garnish

Helpful Hint

Although there are many different types of chili, they all have a hot, spicy flavor. Take care when preparing chilies, as the volatile oils in the seeds and the membrane can cause irritation—wash your hands thoroughly afterward.

Moroccan Penne

1 Preheat the oven to 400° F. Heat the sunflower oil in a large flameproof casserole dish. Add the chopped onion and fry for 5 minutes or until softened.

2 Using a mortar and pestle, pound the garlic, coriander seeds, cumin seeds, and grated nutmeg together into a paste. Add to the onion and cook for 3 minutes.

3 Add the ground lamb to the casserole and fry, stirring with a wooden spoon for 4–5 minutes or until the meat has broken up and browned.

4 Add the eggplant to the meat and fry for 5 minutes. Stir in the chopped tomatoes and vegetable stock, and bring to a boil. Add the apricots and olives, then season well with salt and pepper. Return to a boil, lower the heat, and simmer for 15 minutes.

5 Add the penne to the casserole, stir well, then cover and place in the preheated oven. Cook for 10 minutes, then stir and return to the oven uncovered for an additional 15–20 minutes or until the pasta is al dente. Remove from the oven, sprinkle with toasted pine nuts, and serve immediately.

INGREDIENTS
Serves 4

1 tbsp. sunflower oil
1 red onion, peeled and chopped
2 garlic cloves, peeled and crushed
1 tbsp. coriander seeds
¼ tsp. cumin seeds
¼ tsp. freshly grated nutmeg
5 cups ground lean lamb
1 eggplant, trimmed and diced
14-oz. can chopped tomatoes
1¼ cups vegetable stock
½ cup chopped dried apricots
12 black olives, pitted
salt and freshly ground black pepper
3 cups penne
1 tbsp. toasted pine nuts, to garnish

Helpful Hint

You can sometimes buy toasted pine nuts, but if you cannot find any, they are easy to toast. Sprinkle them on a foil-lined broiler pan and place under a medium broiler for 3–4 minutes, turning frequently until they are golden brown. Alternatively, fry them in a nonstick skillet, tossing the nuts every few seconds. Always watch nuts when cooking, as they can burn easily.

Spicy Chili Beef

1 Heat the olive oil in a large heavy-based pan. Add the onion and red bell pepper, and cook for 5 minutes or until beginning to soften. Add the ground beef and cook over a high heat for 5–8 minutes or until the meat is browned. Stir with a wooden spoon during cooking to break up any lumps in the meat. Add the garlic and chilies, fry for 1 minute, then season to taste.

2 Add the chopped tomatoes, tomato paste, and the kidney beans to the pan. Bring to a boil, lower the heat, and simmer covered for at least 40 minutes, stirring occasionally. Stir in the grated chocolate and cook for 3 minutes or until melted.

3 Meanwhile, bring a large pan of lightly salted water to a rolling boil. Add the fusilli and cook according to the package directions or until al dente.

4 Drain the pasta, return to the pan, and toss with the butter and parsley. Spoon into a warmed serving dish or spoon onto individual plates. Spoon the sauce over the pasta. Sprinkle with paprika and serve immediately with spoonfuls of sour cream.

INGREDIENTS
Serves 4

2 tbsp. olive oil
1 onion, peeled and finely chopped
1 red bell pepper, deseeded and sliced
5 cups ground beef
2 garlic cloves, peeled and crushed
2 red chilies, deseeded and finely sliced
salt and freshly ground black pepper
14-oz. can chopped tomatoes
2 tbsp. tomato paste
14-oz. can red kidney beans, drained
2 squares good-quality dark chocolate, grated
3 cups dried fusilli
1 tsp. butter
2 tbsp. freshly chopped Italian parsley
paprika, to garnish
sour cream, to serve

Food Fact

The chocolate in this traditional spicy Mexican dish adds rich warm undertones, color, and a slight sweetness, but no one will realize it is there unless you tell them. For maximum flavor, use a good quality, dark chocolate with a low sugar content and a high percentage of cocoa solids.

Pasta & Pork Ragù

1 Heat the sunflower oil in a large skillet. Add the sliced leek and cook, stirring frequently, for 5 minutes or until softened. Add the pork and cook, stirring, for 4 minutes or until sealed.

2 Add the crushed garlic and the paprika and cayenne peppers to the pan. Stir until all the pork is lightly coated in the garlic and pepper mixture.

3 Pour in the wine and 1¼ cups of the vegetable stock. Add the cranberry beans and carrots, and season to taste with salt and pepper. Bring the sauce to a boil, then lower the heat and simmer for 5 minutes.

4 Meanwhile, place the egg tagliatelle in a large saucepan of lightly salted boiling water, cover and simmer for 5 minutes or until the pasta is cooked al dente.

5 Drain the pasta, then add to the pork ragù; toss well. Adjust the seasoning, then spoon into a warmed serving dish. Sprinkle with chopped parsley and serve with a little crème fraîche.

INGREDIENTS
Serves 4

1 tbsp. sunflower oil
1 leek, trimmed and thinly sliced
2½ cups diced pork tenderloin
1 garlic clove, peeled and crushed
2 tsp. paprika
¼ tsp. cayenne pepper
⅔ cup white wine
2½ cups vegetable stock
14-oz. can cranberry beans, drained and rinsed
2 carrots, peeled and diced
salt and freshly ground black pepper
8 oz. fresh egg tagliatelle
1 tbsp. freshly chopped parsley, to garnish
crème fraîche, to serve

Helpful Hint

Pork tenderloin, also known as "fillet," is a very lean and tender cut of pork. It needs little cooking time, so is perfect for this quick and simple dish. Sirloin steak or boneless skinned chicken breast, cut into thin strips, could be used instead, if preferred.

Sausage & Red Currant Pasta Bake

1 Preheat the oven to 425° F. Prick the sausages, place in a shallow ovenproof dish, and toss in the sunflower oil. Cook in the oven for 25–30 minutes or until golden brown.

2 Meanwhile, melt the butter in a skillet. Add the sliced onion and fry for 5 minutes or until golden brown. Stir in the flour and cook for 2 minutes. Remove the pan from the heat and gradually stir in the chicken stock with the port or red wine.

3 Return the pan to the heat and bring to a boil, stirring continuously until the sauce starts to thicken. Add the thyme, bay leaf, and red currant jelly, and season well with salt and pepper. Simmer the sauce for 5 minutes.

4 Bring a large pan of salted water to a rolling boil. Add the pasta and cook for about 4 minutes or until al dente. Drain thoroughly and set aside.

5 Lower the oven temperature to 400° F. Remove the sausages from the oven, drain off any excess fat, and return the sausages to the dish. Add the pasta. Pour over the sauce, discarding the bay leaf, and toss together. Sprinkle with the Gruyère cheese and return to the oven for 15–20 minutes or until bubbling and golden brown. Serve immediately, garnished with thyme sprigs.

INGREDIENTS
Serves 4

1 lb. good-quality, thick pork sausages
2 tsp. sunflower oil
2 tbsp. butter
1 onion, peeled and sliced
2 tbsp. all-purpose flour
1¼ cups chicken stock
⅔ cup port or good-quality red wine
1 tbsp. freshly chopped thyme leaves, plus sprigs to garnish
1 bay leaf
4 tbsp. red currant jelly
salt and freshly ground black pepper
3 cups fresh penne
¼ cup grated Gruyère cheese

Tasty Tip

For a change, try specialty sausages for this recipe. Venison or wild boar sausages would work well with the rich sauce, as would Cumberland or spicy Cambridge pork sausages.

Pappardelle Pork with Brandy Sauce

1 Preheat the oven to 400° F. Using a sharp knife, cut two slits in each pork tenderloin, then stuff each slit with chopped sage. Season well with salt and pepper, and wrap each tenderloin with a slice of prosciutto.

2 Heat the olive oil in a large skillet. Add the wrapped pork fillets and cook, turning once, for 1–2 minutes or until the prosciutto is golden brown. Transfer to a roasting pan and cook in the preheated oven for 10–12 minutes.

3 Return the skillet to the heat and add the brandy, scraping the bottom of the pan with a spoon to release all the flavors. Boil for 1 minute, then pour in the chicken stock. Boil for an additional 2 minutes, then pour in the cream and boil again for 2–3 minutes or until the sauce has thickened slightly. Season the brandy sauce to taste.

4 Bring a large pan of lightly salted water to a rolling boil. Add the pasta and cook according to the package directions or until al dente. Drain the pasta thoroughly and return to the pan. Add the butter and chopped parsley, and toss together. Keep the pasta warm.

5 Remove the pork from the oven and pour any juices into the brandy sauce. Pile the pasta on individual plates and season with pepper. Spoon over the brandy sauce and serve immediately with the pork fillets.

INGREDIENTS
Serves 4

4 pork tenderloins, each weighing about 6 oz.
1 tbsp. freshly chopped sage, plus whole leaves to garnish
salt and freshly ground black pepper
4 slices prosciutto
1 tbsp. olive oil
6 tbsp. brandy
1¼ cups chicken stock
¼ cup heavy cream
12 oz. pappardelle
1–2 tsp. butter
2 tbsp. freshly chopped Italian parsley

Tasty Tip

An inexpensive French cooking brandy can be used for this recipe, but for a special occasion, use Calvados. Made from apples, it goes well with pork.

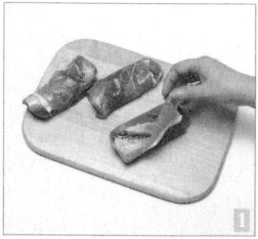

Tagliatelle with Spicy Sausage Ragù

1 Preheat the oven to 400° F. Heat 1 tablespoon of the olive oil in a large skillet. Prick the sausages, add to the pan, and cook for 8–10 minutes or until browned and cooked through. Remove and cut into thin diagonal slices. Set aside.

2 Return the pan to the heat and pour in the remaining olive oil. Add the onion and cook for 8 minutes or until softened. Add the fennel seeds and ground pork, and cook, stirring, for 5–8 minutes or until the meat is sealed and browned.

3 Stir in the tomatoes, tomato paste, and the wine or port. Season to taste with salt and pepper. Bring to a boil, cover, and simmer for 30 minutes, stirring occasionally. Remove the lid and simmer for 10 minutes.

4 Bring a large pan of lightly salted water to a rolling boil. Add the pasta and cook according to the package directions or until al dente. Drain thoroughly and toss with the meat sauce.

5 Place half the pasta in an ovenproof dish, and cover with 4 tablespoons of the white sauce. Top with half the sausages and grated Parmesan cheese. Repeat the layering, finishing with white sauce and Parmesan cheese. Bake in the preheated oven for 20 minutes, until golden brown. Serve immediately.

INGREDIENTS
Serves 4

3 tbsp. olive oil
6 spicy sausages
1 small onion, peeled and finely chopped
1 tsp. fennel seeds
2¼ cups fresh ground pork
8-oz. can chopped tomatoes with garlic
1 tbsp. sun-dried tomato paste
2 tbsp. red wine or port
salt and freshly ground black pepper
12 oz. tagliatelle
1¼ cups prepared white sauce (see page 232)
½ cup freshly grated Parmesan cheese

Helpful Hint

Most supermarkets sell cans of chopped tomatoes with added flavoring; if you cannot find them, simply add a large crushed garlic clove to regular canned tomatoes.

Food Fact

The sweet aniseed flavor of fennel seeds has an affinity with the slight acidity of tomatoes.

Pasta with Beef, Capers, & Olives

1 Heat the olive oil in a large skillet over a high heat. Add the steak and cook, stirring, for 3–4 minutes or until browned. Remove from the pan using a slotted spoon and set aside.

2 Lower the heat, add the scallions and garlic to the pan, and cook for 1 minute. Add the zucchini and bell pepper, and cook for 3–4 minutes.

3 Add the oregano, capers, and olives to the pan with the chopped tomatoes. Season to taste with salt and pepper, then simmer for 7 minutes, stirring occasionally. Return the beef to the pan and simmer for 3–5 minutes or until the sauce has thickened slightly.

4 Meanwhile, bring a large pan of lightly salted water to a rolling boil. Add the pasta and cook according to the package directions or until al dente.

5 Drain the pasta thoroughly. Return to the pan and add the beef sauce. Toss gently until the pasta is lightly coated. Spoon into a warmed serving dish or onto individual plates. Sprinkle with chopped parsley and serve immediately.

INGREDIENTS
Serves 4

2 tbsp. olive oil
11 oz. rump steak, trimmed and cut into strips
4 scallions, trimmed and sliced
2 garlic cloves, peeled and chopped
2 zucchini, trimmed and cut into strips
1 red bell pepper, deseeded and cut into strips
2 tsp. freshly chopped oregano
2 tbsp. capers, drained and rinsed
4 tbsp. pitted black olives, sliced
14-oz. can chopped tomatoes
salt and freshly ground black pepper
1 lb. fettuccine
1 tbsp. freshly chopped parsley, to garnish

Tasty Tip

When cooking the beef, it is important that it fries rather than steams in the pan, giving a beautifully brown and caramelized outside while keeping the middle moist and tender. Make sure that the oil in the pan is hot so that the strips of beef sizzle when added. Pat the beef dry with paper towels, and cook it in two batches so there is plenty of room to move it around the pan. Spoon the first batch onto a plate and set aside while cooking the second, then return to the pan with any juices.

Gnocchi & Prosciutto Bake

1 Heat the oven to 350° F. Heat 2 tablespoons of the olive oil in a large skillet and cook the onion and garlic for 5 minutes or until softened. Stir in the tomatoes, sun-dried tomato paste, and mascarpone cheese. Season to taste with salt and pepper. Add half the tarragon. Bring to a boil, then lower the heat immediately and simmer for 5 minutes.

2 Meanwhile, bring 8 cups water to a boil in a large pan. Add the remaining olive oil and a good pinch of salt. Add the gnocchi and cook for 1–2 minutes or until they rise to the surface.

3 Drain the gnocchi thoroughly and transfer to a large ovenproof dish. Add the tomato sauce and toss gently to coat the pasta. Combine the cheddar or Parmesan cheese with the bread crumbs and remaining tarragon and spread over the pasta mixture. Top with the prosciutto and olives and season again.

4 Cook in the preheated oven for 20–25 minutes, or until golden and bubbling. Serve immediately, garnished with parsley sprigs.

INGREDIENTS
Serves 4

3 tbsp. olive oil
1 red onion, peeled and sliced
2 garlic cloves, peeled
3 plum tomatoes, skinned and quartered
2 tbsp. sun-dried tomato paste
1 cup mascarpone cheese
salt and freshly ground black pepper
1 tbsp. freshly chopped tarragon
11 oz. fresh gnocchi
1 cup grated cheddar or Parmesan cheese
1 cup fresh white bread crumbs
2 oz. prosciutto, sliced
10 pitted green olives, halved
sprigs of Italian parsley, to garnish

Helpful Hint

Make sure that you buy gnocchi potato dumplings for this recipe and not gnocchi sardi, a pasta of a similar name. It is important to use a large pan of boiling water so that the gnocchi have plenty of room to move around, otherwise they will stick together during cooking. If you do not have a large enough pan, cook the gnocchi in two batches.

1

2

3

Chinese Beef with Angel Hair Pasta

1 Crush the peppercorns, using a mortar and pestle. Transfer to a shallow bowl and combine with the chili powder, Szechuan pepper, light soy sauce, and sherry. Add the beef strips and stir until lightly coated. Cover and place in the refrigerator to marinate for 3 hours; stir occasionally during this time.

2 When ready to cook, bring a large pan of lightly salted water to a boil. Add the pasta, and cook according to the package directions or until al dente. Drain and return to the pan. Add the sesame oil and toss lightly. Keep the pasta warm.

3 Heat a wok or large skillet, then add the sunflower oil and heat until very hot. Add the shredded scallions with the sliced red and green bell peppers, and stir-fry for 2 minutes.

4 Drain the beef, saving the marinade, then add the beef to the wok or skillet and stir-fry for 3 minutes. Pour the marinade, and stir-fry for 1-2 minutes or until the beef is tender.

5 Pile the pasta onto 4 warm plates. Top with the beef and bell peppers, then garnish with toasted sesame seeds and shredded scallions. Serve immediately.

Food Fact

Szechuan pepper, which is also known as "Sichwan pepper," "anise pepper," and *fagara*, is not related in any way to black and white pepper. It is the reddish-brown, dried berry of the Chinese prickly ash tree and has a pronounced spicy, woody flavor. It is one of the essential ingredients of Chinese five-spice powder.

INGREDIENTS
Serves 4

1 tbsp. pink peppercorns
1 tbsp. chili powder
1 tbsp. Szechuan pepper
3 tbsp. light soy sauce
3 tbsp. dry sherry
1 lb. sirloin steak, cut into strips
12 oz. angel-hair pasta
1 tbsp. sesame oil
1 tbsp. sunflower oil
1 bunch scallions, trimmed and finely shredded, plus extra to garnish
1 red bell pepper, deseeded and thinly sliced
1 green bell pepper, deseeded and thinly sliced
1 tbsp. toasted sesame seeds, to garnish

Lamb Arrabbiata

1 Heat 2 tablespoons of the olive oil in a large skillet and cook the lamb for 5–7 minutes or until sealed. Remove from the skillet using a slotted spoon and set aside.

2 Heat the remaining oil in the skillet. Add the onion, garlic, and chili, and cook until softened. Add the tomatoes and bring to a boil, then simmer for 10 minutes.

3 Return the browned lamb to the skillet with the olives and pour in the wine. Bring the sauce back to a boil, then reduce the heat and simmer, uncovered, for 15 minutes or until the lamb is tender. Season to taste with salt and pepper.

4 Meanwhile, bring a large pan of lightly salted water to a rolling boil. Add the pasta and cook according to the package directions or until al dente.

5 Drain the pasta. Toss in the butter, then add to the sauce and mix. Stir in 4 tablespoons of the chopped parsley, then spoon into a warmed serving dish. Sprinkle with the remaining parsley and serve immediately.

INGREDIENTS
Serves 4

4 tbsp. olive oil
1 lb. lamb fillets, cubed
1 large onion, peeled and sliced
4 garlic cloves, peeled and finely chopped
1 red chili, deseeded and finely chopped
14-oz. can chopped tomatoes
1½ cups black olives, pitted and halved
⅔ cup white wine
salt and freshly ground black pepper
2½ cups farfalle
1 tsp. butter
4 tbsp. freshly chopped parsley, plus 1 tbsp. to garnish

Food Fact

When cooking pasta, remember to use a very large pan so that the pasta has plenty of space to move around freely. Once the water has come to a boil, add the pasta and stir, then cover with a lid and return to a boil. The lid can then be removed so that the water does not boil over.

Helpful Hint

Lamb fillet can be quite fatty—cut off and discard as much fat as possible. If preferred, leg of lamb can be used instead.

Creamed Lamb & Wild Mushroom Pasta

1 Place the porcini in a small bowl and cover with almost-boiling water. Let soak for 30 minutes. Drain the porcini, saving the soaking liquid. Chop the porcini finely.

2 Bring a large pan of lightly salted water to a rolling boil. Add the pasta and cook according to the package directions or until al dente.

3 Meanwhile, melt the butter with the olive oil in a large skillet and fry the lamb to seal. Add the garlic, mushrooms, and prepared porcini, and cook for 5 minutes or until just soft.

4 Add the wine and the porcini soaking liquid, then simmer for 2 minutes. Stir in the cream with the seasoning and simmer for 1–2 minutes or until just thickened.

5 Drain the pasta thoroughly, setting aside about 4 tablespoons of the cooking water. Return the pasta to the pan. Pour over the mushroom sauce and toss lightly together, adding the pasta water if the sauce is too thick. Spoon into a warmed serving dish or onto individual plates. Garnish with the chopped parsley and serve immediately with grated Parmesan cheese.

INGREDIENTS
Serves 4

⅔ cup dried porcini
4 cups pasta shapes
2 tbsp. butter
1 tbsp. olive oil
12 oz. lamb neck fillet, thinly sliced
1 garlic clove, peeled and crushed
2½ cups brown or wild mushrooms, wiped and sliced
4 tbsp. white wine
½ cup heavy cream
salt and freshly ground black pepper
1 tbsp. freshly chopped parsley, to garnish
freshly grated Parmesan cheese, to serve

Helpful Hint

Dried porcini mushrooms have a rich, intense flavor. After soaking, they should be briefly rinsed to remove any grit or dirt. Strain the soaking liquid through a cheesecloth or a very fine sieve. If you do not have either of these, leave it to settle for about 10 minutes; grit will sink to the bottom and the liquid can be poured off, leaving any sediment behind.

Tagliatelle with Creamy Liver & Basil

1 Season the flour lightly with salt and pepper and place in a large plastic bag. Add the liver and toss gently to coat. Remove the liver from the bag and set aside.

2 Melt the butter with the olive oil in a large skillet. Add the onion and garlic, and fry for 6–8 minutes or until the onions begin to brown. Add the liver and fry until brown on all sides.

3 Stir in the chicken stock, tomato paste, and sun-dried tomatoes. Bring to a boil, then reduce the heat and simmer very gently for 10 minutes.

4 Meanwhile, bring a large pan of lightly salted water to a rolling boil. Add the pasta and cook according to the package directions or until al dente.

5 Stir the chopped basil and cream into the liver sauce and season to taste.

6 Drain the pasta thoroughly, setting aside 2 tablespoons of the cooking water. Spoon the pasta into a warmed serving dish or pile onto individual plates. Stir the reserved cooking water into the liver sauce and pour over the pasta. Toss lightly to coat the pasta. Garnish with basil leaves and serve immediately.

Helpful Hint

Although not as delicately flavored as calf's liver, lamb's liver can be wonderfully tender and moist if gently simmered, as shown here. To tone down the flavor, it can be soaked in a little milk for 1 hour after preparation. Drain the liver and pat it dry on paper towels before cooking.

INGREDIENTS
Serves 4

2 tbsp. all-purpose flour
salt and freshly ground black pepper
1 lb. lamb's liver, thinly sliced and cut into bite-sized pieces (use calf's liver if lamb's liver is unavailable)
2 tbsp. butter
1 tbsp. olive oil
2 red onions, peeled and sliced
1 garlic clove, peeled and sliced
⅔ cup chicken stock
1 tbsp. tomato paste
2 sun-dried tomatoes, finely chopped
1 tbsp. freshly chopped basil
⅔ cup heavy cream
12 oz. tagliatelle verde
fresh basil leaves, to garnish

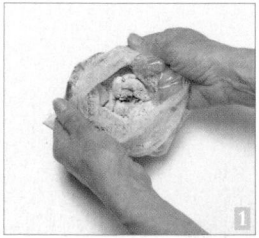

Ham Steak with Red Wine Sauce & Pasta

1 Preheat the broiler to a medium heat before cooking. Heat the butter with the red wine in a large heavy-based pan. Add the onions and cover with a tight-fitting lid. Cook over a very low heat for 30 minutes or until softened and transparent. Remove the lid from the pan then stir in the orange juice and sugar. Increase the heat, and cook for about 10 minutes or until the onions are golden.

2 Meanwhile, cook the ham steak under the preheated broiler, turning at least once, for 4–6 minutes or until tender. Cut the cooked ham into bite-sized pieces. Set aside and keep warm.

3 Meanwhile, bring a large pan of very lightly salted water to a rolling boil. Add the pasta and cook according to the package directions or until al dente. Drain the pasta, then return it to the pan. Season with a little black pepper and keep warm.

4 Stir the whole-grain mustard and chopped parsley into the onion sauce, then pour over the pasta. Add the ham pieces to the pan and toss lightly to thoroughly coat the pasta with the sauce. Pile the pasta mixture onto two warmed serving plates. Garnish with sprigs of Italian parsley and serve immediately.

INGREDIENTS
Serves 2

2 tbsp. butter
⅔ cup red wine
4 red onions, peeled and sliced
4 tbsp. orange juice
1 tsp. soft brown sugar
8 oz. ham steak, trimmed
1½ cups fusilli
freshly ground black pepper
3 tbsp. whole-grain mustard
2 tbsp. freshly chopped Italian parsley, plus sprigs to garnish

Helpful Hint

Ham steak can be slightly salty, so add only a little salt when cooking the pasta. Whole-grain mustard is made from mixed mustard seeds. This gives it a grainy texture and a fruity, spicy flavor that goes particularly well with ham steak.

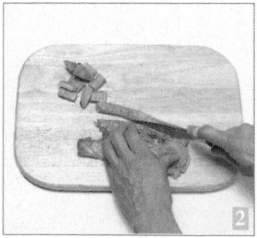

Prosciutto & Gruyère Carbonara

1 Place the egg yolks with 6 tablespoons of the Gruyère cheese in a bowl and mix lightly until well blended, then set aside.

2 Heat the olive oil in a large pan, and cook the garlic and shallots for 5 minutes or until golden-brown. Add the prosciutto ham, then cook for an additional minute. Pour in the dry vermouth and simmer for 2 minutes, then remove from the heat. Season to taste with salt and pepper and keep warm.

3 Meanwhile, bring a large pan of lightly salted water to a rolling boil. Add the pasta and cook according to the package directions or until al dente. Drain thoroughly, setting aside 4 tablespoons of the water, and return the pasta to the pan.

4 Remove from the heat, then add the egg and cheese mixture with the butter to the pasta; toss lightly until coated. Add the prosciutto mixture and toss again, adding the pasta water, if needed, to moisten. Season to taste and sprinkle with the remaining Gruyère cheese and the shredded basil leaves. Garnish with basil sprigs and serve immediately.

INGREDIENTS
Serves 4

3 medium egg yolks
½ cup grated Gruyère cheese
2 tbsp. olive oil
2 garlic cloves, peeled and crushed
2 shallots, peeled and finely chopped
7 oz. prosciutto ham, cut into strips
4 tbsp. dry vermouth
salt and freshly ground black pepper
1 lb. spaghetti
1 tbsp. butter
1 tbsp. freshly shredded basil leaves
basil sprigs, to garnish

Food Fact

Gruyère cheese is now produced in many countries, including the United States and France. It is named after the Swiss mountain village where it originated and is still made. The pale yellow cheese is pitted with pea-sized holes and has a firm texture and a sweet, slightly nutty taste.

Gnocchi with Tuscan Beef Ragù

1 Preheat the oven to 400° F. Place the porcini in a small bowl and cover with almost-boiling water. Let soak for 30 minutes. Drain, setting aside the soaking liquid and straining it through a cheesecloth-lined sieve. Chop the porcini.

2 Heat the olive oil in a large heavy-based pan. Add the onion, carrot, celery, fennel, and garlic, and cook, stirring, for 8 minutes or until soft. Add the ground beef and cook, stirring, for 5–8 minutes or until sealed and any lumps are broken up.

3 Pour in the wine, then add the porcini with half the pine nuts, the rosemary, and tomato paste. Stir in the porcini soaking liquid, then simmer for 5 minutes. Add the chopped tomatoes and simmer gently for about 40 minutes, stirring occasionally.

4 Meanwhile, bring 8 cups of lightly salted water to a rolling boil in a large pan. Add the gnocchi and cook for 1–2 minutes, until they rise to the surface.

5 Drain the gnocchi and place in an ovenproof dish. Stir in three-quarters of the mozzarella cheese with the beef sauce. Season to taste. Top with the remaining mozzarella and pine nuts, then bake in the preheated oven for 20 minutes until golden brown. Serve immediately.

INGREDIENTS
Serves 4

⅔ cup dried porcini
3 tbsp. olive oil
1 small onion, peeled and finely chopped
1 carrot, peeled and finely chopped
1 celery, trimmed and finely chopped
1 fennel bulb, trimmed and sliced
2 garlic cloves, peeled and crushed
1 lb. fresh ground beef
4 tbsp. red wine
⅓ cup pine nuts
1 tbsp. freshly chopped rosemary
2 tbsp. tomato paste
14-oz. can chopped tomatoes
1 cup cubed mozzarella cheese
salt and freshly ground black pepper
8 oz. fresh gnocchi

Food Fact

Pine nuts are small, creamy-colored, tear-shaped nuts from the base of the cone scales of the Mediterranean stone pine. Due to their high oil content, they may become rancid if kept too long, so buy in small amounts and use within 1–2 months.

Saffron Roast Chicken with Crispy Onions

1 Preheat the oven to 400° F. Using your fingertips, gently loosen the skin from the chicken breast by sliding your hand between the skin and flesh. Cream together ½ stick of the butter with the saffron threads, lemon rind, and half the parsley until smooth. Push the butter under the skin. Spread over the breast and the top of the thighs with your fingers. Pull the neck skin to tighten the skin over the breast and tuck under the bird, then secure with a toothpick.

2 Heat the olive oil and remaining butter in a large, heavy skillet, and cook the onions and garlic cloves for 5 minutes or until the onions are soft. Stir in the cumin seeds, cinnamon, pine nuts, and golden raisins, and cook for 2 minutes. Season to taste with salt and pepper, and put in a roasting pan.

3 Place the chicken, breast-side down, on the base of the onions, and roast in the preheated oven for 45 minutes. Reduce the oven temperature to 325° F. Turn the chicken breast-side up and stir the onions. Continue roasting until the chicken is a deep golden yellow and the onions are crisp. Allow to rest for 10 minutes, then sprinkle with the remaining parsley. Before serving, garnish with a sprig of parsley, and serve immediately with the onions and garlic.

INGREDIENTS
Serves 4–6

3½ lb. oven-ready chicken
½ stick butter, softened
1 tsp. saffron strands, lightly toasted
1 tbsp. grated lemon rind
2 tbsp. freshly chopped Italian parsley
2 tbsp. extra-virgin olive oil
2½ cups onions, peeled and cut into thin wedges
8–12 garlic cloves, peeled
1 tsp. cumin seeds
½ tsp. ground cinnamon
½ cup pine nuts
5 tbsp. golden raisins
salt and freshly ground black pepper
sprig of fresh Italian parsley, to garnish

Helpful Hint

Roasting the chicken breast-side down first helps to ensure that the white meat will be moist. Turning the chicken halfway through cooking will give a crisp, golden skin.

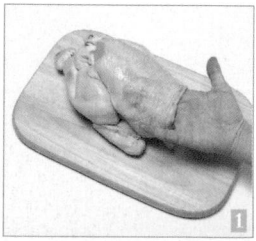

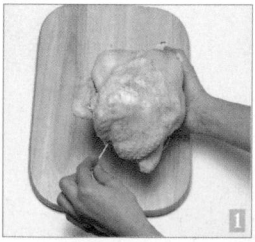

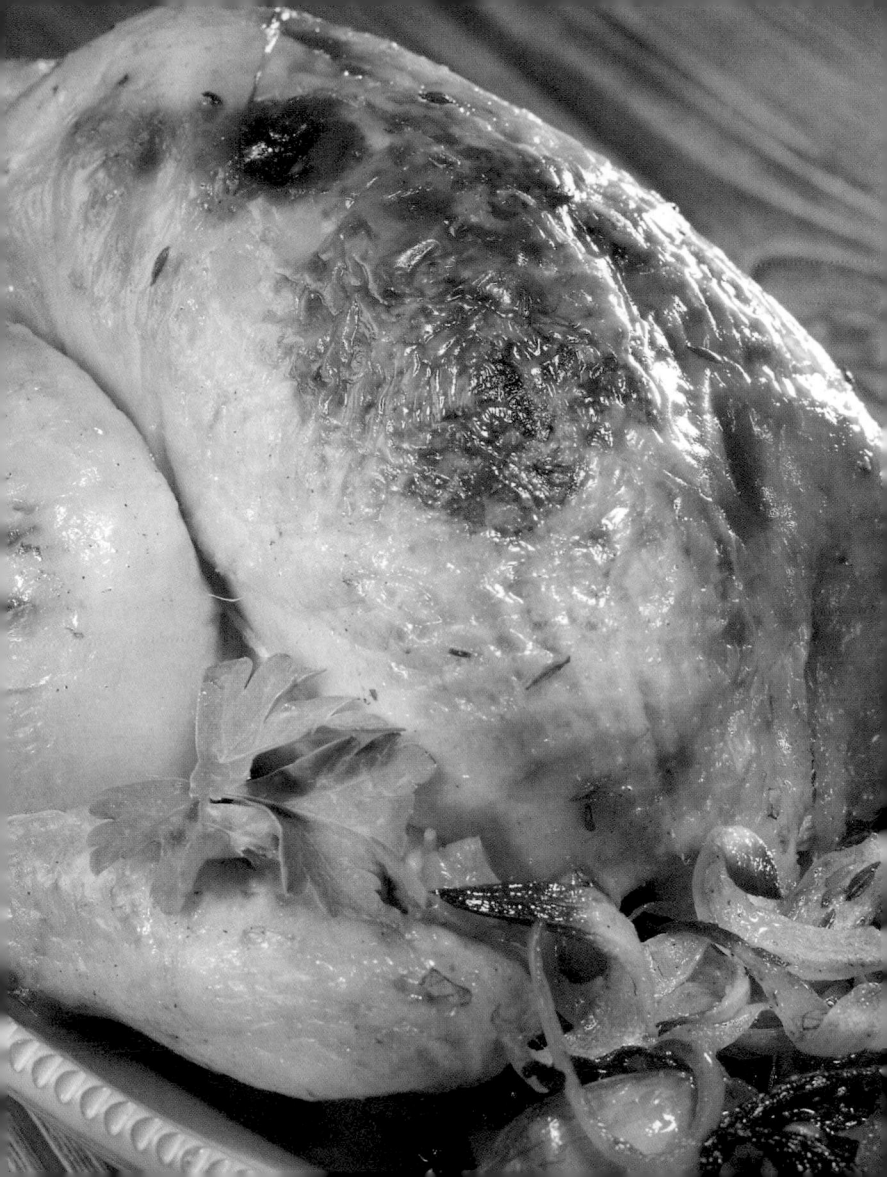

Game Hen with Mushrooms & Red Wine Gravy

1 Preheat the oven to 350° F. Heat the butter and oil in a large saucepan or skillet. Add the game hens and shallots, working in batches, if necessary, and cook for 10 minutes or until golden on all sides, shaking the saucepan to glaze the shallots. Transfer to a casserole dish large enough to hold the pieces in a single layer. Add the mushroom and thyme to the saucepan, and cook for 2–3 minutes or until beginning to brown. Transfer to the dish with the game hen halves.

2 Add the wine to the saucepan; it will bubble and steam. Cook, stirring up any browned bits from the pan and allow to reduce by half. Pour in the stock and bring to a boil, then pour over the game hens. Cover and braise in the preheated oven for 50 minutes or until tender. Remove the game hens and vegetables to a wide, shallow serving dish, and set the casserole or roasting pan over a medium-high heat.

3 Skim off any surface fat and bring to a boil. Blend the cornstarch with the vinegar, and stir into the sauce with the red currant jelly. Boil until the sauce is reduced and thickened slightly. Stir in the parsley, and season to taste with salt and pepper. Pour over the game hens, garnish with sprigs of fresh thyme, and serve immediately.

Helpful Hint

To halve the game hens, cut along one side of the sternum, pulling the breast away from the rib cage in one piece. Cut through the thigh joint where it joins the back to give half a game hen. Repeat along the other side of the sternum.

INGREDIENTS
Serves 4

¼ stick butter
1 tbsp. olive oil
2 small game hens, rinsed, well-dried, and halved
8 shallots, peeled
2¾ cups large mushrooms, thickly sliced
2–3 sprigs of fresh thyme or rosemary, leaves stripped
1¼ cups Valpolicella or fruity red wine
1¼ cups hot chicken stock
1 tbsp. cornstarch
2 tbsp. balsamic vinegar
2 tbsp. red currant jelly, or to taste
2 tbsp. freshly chopped Italian parsley
salt and freshly ground black pepper
sprigs of fresh thyme, to garnish

Game Hen with Sage & Blueberries

1 Preheat the oven to 350° F. Place the oil, shallots, sage, and bay leaf in a bowl, with the juice from the lemon halves. Season with salt and pepper. Put each of the squeezed lemon halves into the game hens with ¼ cup of the blueberries, then rub the game hens with the marinade, and leave for 2–3 hours, basting occasionally.

2 Remove the game hens from the marinade, and cover each with 2 slices of prosciutto. Tie the legs of each game hen with kitchen string, and place in a roasting pan. Pour over the marinade and add the vermouth. Roast in the preheated oven for 1 hour or until golden, and the juices run clear when a thigh is pierced with a sharp knife.

3 Transfer to a warm serving plate, cover with foil, and discard the string. Skim off any surface fat from the pan, and set over a medium-high heat.

4 Add the stock to the pan and bring to a boil, scraping any browned bits from the bottom. Boil until slightly reduced. Beat in the cream or butter, if desired, and simmer until thickened, beating constantly. Stir in the brandy and strain into a gravy jug. Add the remaining blueberries and keep warm.

5 Using a sharp carving knife, cut each of the game hens in half, and arrange on the plate with the prosciutto. Serve immediately with roasted potatoes and gravy.

INGREDIENTS
Serves 4

3 tbsp. olive oil
3 shallots, peeled and coarsely chopped
2 sprigs of fresh sage, coarsely chopped
1 bay leaf
1 lemon, halved
salt and freshly ground black pepper
2 game hens, rinsed and dried
1 cup blueberries
4 slices prosciutto or bacon
½ cup vermouth or dry white wine
1 cup chicken stock
3 tbsp. heavy cream or butter (optional)
1 tbsp. brandy
roasted potatoes and gravy, to serve

1

2

5

Game Hens with Garlic Sage Butter

1 Preheat the broiler or light an outdoor charcoal grill, and line the broiler rack with foil just before cooking. Put the garlic cloves in a small saucepan and cover with cold water. Bring to a boil, then simmer for 5 minutes or until softened. Drain and cool slightly. Cut off the root end of each clove, and squeeze the softened garlic into a bowl.

2 Pound the garlic until smooth, then beat in the butter, chives, sage, lemon rind, and lemon juice. Season to taste with salt and pepper.

3 Using your fingertips, gently loosen the skin from each game hen breast by sliding your hand between the skin and the flesh. Push one quarter of the herb butter under the skin, spreading evenly over the breast and the top of the thighs. Pull the neck skin gently to tighten the skin over the breast and tuck under the bird. Repeat with the remaining birds and herb butter.

4 Thread 2 wooden skewers through each game hen from one wing through the opposite leg, to keep the game hen flat. Repeat with the remaining game hens, brush with the olive oil, and season with salt and pepper.

5 Arrange the game hens on the rack over the foil-lined rack, and broil for 25 minutes, turning occasionally until golden and crisp, and the juices run clear when a thigh is pierced with a sharp knife. Position the rack about 5 inches from the heat source, or the skin will brown before the birds are cooked through. Garnish with chives and sage leaves, and serve immediately with broiled polenta and a few broiled tomatoes.

INGREDIENTS
Serves 4

FOR THE HERB BUTTER:
6 large garlic cloves
1 stick butter, softened
2 tbsp. freshly cut chives
2 tbsp. freshly chopped sage
1 tbsp. grated lemon rind
1 tbsp. lemon juice
salt and freshly ground black pepper

FOR THE GAME HENS:
4 game hens
2 tbsp. extra-virgin olive oil

TO GARNISH:
chives
fresh sage leaves

TO SERVE:
broiled polenta (see p. 358)
broiled tomatoes

2

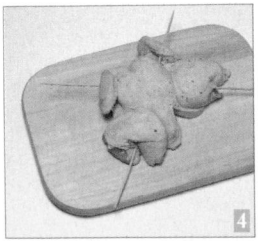
4

5

Chicken Cacciatore

1 Heat 1 tablespoon of the olive oil in a large, deep skillet, and add the diced pancetta or bacon and stir-fry for 2–3 minutes or until crisp and golden brown. Using a slotted spoon, transfer the pancetta or bacon to a plate and set aside.

2 Season the flour with salt and pepper, then use to coat the chicken. Heat the remaining oil in the skillet, and brown the chicken pieces on all sides for about 15 minutes. Remove from the skillet and add to the bacon.

3 Stir the garlic into the skillet and cook for 30 seconds. Add the red wine and cook, stirring and scraping any browned bits from the base of the skillet. Let the wine boil until it is reduced by half. Add the tomatoes, stock, onions, bay leaf, brown sugar, and oregano, and stir well. Season to taste.

4 Return the chicken and bacon to the skillet and bring to a boil. Cover and simmer for 30 minutes, then stir in the bell peppers and mushrooms and simmer for an additional 15–20 minutes or until the chicken and vegetables are tender, and the sauce is reduced and slightly thickened. Stir in the parsley, and serve immediately with tagliatelle.

INGREDIENTS
Serves 4

2–3 tbsp. olive oil
½ cup pancetta or bacon, diced
¼ cup all-purpose flour
salt and freshly ground black pepper
3–3½ lb. chicken, cut into 8 pieces
2 garlic cloves, peeled and chopped
½ cup red wine
14 oz. can chopped tomatoes
⅔ cup chicken stock
12 small onions, peeled
1 bay leaf
1 tsp. brown sugar
1 tsp. dried oregano
1 green bell pepper, seeded and chopped
2 cups chestnut or field mushrooms, thickly sliced
2 tbsp. freshly chopped parsley
freshly cooked tagliatelle, to serve

Tasty Tip

Use chestnut or field mushrooms in this recipe because they have a stronger flavor than button mushrooms and will also help to add color to the sauce.

Lemon Chicken with Potatoes, Rosemary, & Olives

1 Preheat the oven to 400° F. Trim the chicken thighs and place in a shallow baking dish large enough to hold them in a single layer. Remove the rind from the lemon with a zester, or if using a peeler, julienne. Set half aside and add the remainder to the chicken. Squeeze the lemon juice over the chicken, toss to coat well, and let stand for 10 minutes.

2 Transfer the chicken to a large roasting pan. Add the remaining lemon zest or strips, olive oil, sliced garlic, onions, and half of the rosemary sprigs. Toss gently and leave for about 20 minutes.

3 Cover the potatoes with lightly salted water and bring to a boil. Cook for 2 minutes, then drain well and add to the chicken. Season to taste with salt and pepper.

4 Roast the chicken in the preheated oven for 50 minutes, turning frequently and basting, or until the chicken is cooked. Just before the end of cooking time, discard the rosemary, and add fresh sprigs of rosemary. Add the olives and stir. Serve immediately with steamed carrots and zucchini.

INGREDIENTS
Serves 6

12 skinless boneless chicken thighs
1 large lemon
½ cup extra-virgin olive oil
6 garlic cloves, peeled and sliced
2 onions, peeled and thinly sliced
1 bunch fresh rosemary
2½ lbs. potatoes, peeled and cut into 1½-inch pieces
salt and freshly ground black pepper
18–24 pitted ripe olives

TO SERVE:
steamed carrots
zucchini

Helpful Hint

It is worth seeking out unwaxed lemons for this recipe, or for any recipe in which the lemon zest is to be eaten. If unwaxed fruit is unavailable, pour hot water over and scrub well before removing the zest.

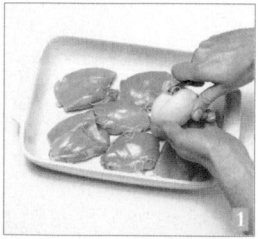

Chicken with Porcini Mushrooms & Cream

1 Heat the olive oil in a large, heavy skillet, then add the chicken breasts, skin-side down, and cook for about 10 minutes or until they are well browned. Remove the chicken breasts and set aside. Add the garlic, stir into the juices, and cook for 1 minute.

2 Pour the vermouth or white wine into the skillet, and season to taste with salt and pepper. Return the chicken to the skillet. Bring to a boil, reduce the heat to low, and simmer for about 20 minutes or until tender.

3 In another large skillet, heat the butter and add the sliced porcini or wild mushrooms. Stir-fry for about 5 minutes or until the mushrooms are golden and tender.

4 Add the porcini or wild mushrooms and any juices to the chicken. Season to taste with salt and pepper, then add the chopped oregano. Stir together gently and cook for 1 minute longer. Transfer to a large serving plate, and garnish with sprigs of fresh basil, if desired. Serve immediately with rice.

INGREDIENTS
Serves 4

2 tbsp. olive oil
4 boneless chicken breasts
2 garlic cloves, peeled and crushed
⅔ cup dry vermouth or dry white wine
salt and freshly ground black pepper
¼ stick butter
4 cups porcini or wild mushrooms, thickly sliced
1 tbsp. freshly chopped oregano
sprigs of fresh basil, to garnish
freshly cooked rice, to serve

Tasty Tip

Porcini mushrooms grow wild and are relatively easy to find, if you know where to look. They can, however, be very expensive to buy fresh. If they are unavailable, substitute with fresh button or chestnut mushrooms and 5 tablespoons reconstituted dried porcini instead.

Helpful Hint

If using dried mushrooms, cover with almost-boiling water, leave for 20 minutes, then drain, straining the soaking liquid to use.

Turkey Cutlets Marsala with Wilted Watercress

1 Place each turkey cutlet between 2 sheets of nonstick baking parchment, and, using a meat mallet or rolling pin, pound to make a cutlet about ⅛ inch thick. Put the flour in a shallow dish, add the thyme, season to taste with salt and pepper, and stir to blend. Coat each cutlet lightly on both sides with the flour mixture, then set aside.

2 Heat the olive oil in a large skillet, then add the watercress, and stir-fry for about 2 minutes until just wilted and brightly colored. Season with salt and pepper. Using a slotted spoon, transfer the watercress to a plate and keep warm.

3 Add half the butter to the skillet, and when melted, add the mushrooms. Stir-fry for 4 minutes or until golden and tender. Remove from the skillet and set aside.

4 Add the remaining butter to the skillet and, working in batches, cook the flour-coated cutlets for 2–3 minutes on each side or until golden and cooked thoroughly, adding the remaining oil if necessary. Remove from the skillet and keep warm.

5 Add the Marsala wine to the skillet and stir, scraping up any browned bits from the bottom of the skillet. Add the stock or water and bring to a boil over a high heat. Season lightly.

6 Return the cutlets and mushrooms to the skillet and reheat gently until piping hot. Divide the warm watercress among 4 serving plates.

7 Arrange one cutlet over each serving of watercress, and spoon over the mushrooms and Marsala sauce. Serve immediately.

INGREDIENTS
Serves 4

4 turkey cutlets, ¼ lb. each
¼ cup all-purpose flour
½ tsp. dried thyme
salt and freshly ground black pepper
1–2 tbsp. olive oil
2½ cups watercress
½ stick butter
2 cups mushrooms, wiped and quartered
¼ cup dry Marsala or Italian fortified wine
¼ cup chicken stock or water

Helpful Hint

Turkey cutlets are thin slices of turkey breast fillets, which have been flattened. If they are unavailable, substitute chicken breasts that have been halved horizontally and flattened between pieces of plastic wrap.

Lemon Chicken with Basil & Linguine

1 Blend the lemon rind and juice, garlic, half the oil, half the basil, and the salt and pepper in a large bowl. Add the chicken pieces and toss well to coat. Let stand for about 1 hour, stirring occasionally.

2 Heat the remaining oil in a large nonstick skillet, then add the sliced onion, and cook for 3–4 minutes or until slightly softened. Using a slotted spoon, drain the chicken pieces and add to the skillet, setting the marinade aside. Cook the chicken for 2–3 minutes or until golden brown, then add the sliced celery and mushroom halves and cook for an additional 2–3 minutes.

3 Sprinkle in the flour and stir until the chicken and vegetables are coated. Gradually stir the wine into the skillet until a thick sauce forms, then stir in the stock and marinade. Bring to a boil, stirring constantly. Cover and simmer for about 10 minutes, then stir in the remaining basil.

4 Meanwhile, bring a large saucepan of lightly salted water to a boil. Slowly add the linguine, and simmer for 7–10 minutes or until al dente. Drain well and turn into a large serving bowl, pour over the sauce, and garnish with the lemon zest and fresh basil leaves. Serve immediately.

Tasty Tip

Make basil-flavored olive oil for this recipe by putting a large handful of chopped basil leaves into the bowl of a small food processor or blender. Add 3–4 tablespoons good-quality olive oil, and blend to a purée. Pass the oil through a fine strainer. This oil will not keep and should be used immediately.

INGREDIENTS
Serves 4

1 tbsp. grated lemon rind
3 tbsp. lemon juice
2 garlic cloves, peeled and crushed
2 tbsp. basil-flavored extra-virgin olive oil
4 tbsp. freshly chopped basil
salt and freshly ground black pepper
1 lb. skinless, boneless chicken breast, cut into bite-size pieces
1 onion, peeled and finely chopped
3 celery stalks, trimmed and thinly sliced
1½ cups mushrooms, wiped and halved
2 tbsp. all-purpose flour
⅔ cup white wine
⅔ cup chicken stock
4–6 cups linguine pasta

TO GARNISH:
lemon zest
fresh basil leaves

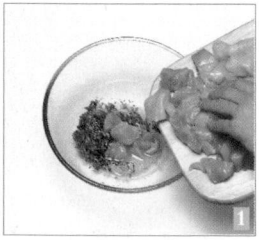

Chicken Liver & Tomato Sauce with Tagliolini

1 Heat half the olive oil in a large, deep, heavy skillet and add the onion. Cook, stirring frequently, for 4–5 minutes or until soft and translucent. Stir in the garlic, and cook for an additional minute.

2 Add the red wine and cook, stirring until the wine is reduced by half, then add the tomatoes, tomato paste, and half the sage or thyme. Bring to a boil, stirring to break up the tomatoes. Simmer for 30 minutes, stirring occasionally or until the sauce has reduced and thickened. Season to taste with salt and pepper.

3 Bring a large saucepan of lightly salted water to a boil. Add the pasta and cook for 7–10 minutes or until al dente.

4 Meanwhile, in a large, heavy skillet, melt the remaining oil and the butter, and heat until very hot. Pat the chicken livers dry, and dust lightly with a little flour. Add to the skillet, a few at a time, and cook for 5 minutes or until crisp and browned, turning carefully—the livers should still be pink inside.

5 Drain the pasta well, and turn into a large, warmed serving bowl. Stir the livers carefully into the tomato sauce, then pour the sauce over the drained pasta, and toss gently to coat. Garnish with a sprig of fresh sage and serve immediately.

Helpful Hint

Many recipes using wine call for it to be simmered until reduced by half. This is to eliminate the alcohol from the wine and to concentrate the flavor. Without this reduction, the sauce would taste of raw wine, which can be quite sour.

INGREDIENTS
Serves 4

¼ cup extra-virgin olive oil
1 onion, peeled and finely chopped
2 garlic cloves, peeled and finely chopped
½ cup dry red wine
2 14-oz. cans Italian peeled plum tomatoes with juice
1 tbsp. tomato paste
1 tbsp. freshly chopped sage or thyme leaves
salt and freshly ground black pepper
4 cups fresh or dried tagliolini, papardelle, or tagliatelle
¼ stick butter
2 cups fresh chicken livers, trimmed and cut in half
all-purpose flour, for dusting
sprigs of fresh sage, to garnish

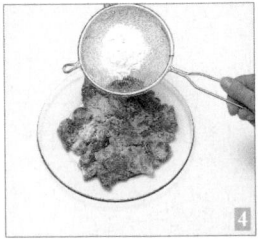

Creamy Chicken Cannelloni

1 Preheat the oven to 375° F. Lightly butter a 9 x 11 inch ovenproof baking dish. Heat half the butter in a large, heavy skillet, add the garlic and mushrooms, and cook gently for 5 minutes. Stir in the basil and the spinach, and cook covered until the spinach is wilted and tender, stirring frequently. Season with salt and pepper, then spoon into the dish and set aside.

2 Melt the remaining butter in a small saucepan, then stir in the flour and cook for about 2 minutes, stirring constantly. Remove from the heat, stir in the stock, the white wine, and the cream. Return to the heat, bring to a boil, and simmer, until the sauce is thick and smooth, then season to taste.

3 Measure ½ cup of the cream sauce into a bowl. Add the chopped chicken, prosciutto, and the dried thyme. Season to taste, then spoon the chicken mixture into the cannelloni tubes, arranging them in 2 long rows on top of the spinach layer.

4 Add half the shredded Gruyère cheese to the cream sauce and heat, stirring, until the cheese melts. Pour over the sauce and top with the remaining Gruyère and the Parmesan cheeses. Cook in the preheated oven for 35 minutes or until golden and bubbling. Garnish with a sprig of fresh basil and serve immediately.

Tasty Tip

This rich sauce demands a salad to accompany it. Beat together 1 teaspoon mustard, 2 teaspoons lemon juice, a pinch of sugar, and salt and pepper to taste. When blended, beat in 3–4 tablespoons good-quality olive oil. Add a package of mixed salad and toss to coat.

INGREDIENTS
Serves 6

½ stick butter
2 garlic cloves, peeled and finely crushed
2 cups button mushrooms, thinly sliced
2 tbsp. freshly chopped basil
10 cups fresh spinach, blanched
salt and freshly ground black pepper
2 tbsp. all-purpose flour
1¼ cups chicken stock
⅔ cup dry white wine
⅔ cup heavy cream
3¼ cups skinless, boneless, cooked chicken, chopped
¼ cup prosciutto, finely chopped
½ tsp. dried thyme
16 precooked cannelloni tubes
1½ cups Gruyère cheese, shredded
½ cup Parmesan cheese, shredded
sprig of fresh basil, to garnish

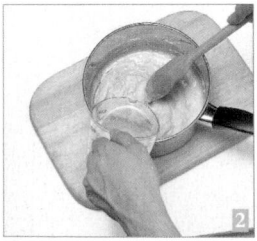

Duck Lasagna with Porcini & Basil

1 Preheat the oven to 350° F. Put the duck with the vegetables, garlic, peppercorns, bay leaves, and thyme into a large stock pot, and cover with cold water. Bring to a boil, skimming off any fat, then reduce the heat and simmer for 1 hour. Transfer the duck to a bowl and cool slightly.

2 When cool enough to handle, remove the meat from the duck and dice. Return all the bones and trimmings to the simmering stock and continue to simmer for 1 hour. Strain the stock into a large bowl and leave until cool. Remove and discard the fat that has risen to the top of the stock.

3 Put the porcini in a strainer and rinse under cold running water. Leave for 1 minute to dry off, then turn out onto a chopping board and chop finely. Place in a bowl, then pour over the sherry, and leave for about 1 hour or until the porcini are plump and all the sherry is absorbed.

4 Heat ¼ stick of the butter in a skillet. Shred the basil leaves and add to the hot butter, stirring until wilted. Add the soaked porcini and any liquid, mix well, and set aside.

5 Grease a 9 x 12 inch baking dish, and pour a little stock into the base. Cover with 6–8 lasagna sheets, making sure that the sheets slightly overlap. Continue to layer the pasta with a little stock, the duck, the mushroom-basil mixture, and Parmesan. Add a little butter every other layer.

6 Cover with foil and cook in the preheated oven for 40–45 minutes or until cooked. Let stand for 10 minutes before serving. Garnish with a sprig of parsley and serve with salad.

INGREDIENTS
Serves 6

3–4 lb. duck, quartered
1 onion, unpeeled and quartered
2 carrots, peeled and cut into pieces
1 celery stalk, cut into pieces
1 leek, trimmed and cut into pieces
2 garlic cloves, unpeeled and smashed
1 tbsp. black peppercorns
2 bay leaves
6–8 sprigs of fresh thyme
½ cup dried porcini mushrooms
½ cup dry sherry
½ stick butter, diced
1 bunch fresh basil leaves, stripped from stems
24 precooked lasagna sheets
1 cup Parmesan cheese, shredded
sprig of parsley, to garnish
mixed salad, to serve

1

2

3

Turkey Tetrazzini

1 Preheat the oven to 350° F. Lightly grease a large ovenproof dish. Bring a large saucepan of lightly salted water to a boil. Add the tagliatelle and cook for 7–9 minutes or until al dente. Drain well and set aside.

2 In a heavy saucepan, heat the butter and add the bacon. Cook for 2–3 minutes or until crisp and golden. Add the onion and mushrooms, and cook for 3–4 minutes or until the vegetables are tender.

3 Stir in the flour and cook for 2 minutes. Remove from the heat and slowly stir in the stock. Return to the heat and cook, stirring, until a smooth, thick sauce has formed. Add the tagliatelle, then pour in the cream and sherry. Add the turkey and parsley. Season to taste with the nutmeg, salt, and pepper. Toss well to coat.

4 Turn the mixture into the prepared dish, spreading evenly. Sprinkle the top with the Parmesan cheese, and cook in the preheated oven for 30–35 minutes or until crisp, golden, and bubbling. Garnish with chopped parsley and Parmesan cheese. Serve straight from the dish.

INGREDIENTS
Serves 4

3¼ cups green and white tagliatelle
½ stick butter
4 slices bacon, diced
1 onion, peeled and finely chopped
1½ cups mushrooms, thinly sliced
½ cup all-purpose flour
2 cups chicken stock
½ cup heavy cream
2 tbsp. sherry
5 cups cooked turkey meat, cut into bite-sized pieces
1 tbsp. freshly chopped parsley
freshly grated nutmeg
salt and freshly ground black pepper
¼ cup Parmesan cheese, shredded

TO GARNISH:
freshly chopped parsley
Parmesan cheese, shredded

Tasty Tip

This is a great way to use Thanksgiving leftovers—it's worth putting extra meat in the freezer. Use frozen leftovers within 1 month.

Poached Chicken with Salsa Verde Herb Sauce

1 Place the chicken breasts with the stock in a large skillet, and bring to a boil. Reduce the heat and simmer for 10–15 minutes or until cooked. Let cool in the stock.

2 To make the salsa verde, turn on the food processor, then drop in the garlic cloves and chop finely. Add the parsley and mint, and using the pulse button, pulse 2–3 times. Add the capers and, if using, add the gherkins, anchovies, and arugula. Pulse 2–3 times until the sauce is evenly textured.

3 With the machine still running, pour in the lemon juice or red wine vinegar, then add the olive oil in a slow, steady stream until the sauce is smooth. Season to taste with salt and pepper, then transfer to a large serving bowl and set aside.

4 Carve each chicken breast into thick slices and arrange on serving plates, fanning out the slices slightly. Spoon a little of the salsa verde onto each chicken breast, garnish with sprigs of mint, and serve immediately with freshly cooked vegetables.

INGREDIENTS
Serves 6

6 boneless chicken breasts
2½ cups chicken stock, preferably homemade

FOR THE SALSA VERDE:
2 garlic cloves, peeled and chopped
4 tbsp. freshly chopped parsley
3 tbsp. freshly chopped mint
2 tsp. capers
2 tbsp. chopped gherkins (optional)
2–3 anchovy fillets in olive oil, drained and finely chopped (optional)
1 handful arugula, chopped (optional)
2 tbsp. lemon juice or red wine vinegar
½ cup extra-virgin olive oil
salt and freshly ground black pepper
sprigs of mint, to garnish
freshly cooked vegetables, to serve

Helpful Hint

The salsa verde can be made ahead of time and stored in an airtight container for a day. Bring to room temperature and stir well before serving.

Chicken en Papillote with Zucchini & Pasta

1 Preheat the oven to 400° F. Lightly brush 4 large sheets of nonstick baking parchment with half the oil. Bring a saucepan of lightly salted water to a boil, and cook the pasta for 10 minutes or until al dente. Drain and set aside.

2 Heat the remaining oil in a skillet and cook the onion for 2–3 minutes. Add the garlic and cook for 1 minute. Add the zucchini and cook for 1 minute, then remove from the heat, season to taste with salt and pepper, and add half the oregano.

3 Divide the cooked pasta equally among the 4 sheets of baking parchment, positioning the pasta in the center. Top the pasta with equal amounts of the vegetable mixture, and sprinkle a quarter of the chopped tomatoes over each.

4 Score the surface of each chicken breast about ½ inch deep. Place a chicken breast on top of the pasta, and sprinkle each with the remaining oregano and the white wine. Fold the edges of the paper along the top and then along each side, creating a sealed envelope.

5 Cook in the preheated oven for 30–35 minutes or until cooked. Serve immediately. Be careful when opening the pouches, as the steam will be very hot.

INGREDIENTS
Serves 4

2 tbsp. olive oil
1 cup farfalle pasta or pasta shapes
1 onion, peeled and thinly sliced
1 garlic clove, peeled and finely chopped
2 medium zucchini, trimmed and thinly sliced
salt and freshly ground black pepper
2 tbsp. freshly chopped oregano
4 plum tomatoes, seeded and coarsely chopped
4 boneless, skinless chicken breasts
⅔ cup Italian white wine

Helpful Hint

This is a great recipe for entertaining. The pockets can be prepared ahead and cooked when needed. For a dramatic presentation, serve in the paper.

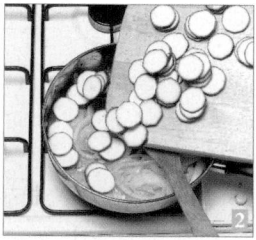

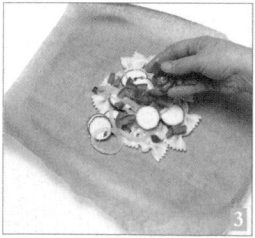

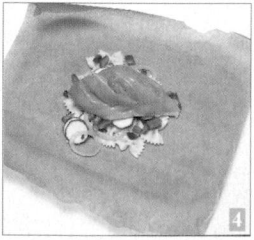

Chicken Under a Brick

1 Rinse the chicken and dry well, inside and out. Using poultry shears or kitchen scissors, cut along each side of the backbone of the chicken and discard or use for stock. Place the chicken skin-side up on a work surface, and using the palm of your hand, press down firmly to break the sternum and flatten the bird.

2 Turn the chicken breast-side up, and use a sharp knife to slit the skin between the breast and thigh on each side. Fold the legs in and push the drumstick bones through the slits. Tuck the wing under so that the chicken should be as flat as possible.

3 Heat the olive oil in a large, heavy skillet until very hot, but not smoking. Place the chicken in the skillet, skin-side down, and place a flat lid or plate directly on top of the chicken. Top with a brick (hence the recipe name) or a 5-lb. weight. Cook for 12–15 minutes or until golden brown.

4 Remove the weights and lid, and using a pair of tongs, turn the chicken carefully, then season to taste with salt and pepper. Cover and weigh the lid again, then cook for 12–15 minutes longer until the chicken is tender and the juices run clear when a thigh is pierced with a sharp knife.

5 Transfer the chicken to a serving plate and cover loosely with foil to keep warm. Allow to rest for at least 10 minutes before carving. Garnish with sprigs of basil and chives, and serve with lettuce leaves.

INGREDIENTS
Serves 4–6

4 lb. oven-ready chicken
4 tbsp. olive oil
sea salt and freshly ground black pepper

TO GARNISH:
sprigs of fresh basil
chives
tossed, bitter lettuce leaves, to serve

Tasty Tip

In a large bowl, beat together 1 teaspoon of mustard, 1 crushed garlic clove, 2 teaspoons of balsamic vinegar, and seasoning. When combined thoroughly, beat in 3–4 tablespoons of good-quality olive oil to taste. Toss with a mixture of bitter lettuce leaves, such as Italian red lettuce, radicchio, and chicory, and serve with the chicken.

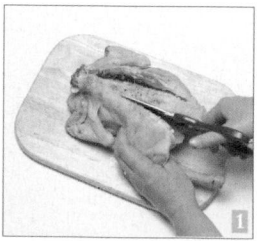

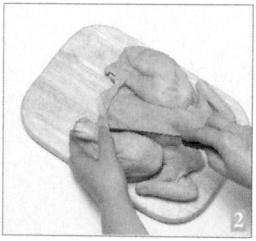

Chicken & Asparagus with Tagliatelle

1 Using a swivel-bladed vegetable peeler, lightly peel the asparagus stalks and then cook in lightly salted, boiling water for 2–3 minutes or until just tender. Drain and rinse in cold water, then cut into 1½-inch pieces and set aside.

2 Melt the butter in a large skillet, then add the scallions and the chicken slices, and cook for 4 minutes. Add the vermouth and allow to reduce until the liquid has evaporated. Pour in the cream and half the chives. Cook gently for 5–7 minutes until the sauce has thickened and the chicken is tender.

3 Bring a large saucepan of lightly salted water to a boil and cook the tagliatelle for 4–5 minutes or until al dente. Drain and immediately add to the chicken and cream sauce.

4 Using a pair of spaghetti tongs or kitchen forks, lightly toss the sauce and pasta until it is mixed thoroughly. Add the remaining chives and the Parmesan cheese, and toss gently. Garnish with cut chives and serve immediately, with extra Parmesan cheese, if desired.

INGREDIENTS
Serves 4

2 cups fresh asparagus stalks
½ stick butter
4 scallions, trimmed and coarsely chopped
¼ lb. boneless, skinless chicken breast, thinly sliced
2 tbsp. white vermouth
1 cup heavy cream
2 tbsp. freshly chopped chives
4½ cups fresh tagliatelle
½ cup Parmesan or pecorino cheese, shredded
cut chives, to garnish

Tasty Tip

Freshly made pasta will cook in 30–60 seconds. It is cooked when it rises to the surface. Fresh pasta purchased in the store will take between 2–3 minutes. Dried pasta takes longer to cook (between 4–10 minutes) depending on the variety—check the package instructions.

Marinated Game Hen Breasts with Broiled Polenta

1 Preheat the broiler just before cooking. Blend 2 tablespoons of the olive oil with the rosemary or sage, cinnamon, and orange zest. Season to taste with salt and pepper.

2 Place the game hen breasts in a large, shallow dish, pour over the oil, and marinate until needed, turning occasionally.

3 Bring the water and 1 teaspoon of salt to a boil in a large, heavy saucepan. Slowly beat in the polenta in a thin, steady stream. Reduce the heat and simmer for 5–10 minutes or until thick, stirring constantly.

4 Stir the butter and cheese into the polenta, along with the parsley and a little black pepper.

5 Turn the polenta out onto a lightly greased, nonstick baking sheet and spread into an even layer about ¾ inch thick. Allow to cool, then chill in the refrigerator for about 1 hour or until the polenta is chilled.

6 Turn the cold polenta onto a work surface. Cut into 4-inch squares. Brush with olive oil and arrange on a broiler rack. Broil for 2–3 minutes on each side until crisp and golden, then cut each square into triangles and keep warm.

7 Transfer the marinated game hen breasts to the broiler rack, and broil for 5 minutes or until crisp and beginning to brown, turning once. Serve the game hens immediately with the polenta and lettuce leaves.

INGREDIENTS
Serves 4

3 tbsp. extra-virgin olive oil
1 tbsp. freshly chopped rosemary or sage leaves
½ tsp. ground cinnamon
1 tbsp. grated orange zest
salt and freshly ground black pepper
8 game hen breasts
2½ cups water
1 cup quick-cook polenta
2 tbsp. butter, diced
½ cup Parmesan cheese, shredded
1–2 tbsp. freshly chopped parsley
assorted lettuce leaves, to serve

Tasty Tip

Heat a frying pan and fry the game hen breasts, skin-side down, for 2–3 minutes. Turn and fry 2 minutes longer for rare, 3–4 minutes longer if you prefer them well done.

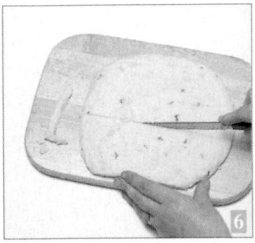

Braised Chicken with Red Bell Peppers

1 Place the chicken pieces in a shallow dish with half the olive oil, the lemon zest and juice, thyme, and some black pepper. Turn until well coated, then cover and let marinate for about 1 hour.

2 Heat half the remaining oil in a large, heavy casserole dish, add the onion, and cook for 5 minutes, then add the bell peppers and cook for an additional 12–15 minutes or until softened, stirring occasionally. Stir in the garlic, tomatoes, and sugar, and cook covered until soft, stirring occasionally.

3 Heat the remaining oil in a large skillet, drain the chicken—setting the marinade aside—and pat the chicken dry with paper towels. Add the chicken to the skillet, and cook until golden. Transfer the chicken to the casserole dish and mix with the tomato sauce.

4 Add the marinade to the skillet and cook, stirring to loosen any browned bits from the skillet. Add to the chicken and stir gently.

5 Cover the dish and simmer for 30 minutes. Serve the chicken and the vegetable mixture with polenta or creamy mashed potatoes.

INGREDIENTS
Serves 4

2½ lbs. chicken pieces
½ cup olive oil
1 tbsp. grated lemon zest
2 tbsp. lemon juice
2–3 tbsp. freshly chopped thyme
salt and freshly ground black pepper
1 onion, peeled and thinly sliced
4 red bell peppers, seeded and cut into 1-inch pieces
2 garlic cloves, peeled and crushed
14-oz. can strained, crushed tomatoes
1 tsp. brown sugar
freshly cooked polenta or creamy mashed potatoes, to serve

Helpful Hint

Using a casserole dish is an excellent way to cook chicken, as it has a tendency to be dry. Buy from a good butcher, who will also be able to joint it for you.

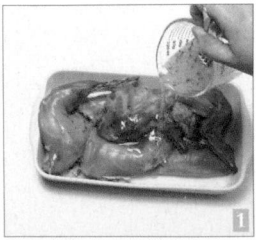

Chicken & Pasta Salad

1 Bring a large saucepan of lightly salted water to a boil. Add the pasta and cook for 10 minutes or until al dente.

2 Drain the pasta and rinse under cold running water, then drain again. Place in a large serving bowl and toss with the olive oil.

3 Add the chicken, diced red and yellow bell peppers, sliced sun-dried tomatoes, capers, olives, scallions, and mozzarella to the pasta, and toss gently until mixed. Season to taste with salt and pepper.

4 To make the dressing, put the vinegar, mustard, and sugar into a small bowl or jug, and beat until well blended and the sugar is dissolved. Season with some pepper, then gradually beat in the olive oil in a slow, steady stream until a thickened vinaigrette forms.

5 Put the mayonnaise in a bowl and gradually beat in the dressing until smooth. Pour over the pasta mixture, and mix gently until all the ingredients are coated. Turn into a large, shallow serving bowl and serve at room temperature.

INGREDIENTS
Serves 6

6 cups short pasta
2–3 tbsp. extra-virgin olive oil
3 cups cold, cooked chicken, cut into bite-sized pieces (preferably roasted)
1 red bell pepper, seeded and diced
1 yellow bell pepper, seeded and diced
4–5 sun-dried tomatoes, sliced
2 tbsp. capers, rinsed and drained
⅓ cup pitted Italian ripe olives
4 scallions, chopped
2 cups mozzarella cheese, preferably buffalo, diced
salt and freshly ground black pepper

FOR THE DRESSING:
4 tbsp. red or white wine vinegar
1 tbsp. mild mustard
1 tsp. sugar
½ cup extra-virgin olive oil
½ cup mayonnaise

Tasty Tip

In the bowl of a food processor or blender, beat together 1 egg yolk, 1 teaspoon mustard, 2 tablespoons lemon juice, and some seasoning until it is foaming. Add 1 cup light olive oil in a slow but steady stream until the mayonnaise is thick and all the oil has been added. Season to taste and use to dress the salad. Keep the remainder in the refrigerator for other uses.

3

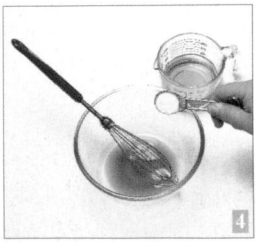
4

4

Hot Duck Pasta Salad

1 Preheat the oven to 400° F. Place the duck breasts on a cookie sheet lined with foil. Mix together the mustard and honey, and season lightly with salt and pepper, then spread over the duck breasts. Roast in the preheated oven for 20–30 minutes or until tender. Remove from the oven and keep warm.

2 Meanwhile, place the eggs in a small pan, then cover with water and bring to a boil. Simmer for 8 minutes, then drain. Bring a large pan of lightly salted water to a rolling boil. Add the beans and pasta, then return to a boil and cook according to the package directions or until al dente. Drain the pasta and beans and refresh under cold running water.

3 Place the pasta and beans in a bowl. Add the carrot, corn, and spinach leaves, and toss lightly. Shell the eggs, then cut into wedges and arrange on top of the pasta. Slice the duck breasts, then place them on top of the salad. Beat the dressing ingredients together in a bowl until well blended, then drizzle over the salad. Serve immediately.

INGREDIENTS
Serves 6

3 boneless and skinless duck breasts
1 tbsp. whole-grain mustard
1 tbsp. clear honey
salt and freshly ground black pepper
4 medium eggs
4 cups fusilli
⅔ cup trimmed green beans
1 large carrot, peeled and thinly sliced
1 cup corn kernels, cooked if frozen
1 cup shredded fresh baby spinach leaves

FOR THE DRESSING:
8 tbsp. French dressing
1 tsp. horseradish sauce
4 tbsp. crème fraîche

Helpful Hint

Eggs should never be boiled rapidly, since this may cause the shells to crack and make the egg white rubbery. When cooking hard-boiled eggs for salads, turn the eggs gently once or twice in the first few minutes of cooking, so that the yolks stay in the middle. As soon as the eggs are cooked, remove them from the pan and place in a bowl of very cold water to prevent dark rings from forming around the yolk.

1

2

3

Chicken Tagliatelle

1 Bring a large pan of lightly salted water to a rolling boil. Add the pasta and cook according to the package directions or until al dente. Add the peas to the pan 5 minutes before the end of cooking time and cook until tender. Drain the pasta and peas, then return to the pan and keep warm.

2 Trim the chicken if necessary, then cut into bite-sized pieces. Heat the olive oil in a large skillet, then add the chicken and cook for 8 minutes or until golden, stirring occasionally.

3 Add the cucumber and cook for 2 minutes or until slightly softened, stirring occasionally. Stir in the vermouth and bring to a boil, then lower the heat and simmer for 3 minutes or until reduced slightly.

4 Add the cream to the pan. Bring to a boil, stirring constantly, then stir in the Stilton cheese and cut chives. Season to taste with salt and pepper. Heat through well, stirring occasionally, until the cheese begins to melt.

5 Toss the chicken mixture into the pasta. Spoon into a warmed serving dish or onto individual plates. Garnish and serve immediately.

INGREDIENTS
Serves 4

12 oz. tagliatelle
1 cup frozen peas
4 boneless and skinless chicken breasts
2 tbsp. olive oil
¼ cucumber, cut into strips
⅔ cup dry vermouth
⅔ cup heavy cream
1 cup crumbled Stilton cheese
3 tbsp. freshly cut chives, plus extra to garnish
salt and freshly ground black pepper
fresh herbs, to garnish

Helpful Hint

Chives add a mild onion flavor and attractive color to this dish. If you do not have any, finely shred the green tops of scallions and use them instead. If preferred, a mixture of dry white wine and 1–2 tablespoons of dry sherry can be substituted for the vermouth.

Mixed Vegetable & Chicken Pasta

1 Preheat the broiler just before using. Cut the chicken into thin strips. Trim the leeks, leaving some of the dark green tops, then shred and wash in cold water. Peel the onion and cut into thin wedges.

2 Bring a large pan of lightly salted water to a rolling boil. Add the pasta and cook according to the package directions or until al dente.

3 Meanwhile, melt the butter with the olive oil in a large heavy-based pan. Add the chicken and cook, stirring occasionally, for 8 minutes or until browned all over. Add the leeks and onion, and cook for 5 minutes or until softened. Add the garlic and cherry tomatoes, and cook for an additional 2 minutes.

4 Stir the cream and asparagus tips into the chicken and vegetable mixture, and bring to a boil slowly, then remove from the heat. Drain the pasta and return to the pan. Pour the sauce over the pasta, and season to taste with salt and pepper, then toss lightly.

5 Spoon the mixture into a gratin dish and sprinkle with the cheese. Cook under the preheated broiler for 5 minutes or until bubbling and golden, turning the dish occasionally. Serve with a green salad.

INGREDIENTS
Serves 4

3 boneless and skinless chicken breasts
2 leeks
1 red onion
3 cups pasta shells
2 tbsp. butter
2 tbsp. olive oil
1 garlic clove, peeled and chopped
6 oz. cherry tomatoes, halved
¼ cup heavy cream
15-oz. can asparagus tips, drained
salt and freshly ground black pepper
1 cup crumbled Double Gloucester cheese with chives
green salad, to serve

Tasty Tip

Fresh asparagus is in season during May and June, and can be used in place of canned asparagus. Tie in small bundles and cook in lightly salted, boiling water for 5–8 minutes.

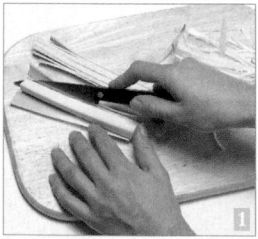

Herb-Baked Chicken with Tagliatelle

1 Preheat the oven to 400° F. Mix together the bread crumbs, 1 tablespoon of the olive oil, the oregano, and tomato paste. Season to taste with salt and pepper. Place the chicken breasts well apart in a roasting pan, and coat with the bread-crumb mixture.

2 Mix the plum tomatoes with the chopped basil and white wine. Season to taste, then spoon evenly around the chicken.

3 Drizzle the remaining olive oil over the chicken breasts and cook in the preheated oven for 20–30 minutes or until the chicken is golden and the juices run clear when a skewer is inserted into the flesh.

4 Meanwhile, bring a large pan of lightly salted water to a rolling boil. Add the pasta and cook according to the package directions or until al dente.

5 Drain the pasta thoroughly and transfer to warmed serving plates. Arrange the chicken breasts on top of the pasta and spoon over the sauce. Garnish with sprigs of basil and serve immediately.

INGREDIENTS
Serves 4

1½ cups fresh white bread crumbs
3 tbsp. olive oil
1 tsp. dried oregano
2 tbsp. sun-dried tomato paste
salt and freshly ground black pepper
4 boneless and skinless chicken breasts, each about 5 oz.
2 14-oz. cans plum tomatoes
4 tbsp. freshly chopped basil
2 tbsp. dry white wine
12 oz. tagliatelle
fresh basil sprigs, to garnish

Food Fact

Sun-dried tomatoes are ripened on the vine, then split open and dried in the sun to give a deep, concentrated caramelized flavor. Sun-dried tomato paste usually comes in glass jars, but can also be found in tubes. Once opened, store in the refrigerator, and if in a jar, cover the surface with a teaspoon of olive oil to keep fresh.

Creamy Chicken & Sausage Penne

1 Heat the olive oil in a large skillet, then add the shallots and cook for 3 minutes or until golden. Remove and drain on paper towels. Add the chicken thighs to the skillet and cook for 5 minutes, turning frequently until browned. Drain on paper towels.

2 Add the smoked sausage and chestnut mushrooms to the skillet and cook for 3 minutes or until browned. Drain separately on paper towels.

3 Return the shallots, chicken, and sausage to the skillet, then add the garlic, paprika, and thyme, and cook for 1 minute, stirring. Pour in the wine and stock and season to taste with the pepper. Bring to a boil, then lower the heat and simmer covered for 15 minutes.

4 Add the mushrooms to the skillet and simmer covered for 15 minutes or until the chicken is tender.

5 Meanwhile, bring a large pan of lightly salted water to a rolling boil. Add the penne and cook according to the package directions or until al dente. Drain thoroughly.

6 Stir the mascarpone cheese into the chicken sauce and heat through, stirring gently. Spoon the pasta onto a warmed serving dish, and add the sauce. Garnish and serve immediately.

INGREDIENTS
Serves 4

2 tbsp. olive oil
8 oz. shallots, peeled
8 chicken thighs
6 oz. smoked sausage, thickly sliced
1¼ cups chestnut mushrooms, wiped and halved
2 garlic cloves, peeled and chopped
1 tbsp. paprika
1 small bunch fresh thyme, chopped, plus leaves to garnish
⅔ cup red wine
1¼ cups chicken stock
freshly ground black pepper
3 cups penne
1 cup mascarpone cheese

Food Fact

Mascarpone is a rich, soft, white cheese, more like cream than cheese. Its slightly sweet flavor means that it is frequently used in desserts, but it also makes a wonderfully smooth, quick sauce for cooked pasta since it simply melts in the heat.

Creamy Turkey & Tomato Pasta

1 Preheat the oven to 400° F. Heat 2 tablespoons of the olive oil in a large skillet. Add the turkey and cook for 5 minutes or until sealed, turning occasionally. Transfer to a roasting pan and add the remaining olive oil, the vine tomatoes, garlic, and balsamic vinegar. Stir well and season to taste with salt and pepper. Cook in the preheated oven for 30 minutes or until the turkey is tender, turning the tomatoes and turkey once.

2 Meanwhile, bring a large pan of lightly salted water to a rolling boil. Add the pasta and cook according to the package directions or until al dente. Drain, return to the pan, and keep warm. Stir the basil and seasoning into the crème fraîche.

3 Remove the roasting pan from the oven and discard the vines. Stir the crème fraîche and basil mix into the turkey and tomato mixture and return to the oven for 1–2 minutes or until thoroughly heated through.

4 Stir the turkey and tomato mixture into the pasta and toss lightly together. Spoon into a warmed serving dish. Garnish with Parmesan cheese shavings and serve immediately.

INGREDIENTS
Serves 4

4 tbsp. olive oil
1 lb. turkey breasts, cut into bite-sized pieces
1¼ lb. cherry tomatoes, on the vine
2 garlic cloves, peeled and chopped
4 tbsp. balsamic vinegar
12 oz. tagliatelle
salt and freshly ground black pepper
4 tbsp. freshly chopped basil
¼ cup crème fraîche
shaved Parmesan cheese, to garnish

Helpful Hint

Balsamic vinegar is dark in color with a mellow, sweet-and-sour flavor. It is made from concentrated grape juice and fermented in wooden barrels. Like good wine, the vinegar improves and becomes darker and more syrupy the longer it is aged. Less expensive vinegars bought from supermarkets have been matured for only three or four years. The flavor is nonetheless wonderful and perfect for this recipe.

Prosciutto-Wrapped Chicken with Ribbon Pasta

1 Cut each chicken breast into three pieces and season well with salt and pepper. Wrap each chicken piece in a slice of prosciutto to enclose completely, securing if necessary with either fine twine or toothpicks.

2 Heat the oil in a large skillet and cook the chicken, turning occasionally, for 12–15 minutes or until well cooked. Remove from the skillet with a slotted spoon and set aside.

3 Meanwhile, bring a large pan of lightly salted water to a rolling boil. Add the pasta and cook according to the package directions or until al dente.

4 Add the garlic and scallions to the skillet and cook, stirring occasionally, for 2 minutes or until softened. Stir in the tomatoes, lemon juice, and crème fraîche. Bring to a boil, then lower the heat and simmer, covered, for 3 minutes. Stir in the parsley and sugar, then season to taste. Return the chicken to the skillet and heat for 2–3 minutes or until piping hot.

5 Drain the pasta thoroughly and mix in the chopped parsley, then spoon onto a warmed serving dish or individual plates. Arrange the chicken and sauce over the pasta. Garnish and serve immediately.

INGREDIENTS
Serves 4

4 boneless and skinless chicken breasts
salt and freshly ground black pepper
12 slices prosciutto
2 tbsp. olive oil
12 oz. ribbon pasta
1 garlic clove, peeled and chopped
1 bunch scallions, trimmed and diagonally sliced
14-oz. can chopped tomatoes
juice of 1 lemon
⅔ cup crème fraîche
3 tbsp. freshly chopped parsley
pinch of sugar
freshly grated Parmesan cheese, to garnish

Food Fact

Crème fraîche has a slightly sour taste and a thick, spoonable texture. It is made in a similar way to yogurt, by introducing a bacterial culture to cream. This produces lactic acid, which makes the cream curdle and thicken. The half-fat version is best avoided for cooking; it sometimes separates when boiled.

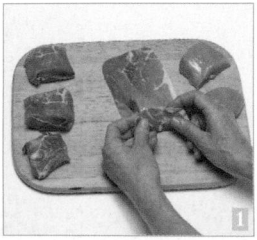

Baked Eggplant with Tomato & Mozzarella

1 Preheat the oven to 400° F. Place the eggplant slices in a colander and sprinkle with salt. Let stand for 1 hour or until the juices run clear. Rinse and dry on paper towels.

2 Heat 3–5 tablespoons of the oil in a large skillet, and cook the prepared eggplants in batches for 2 minutes on each side or until softened. Remove and drain on paper towels.

3 Heat 1 tablespoon of olive oil in a pan, then add the ground turkey and cook for 5 minutes or until browned and sealed.

4 Add the onion to the pan and cook for 5 minutes or until softened. Add the chopped garlic, tomatoes, and mixed herbs. Pour in the wine and season to taste with salt and pepper. Bring to a boil, then lower the heat and simmer for 15 minutes or until thickened.

5 Meanwhile, bring a large pan of lightly salted water to a rolling boil. Add the macaroni, and cook according to the package directions or until al dente. Drain thoroughly.

6 Spoon half the tomato mixture into a lightly greased ovenproof dish. Top with half the eggplant, pasta, and chopped basil, then season lightly. Repeat the layers, finishing with a layer of eggplant. Sprinkle with the mozzarella and Parmesan cheeses, then bake in the preheated oven for 30 minutes or until golden and bubbling. Serve immediately.

INGREDIENTS
Serves 4

3 medium eggplants, trimmed and sliced
salt and freshly ground black pepper
4–6 tbsp. olive oil
1 lb. fresh ground turkey
1 onion, peeled and chopped
2 garlic cloves, peeled and chopped
2 14-oz. cans cherry tomatoes
1 tbsp. fresh mixed herbs
¼ cup red wine
3 cups macaroni
5 tbsp. freshly chopped basil
1 cup mozzarella cheese
½ cup freshly grated Parmesan cheese

Helpful Hint

Eggplants are salted to remove bitterness, although they are now less bitter. Salting also removes moisture so they absorb less oil when fried.

Mini Chicken Balls with Tagliatelle

1 Mix the chicken and tomatoes together and season with salt and pepper. Divide the mixture into 32 pieces and roll into balls. Transfer to a cookie sheet, then cover and refrigerate for 1 hour.

2 Melt the butter in a large skillet. Add the chicken balls and cook for 5 minutes or until golden, turning occasionally. Remove, drain on paper towels, and keep warm.

3 Add the leeks and fava beans to the skillet and cook, stirring, for 10 minutes or until tender. Return the chicken balls to the skillet, then stir in the cream and Parmesan cheese and heat through.

4 Meanwhile, bring a large pan of lightly salted water to a boil. Add the pasta and cook according to the package directions or until al dente.

5 Bring a separate skilletful of water to a boil, then crack in the eggs and simmer for 2–4 minutes or until poached to personal preference.

6 Meanwhile, drain the pasta and return to the pan. Pour the chicken ball and vegetable sauce over the pasta, then toss lightly and heat for 1–2 minutes. Arrange on warmed individual plates and top with the poached eggs. Garnish with fresh herbs and serve immediately.

INGREDIENTS
Serves 4

1 lb. fresh ground chicken
½ cup sun-dried tomatoes, drained and finely chopped
salt and freshly ground black pepper
2 tbsp. butter
12 oz. leeks, trimmed and diagonally sliced
1 cup frozen fava beans
1¼ cups light cream
½ cup freshly grated Parmesan cheese
12 oz. tagliatelle
4 medium eggs
fresh herbs, to garnish

Helpful Hint

Chilling the chicken balls firms them, so that they retain their shape when cooked. They need plenty of room for turning; if necessary, cook in two batches, halving the butter for each. The butter must be sizzling before the chicken balls are added.

Pasta & Bell Pepper Salad

1 Preheat the oven to 400° F. Spoon the olive oil into a roasting pan and heat in the oven for 2 minutes or until almost smoking. Remove from the oven, then add the bell peppers, zucchini, and eggplant, and stir until coated. Bake for 30 minutes or until charred, stirring occasionally.

2 Bring a large pan of lightly salted water to a boil. Add the pasta and cook according to the package directions or until al dente. Drain and refresh under cold running water. Drain thoroughly, then place in a large salad bowl and set aside.

3 Remove the cooked vegetables from the oven and let cool. Add to the cooled pasta, together with the quartered tomatoes, chopped basil leaves, pesto, garlic, and lemon juice. Toss lightly to mix.

4 Shred the chicken coarsely into small pieces and stir into the pasta and vegetable mixture. Season to taste with salt and pepper, then sprinkle the crumbled feta cheese over the pasta and stir gently. Cover the dish and let marinate for 30 minutes, stirring occasionally. Serve the salad with fresh, crusty bread.

INGREDIENTS
Serves 4

4 tbsp. olive oil
1 each red, orange, and yellow bell pepper, deseeded and cut into chunks
1 large zucchini, trimmed and cut into chunks
1 medium eggplant, trimmed and diced
2½ cups fusilli
4 plum tomatoes, quartered
1 bunch fresh basil leaves, coarsely chopped
2 tbsp. pesto
2 garlic cloves, peeled and coarsely chopped
1 tbsp. lemon juice
8 oz. boneless and skinless roasted chicken breast
salt and freshly ground black pepper
1 cup crumbled feta cheese
fresh, crusty bread, to serve

Helpful Hint

If you have one, use a large nonstick roasting pan for cooking the vegetables, and check and move them around frequently so that they brown evenly. For extra flavor, use a garlic- or chili-flavored olive oil and tuck a sprig or two of fresh herbs, such as rosemary or thyme, under the vegetables.

Chicken Marengo

1 Season the flour with salt and pepper and toss the chicken in the flour to coat. Heat 2 tablespoons of the olive oil in a large skillet and cook the chicken for 7 minutes or until browned, turning occasionally. Remove from the skillet using a slotted spoon and keep warm.

2 Add the remaining oil to the skillet, then add the onion and cook, stirring occasionally, for 5 minutes or until softened and starting to brown. Add the garlic, tomatoes, tomato paste, basil, and thyme. Pour in the wine or chicken stock and season well. Bring to a boil. Stir in the chicken pieces, and simmer for 15 minutes or until the chicken is tender and the sauce has thickened.

3 Meanwhile, bring a large pan of lightly salted water to a boil. Add the rigatoni and cook according to the package directions or until al dente.

4 Drain the rigatoni thoroughly, then return to the pan and stir in the chopped parsley. Tip the pasta into a large, warmed serving dish or spoon onto individual plates. Spoon the chicken sauce over the pasta and serve immediately.

INGREDIENTS
Serves 4

2 tbsp. all-purpose flour
salt and freshly ground black pepper
4 boneless and skinless chicken breasts, cut into bite-sized pieces
4 tbsp. olive oil
1 Spanish onion, peeled and chopped
1 garlic clove, peeled and chopped
14-oz. can chopped tomatoes
2 tbsp. sun-dried tomato paste
3 tbsp. freshly chopped basil
3 tbsp. freshly chopped thyme
½ cup dry white wine or chicken stock
3 cups rigatoni
3 tbsp. freshly chopped Italian parsley

Helpful Hint

Spanish onions have a milder flavor and tend to be larger than others. Cook the onion over a fairly low heat until really soft, stirring frequently toward the end to keep it from sticking. Let it caramelize and brown very slightly, as this adds a richer flavor and golden color to the final dish.

1

2

4

Turkey & Oven-Roasted Vegetable Salad

1 Preheat the oven to 400° F. Line a large roasting pan with foil, then pour in half the olive oil and place in the oven for 3 minutes or until very hot. Remove from the oven, add the zucchini and bell peppers, and stir until evenly coated. Bake for 30–35 minutes or until slightly charred, turning occasionally.

2 Add the pine nuts to the pan. Return to the oven and bake for 10 minutes or until the pine nuts are toasted. Remove from the oven and let the vegetables cool completely.

3 Bring a large pan of lightly salted water to a rolling boil. Add the macaroni and cook according to the package directions or until al dente. Drain and rinse the pasta under cold running water, then drain thoroughly and place in a large salad bowl.

4 Cut the turkey into bite-size pieces and add to the macaroni. Add the artichokes and tomatoes with the cooled vegetables and pan juices to the pan. Blend together the cilantro, garlic, remaining oil, vinegar, and seasoning. Pour over the salad, then toss lightly and serve.

INGREDIENTS
Serves 4

6 tbsp. olive oil
3 medium zucchini, trimmed and sliced
2 yellow bell peppers, deseeded and sliced
½ cup pine nuts
2½ cups macaroni
12 oz. cooked turkey
10 oz. jar or can of chargrilled artichokes, drained and sliced
8 oz. baby plum tomatoes, quartered
4 tbsp. freshly chopped cilantro
1 garlic clove, peeled and chopped
3 tbsp. balsamic vinegar
salt and freshly ground black pepper

Helpful Hint

Other vegetables would be equally delicious. Try baby eggplants, trimmed and quartered lengthwise, or scrubbed new potatoes. If you cannot find chargrilled artichokes, use ordinary ones: drain and pat dry, then add to 1 tablespoon of hot olive oil in a skillet and cook for 2–3 minutes or until lightly charred.

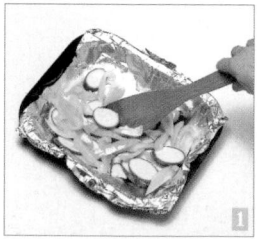

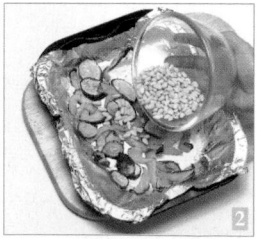

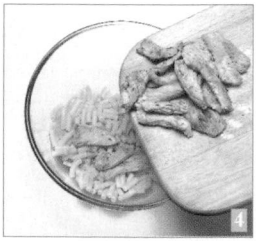

Spicy Chicken & Pasta Salad

1 Bring a large pan of lightly salted water to a rolling boil. Add the pasta shells and cook according to the package directions or until al dente. Drain and refresh under cold running water, then drain thoroughly and place in a large serving bowl.

2 Meanwhile, melt the butter in a heavy-based pan, then add the onion and cook for 5 minutes or until softened. Add the curry paste and cook, stirring, for 2 minutes. Stir in the apricots and tomato paste, then cook for 1 minute. Remove from the heat and let cool.

3 Blend the mango chutney and mayonnaise together in a small bowl. Drain the pineapple slices, adding 2 tablespoons of the pineapple juice to the mayonnaise mixture; set aside the pineapple slices. Season the mayonnaise to taste with salt and pepper.

4 Cut the pineapple slices into chunks and stir into the pasta together with the mayonnaise mixture, curry paste, and cooked chicken pieces. Toss lightly together to coat the pasta. Sprinkle with the almond slivers, then garnish with cilantro sprigs and serve.

INGREDIENTS
Serves 6

4 cups pasta shells
4 tbsp. butter
1 onion, peeled and chopped
2 tbsp. mild curry paste
1 cup chopped dried apricots
2 tbsp. tomato paste
3 tbsp. mango chutney
1¼ cups mayonnaise
15-oz. can pineapple slices in juice
salt and freshly ground black pepper
1 lb. skinned, boned, cooked chicken, cut into bite-size pieces
2 tbsp. almond slivers, flaked and toasted
cilantro sprigs, to garnish

Helpful Hint

If you cannot buy slivered almonds, prepare your own. Place whole or half-blanched almonds in a small bowl and pour in plenty of boiling water. Let soak for 20 minutes, then drain the almonds and cut into slivers using a sharp knife. Spread on a foil-lined broiler pan and toast under a low broiler for 1–2 minutes to make them dry and crunchy again.

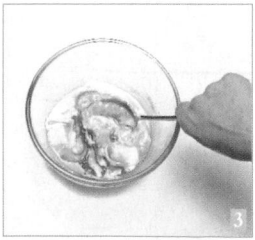

Chicken, Gorgonzola, & Mushroom Macaroni

1 Bring a large pan of lightly salted water to a rolling boil. Add the macaroni and cook according to the package directions or until al dente.

2 Meanwhile, melt the butter in a large skillet, then add the chestnut and button mushrooms and cook for 5 minutes or until golden, stirring occasionally. Add the chicken to the skillet and cook for 4 minutes or until heated through and slightly golden, stirring occasionally.

3 Blend the cornstarch with a little of the milk in a pitcher to form a smooth paste, then gradually blend in the remaining milk and pour into the skillet. Bring to a boil slowly, stirring constantly. Add the Gorgonzola cheese and cook for 1 minute, stirring frequently until melted.

4 Stir the sage and chives into the skillet. Season to taste with salt and pepper, then heat through. Drain the macaroni and return to the pan. Pour the chicken and mushroom sauce over the macaroni and toss lightly to coat. Spoon into a warmed serving dish, and serve immediately with extra Gorgonzola cheese.

INGREDIENTS
Serves 4

4 cups macaroni
¼ stick butter
2½ cups chestnut mushrooms, wiped and sliced
2½ cups baby button mushrooms, wiped and halved
12 oz. cooked chicken, skinned and chopped
2 tsp. cornstarch
1¼ cups low-fat milk
1/2 cup chopped Gorgonzola cheese, plus extra to serve
2 tbsp. freshly chopped sage
1 tbsp. freshly chopped chives, plus extra chive leaves to garnish
salt and freshly ground black pepper

Food Fact

First mentioned in A.D. 879, Gorgonzola is the oldest named cheese in the world. It was named after the Italian town where cattle rested on their annual return from their summer pastures to their winter stalls. The original *piccante* is firm and heavily blue-veined with a strong flavor, while *dolce*, often simply labeled "extra creamy," has a milder taste and a softer texture.

Spaghetti with Turkey & Bacon Sauce

1 Bring a large pan of lightly salted water to a rolling boil. Add the spaghetti and cook according to the package directions or until al dente.

2 Meanwhile, melt the butter in a large skillet. Using a sharp knife, dice the bacon into small pieces. Add the bacon to the skillet with the turkey strips and cook for 8 minutes or until browned, stirring occasionally to prevent sticking. Add the onion and garlic, and cook for 5 minutes or until softened, stirring occasionally.

3 Place the eggs and cream in a bowl and season to taste with salt and pepper. Beat together, then pour into the skillet and cook, stirring, for 2 minutes or until the mixture begins to thicken but does not scramble.

4 Drain the spaghetti thoroughly and return to the pan. Pour over the sauce, then add the Parmesan cheese and toss lightly. Heat through for 2 minutes or until piping hot. Spoon into a warmed serving dish and sprinkle with freshly chopped cilantro. Serve immediately.

INGREDIENTS
Serves 4

1 lb. spaghetti
2 tbsp. butter
8 oz. smoked bacon
12 oz. fresh turkey strips
1 onion, peeled and chopped
1 garlic clove, peeled and chopped
3 medium eggs, beaten
1¼ cups heavy cream
salt and freshly ground black pepper
½ cup freshly grated Parmesan cheese
2–3 tbsp. freshly chopped cilantro, to garnish

Helpful Hint

It is a good idea to remove the skillet from the heat before adding the beaten eggs, since there should be enough residual heat in the sauce to cook them. If the sauce does not start to thicken after 2 minutes, return to a very low heat and continue cooking gently until it does.

Cheesy Baked Chicken Macaroni

1 Preheat the broiler just before cooking. Heat the oil in a large skillet, and cook the chicken for 8 minutes or until browned, stirring occasionally. Drain on paper towels and set aside. Add the diced pancetta to the skillet, and fry until browned and crispy. Remove from the skillet and set aside.

2 Add the onion and garlic to the skillet, and cook for 5 minutes or until softened. Stir in the tomato sauce, chopped tomatoes, and basil, and season to taste with salt and pepper. Bring to a boil, lower the heat, and simmer the sauce for about 5 minutes.

3 Meanwhile, bring a large pan of lightly salted water to a boil. Add the macaroni and cook according to the package directions or until al dente.

4 Drain the macaroni thoroughly, then return to the pan and stir in the sauce, chicken, and mozzarella. Spoon into a shallow ovenproof dish.

5 Sprinkle the pancetta over the macaroni. Sprinkle the Gruyère and Parmesan cheeses on top. Place under the preheated broiler and cook for 5–10 minutes or until golden-brown; turn the dish occasionally. Garnish and serve immediately.

INGREDIENTS
Serves 4

1 tbsp. olive oil
3¼ cups diced boneless and skinless chicken breasts
⅓ cup diced pancetta
1 onion, peeled and chopped
1 garlic clove, peeled and chopped
1½ cups tomato sauce
14-oz. can chopped tomatoes
2 tbsp. freshly chopped basil, plus leaves to garnish
salt and freshly ground black pepper
3 cups macaroni
1¼ cups drained and chopped mozzarella cheese
½ cup grated Gruyère cheese
½ cup freshly grated Parmesan cheese

Tasty Tip

This dish can be made with any pasta shape or flavor; try green spinach pasta for a change. Check the contents of the package of fresh tomato sauce carefully; it may already contain herbs and spices, so you may need to cut out or reduce the garlic and fresh basil accordingly.

Food Fact

Pancetta (unsmoked bacon) imparts a wonderful flavor to a dish; it is available from Italian delicatessens.

Spicy Mexican Chicken

1 Heat the oil in a large skillet, then add the ground chicken and cook for 5 minutes, stirring frequently with a wooden spoon to break up any lumps. Add the onion, garlic, and bell pepper, and cook for 3 minutes, stirring occasionally. Stir in the chili powder and cook for an additional 2 minutes.

2 Stir in the tomato paste, then pour in the chicken stock and season to taste with salt and pepper. Bring to a boil, then reduce the heat and simmer covered for 20 minutes.

3 Add the kidney and chili beans, and cook, stirring occasionally, for 10 minutes or until the chicken is tender.

4 Meanwhile, bring a large pan of lightly salted water to a boil. Add the spaghetti and cook according to the package directions or until al dente.

5 Drain the spaghetti. Arrange on warmed plates, and spoon over the chicken and bean mixture. Serve with the grated cheese, guacamole, and salsa.

INGREDIENTS
Serves 4

2 tbsp. olive oil
1 lb. ground chicken
1 red onion, peeled and chopped
2 garlic cloves, peeled and chopped
1 red bell pepper, deseeded and chopped
1–2 tsp. hot chili powder
2 tbsp. tomato paste
1 cup chicken stock
salt and freshly ground black pepper
15-oz. can red kidney beans, drained
15-oz. can chili beans, drained
12 oz. spaghetti

TO SERVE:
Monterey Jack or cheddar cheese, grated
guacamole
hot chili salsa

Helpful Hint

A variety of chili powders are available. The most common is the red powder made from dried red chilies, which may be mild or hot. A darker powder, which contains a mixture of ground chili and herbs, is specifically for use in Mexican and Southwest dishes.

Pesto Chicken Tagliatelle

1 Heat the oil in a large skillet, then add the chicken and cook for 8 minutes or until golden brown, stirring occasionally. Using a slotted spoon, remove the chicken from the pan, then drain on paper towels and set aside.

2 Melt the butter in the skillet. Add the leeks and cook for 3–5 minutes or until slightly softened, stirring occasionally. Add the oyster and chestnut mushrooms, and cook for 5 minutes or until browned, stirring occasionally.

3 Bring a large pan of lightly salted water to a boil. Add the tagliatelle, then return to a boil and cook for 4 minutes or until al dente.

4 Add the chicken, pesto, and crème fraîche to the mushroom mixture. Stir, then heat through completely. Stir in the grated Parmesan cheese and season to taste with salt and pepper.

5 Drain the tagliatelle thoroughly and pile onto warmed plates. Spoon over the sauce and serve immediately.

INGREDIENTS
Serves 4

2 tbsp. olive oil
12 oz. boneless and skinless chicken breasts, cut into chunks
¼ stick butter
2 medium leeks, trimmed and thinly sliced
1¼ cups oyster mushrooms, trimmed and halved
2¼ cups small open chestnut mushrooms, wiped and halved
1 lb. fresh tagliatelle
4–6 tbsp. red pesto
¼ cup crème fraîche
½ cup freshly grated Parmesan cheese
salt and freshly ground black pepper

Food Fact

Classic pesto is green because it is made from basil. Red pesto is made from a purée of sun-dried tomatoes. Both types of pesto make great pantry standbys since they can be simply tossed with cooked pasta for the speediest of meals. They are even more wonderful livened up with a little crème fraîche, as here, or with mascarpone cheese.

Chicken & Shrimp-Stacked Ravioli

1 Heat the olive oil in a large skillet, then add the onion and garlic and cook for 5 minutes or until softened, stirring occasionally. Add the chicken pieces and fry for 4 minutes or until heated through, turning occasionally.

2 Stir in the chopped tomato, wine, and cream and bring to a boil. Lower the heat and simmer for about 5 minutes or until reduced and thickened. Stir in the shrimp and tarragon, and season to taste with salt and pepper. Heat the sauce through gently.

3 Meanwhile, bring a large pan of lightly salted water to a boil and add 2 lasagna sheets. Return to a boil and cook for 2 minutes, stirring gently to avoid sticking. Remove from the pan using a slotted spoon and keep warm. Repeat with the remaining sheets.

4 Cut each sheet of lasagna in half. Place two pieces on each of the warmed plates and divide half of the chicken mixture among them. Top each serving with a second sheet of lasagna and divide the remainder of the chicken mixture among them. Top with a final layer of lasagna. Garnish with tarragon sprigs and serve immediately.

INGREDIENTS
Serves 4

1 tbsp. olive oil
1 onion, peeled and chopped
1 garlic clove, peeled and chopped
1 lb. boned and skinned cooked chicken, cut into large pieces
1 beefsteak tomato, deseeded and chopped
⅔ cup dry white wine
⅔ cup heavy cream
9 oz. peeled cooked shrimp, thawed if frozen
2 tbsp. freshly chopped tarragon, plus sprigs to garnish
salt and freshly ground black pepper
8 sheets fresh lasagna

Helpful Hint

Always check the package directions when cooking lasagna; some brands may need longer cooking than others. It should be cooked until al dente—tender, but firm to the bite. Dried lasagna—either plain or verde—may be used instead of fresh if preferred, but it will take longer to cook.

Penne with Pan-fried Chicken & Capers

1 Trim the chicken and cut into bite-sized pieces. Season the flour with salt and pepper, then toss the chicken in the seasoned flour and set aside.

2 Bring a large pan of lightly salted water to a rolling boil. Add the penne and cook according to the package directions or until al dente.

3 Meanwhile, heat the oil in a large skillet. Add the chicken and cook for 8 minutes or until golden on all sides, stirring frequently. Transfer the chicken to a plate and set aside.

4 Add the onion and garlic to the oil remaining in the skillet and cook for 5 minutes or until softened, stirring frequently.

5 Return the chicken to the skillet. Stir in the pesto and mascarpone cheese and heat through, stirring gently, until smooth. Stir in the whole-grain mustard, lemon juice, basil, and capers. Season to taste, then continue to heat through until piping hot.

6 Drain the penne thoroughly and return to the pan. Pour over the sauce and toss well to coat. Arrange the pasta on individual warmed plates. Sprinkle the cheese on top and serve immediately.

INGREDIENTS
Serves 4

4 boneless and skinless chicken breasts
2 tbsp. all-purpose flour
salt and freshly ground black pepper
3 cups penne
2 tbsp. olive oil
1 red onion, peeled and sliced
1 garlic clove, peeled and chopped
4–6 tbsp. pesto
1 cup mascarpone cheese
1 tsp. whole-grain mustard
1 tbsp. lemon juice
2 tbsp. freshly chopped basil
3 tbsp. capers in brine, rinsed and drained
freshly shaved Pecorino Romano cheese

Food Fact

Pecorino Romano is a cooked, pressed cheese made in dairies in and around Rome. It is similar to Parmesan (which may be used instead, if preferred) with a dense texture, pale yellow color, and almost smoky aroma. Its flavor is very salty, so take care when seasoning the pasta and chicken when cooking.

Risi e Bisi

1 Melt the butter and olive oil together in a large, heavy saucepan. Add the chopped pancetta or bacon, the chopped onion and garlic, and gently cook for about 10 minutes or until the onion is softened and is just beginning to brown.

2 Pour in the vegetable stock, then add the sugar, lemon juice, and bay leaf. Add the fresh peas, if using. Bring the mixture to a fast boil.

3 Add the rice, stir, and simmer uncovered for about 20 minutes or until the rice is tender. Occasionally, stir the mixture gently while it cooks. If using frozen peas, stir them into the rice about 2 minutes before the end of the cooking time.

4 When the rice is cooked, remove the bay leaf and discard. Stir in 2½ tablespoons of the chopped parsley and the Parmesan cheese. Season to taste with salt and pepper.

5 Transfer the rice to a large serving dish. Garnish with the remaining chopped parsley, a sprig of fresh parsley, and julienned strips of orange rind. Serve immediately while piping hot.

INGREDIENTS
Serves 4

1½ cups peas, thawed if frozen
¼ stick unsalted butter
1 tsp. olive oil
3 slices pancetta or bacon, chopped
1 small onion, peeled and finely chopped
1 garlic clove, peeled and finely chopped
5¼ cups vegetable stock
pinch of sugar
1 tsp. lemon juice
1 bay leaf
1 cup risotto rice
3 tbsp. freshly chopped parsley
½ cup Parmesan cheese, finely shredded
salt and freshly ground black pepper

TO GARNISH:
sprig of fresh parsley
julienned strips of orange rind

Food Fact

This dish of risi e bisi (rice with peas) comes from Venice. It's much moister than a risotto and should be like a very thick soup.

Rice & Vegetable Timbale

1 Preheat the oven to 375° F. Sprinkle the bread crumbs over the base and sides of a thickly buttered 8-inch round springform pan.

2 Heat the olive oil in a large skillet and gently cook the zucchini, eggplant, mushrooms, and garlic for 5 minutes or until beginning to soften. Stir in the vinegar. Tip the vegetables into a large strainer placed over a bowl to catch the juices.

3 Cook the onion gently in the butter for 10 minutes until soft. Add the rice and stir for a minute to coat. Add a ladleful of stock and any juices from the vegetables, and simmer, stirring, until the rice has absorbed all of the liquid.

4 Continue adding the stock in this way until the rice is just tender. This should take about 20 minutes. Remove from the heat and allow to cool for 5 minutes. Stir in the eggs, cheese, and basil. Season to taste with salt and pepper.

5 Spoon a quarter of the rice into the prepared pan. Top with one third of the vegetable mixture. Continue layering up in this way, finishing with a layer of rice.

6 Level the top of the layer of rice, gently pressing down the mixture. Cover with a piece of foil. Put on a baking sheet and cook in the preheated oven for 50 minutes or until firm.

7 Let the timbale stand in the pan for 10 minutes, still covered with foil, then turn out onto a warmed serving platter. Garnish with a sprig of fresh basil and slices of radish, and serve immediately.

INGREDIENTS
Serves 6

¼ cup dried white bread crumbs
3 tbsp. olive oil
2 zucchini, sliced
1 small eggplant, diced
1½ cups mushrooms, sliced
1 garlic clove, peeled and crushed
1 tsp. balsamic vinegar
1 onion, peeled and finely chopped
¼ stick unsalted butter
1¼ cups risotto rice
5¼ cups boiling vegetable stock
2 medium eggs, lightly beaten
¼ cup Parmesan cheese, finely shredded
2 tbsp. freshly chopped basil
salt and freshly ground black pepper

TO GARNISH:
sprig of fresh basil
1 radish, thinly sliced

Vegetables Braised in Olive Oil & Lemon

1 Put the pared lemon rind and juice into a large saucepan. Add the olive oil, bay leaf, thyme, and water. Bring to a boil. Add the scallions and mushrooms. Top with the broccoli and cauliflower, their stalks down. Cover and simmer for 3 minutes.

2 Sprinkle the zucchini on top, so that they are steamed rather than boiled. Cook covered for an additional 3–4 minutes until all the vegetables are tender. Using a slotted spoon, transfer the vegetables from the liquid into a warmed serving dish. Increase the heat and boil rapidly for 3–4 minutes or until the liquid is reduced to about 8 tablespoons. Remove the lemon rind, bay leaf, and thyme sprig, and discard.

3 Stir the chives into the reduced liquid, season to taste with salt and pepper, and pour over the vegetables. Sprinkle with lemon zest and serve immediately.

INGREDIENTS
Serves 4

small strip of pared lemon rind
1 tbsp. lemon juice
4 tbsp. olive oil
1 bay leaf
large sprig of thyme
⅔ cup water
4 scallions, trimmed and finely chopped
1½ cups baby button mushrooms
2 cups broccoli, cut into small florets
2 cups cauliflower, cut into small florets
1 medium zucchini, sliced diagonally
2 tbsp. freshly cut chives
salt and freshly ground black pepper
lemon zest, to garnish

Tasty Tip

Serve these vegetables as an accompaniment to roasted or broiled chicken, fish, or turkey. Alternatively, toast some crusty bread, rub with a garlic clove, drizzle with a little olive oil, and top with a spoonful of vegetables.

Melanzane Parmigiana

1 Preheat the oven to 400° F. Cut the eggplants lengthwise into thin slices. Sprinkle with salt and allow to drain in a strainer over a bowl for 30 minutes.

2 Meanwhile, heat 1 tablespoon of the olive oil in a saucepan, and cook the onion for 10 minutes until softened. Add the paprika and cook for 1 minute. Stir in the wine, stock, tomatoes, and tomato paste. Simmer uncovered for 25 minutes or until fairly thick. Stir in the oregano, and season to taste with salt and pepper. Remove from the heat.

3 Rinse the eggplant slices thoroughly under cold water and pat dry on paper towels. Heat 2 tablespoons of the oil in a frying pan, and cook the eggplants in batches for 3 minutes on each side until golden. Drain well on paper towels.

4 Pour half of the tomato sauce into the base of a large ovenproof dish. Cover with half the eggplant slices, then top with the mozzarella. Cover with the remaining eggplant slices, and pour over the remaining tomato sauce. Sprinkle with the shredded Parmesan cheese.

5 Cook in the preheated oven for 30 minutes or until the eggplants are tender and the sauce is bubbling. Garnish with a sprig of fresh basil, and cool for a few minutes before serving.

INGREDIENTS
Serves 4

2 lbs. eggplant
salt and freshly ground black pepper
⅓ cup olive oil
1 red onion, peeled and chopped
½ tsp. mild paprika pepper
⅔ cup dry red wine
⅔ cup vegetable stock
14-oz. can chopped tomatoes
1 tsp. tomato paste
1 tbsp. freshly chopped oregano
1½ cups mozzarella cheese, thinly sliced
½ cup Parmesan cheese, coarsely shredded
sprig of fresh basil, to garnish

Helpful Hint

Salting the eggplants draws out some of the moisture, so you'll need less oil when cooking.

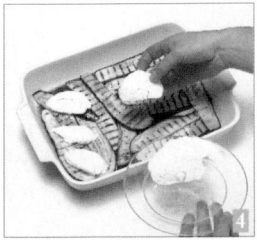

Stuffed Tomatoes with Broiled Polenta

1 Preheat the broiler just before cooking. To make the polenta, pour the stock into a saucepan. Add a pinch of salt and bring to a boil. Pour in the polenta in a fine stream, stirring all the time. Simmer for about 15 minutes or until very thick. Stir in the butter and add a little pepper. Turn the polenta out onto a chopping board and spread to a thickness of just over ½ inch. Cool, cover with plastic wrap, and chill in the refrigerator for 30 minutes.

2 To make the stuffed tomatoes, cut the tomatoes in half, then scoop out the seeds, and press through a fine strainer to extract the juices. Season the insides of the tomatoes with salt and pepper, and set aside.

3 Heat the olive oil in a saucepan, and gently cook the garlic and scallions for 3 minutes. Add the tomato juice and boil for 3–4 minutes until most of the liquid has evaporated. Stir in the herbs, prosciutto, and black pepper with half the bread crumbs. Spoon into the hollowed-out tomatoes and set aside.

4 Cut the polenta into 2-inch squares, then cut each in half diagonally to make triangles. Put the triangles on a piece of foil on the broiler rack, and broil for 4–5 minutes on each side until golden. Cover and keep warm.

5 Broil the tomatoes for 4 minutes—any exposed prosciutto will become crisp. Sprinkle with the remaining bread crumbs, and broil for 1–2 minutes or until the bread crumbs are golden brown. Garnish with cut chives, and serve immediately with the broiled polenta.

INGREDIENTS
Serves 4

FOR THE POLENTA:
1¼ cups vegetable stock
salt and freshly ground black pepper
½ cup quick-cook polenta
1 tbsp. butter

FOR THE STUFFED TOMATOES:
4 large tomatoes
1 tbsp. olive oil
1 garlic clove, peeled and crushed
1 bunch scallions, trimmed and finely chopped
2 tbsp. freshly chopped parsley
2 tbsp. freshly chopped basil
2 slices prosciutto, cut into thin slivers
½ cup fresh white bread crumbs
cut chives, to garnish

Rigatoni with Roasted Beets & Arugula

1 Preheat the oven to 300° F. Wrap the beets individually in foil, and cook for 1–1½ hours or until tender. Test by opening one of the pockets and scraping the skin away from the stem end—it should come off very easily.

2 Leave the beets until cool enough to handle, then peel and cut each beet into 6–8 wedges, depending on the size. Mix the garlic, orange rind, orange juice, lemon juice, walnut or olive oil, salt, and pepper together, then drizzle over the beets and toss to coat well.

3 Meanwhile, bring a large saucepan of lightly salted water to a boil. Cook the pasta for 10 minutes or until al dente.

4 Drain the pasta thoroughly, then add the warm beets, arugula, and dolcelatte or blue cheese. Quickly toss together, then divide among serving bowls, and serve immediately before the arugula wilts.

INGREDIENTS
Serves 4

¼ lb. raw baby beets, unpeeled
1 garlic clove, peeled and crushed
½ tsp. finely grated orange rind
1 tbsp. orange juice
1 tsp. lemon juice
2 tbsp. walnut or olive oil
salt and freshly ground black pepper
4 cups dried fettucini
2 cups arugula
1 cup dolcelatte or blue cheese, cut into small cubes

Helpful Hint

Many large supermarkets sell raw beets, but baby beets may be more readily available from specialty stores. Look for beets with the leaves attached. The bulbs should be firm without any soft spots, and the leaves should not be wilted.

Mixed Salad with Anchovy Dressing & Ciabatta Croutons

1 Divide the endive and chicory into leaves and set aside some of the larger ones. Arrange the smaller leaves in a wide salad bowl.

2 Cut the fennel bulb in half from the stalk to the root end, then cut across in fine slices. Quarter the artichokes, then quarter and slice the cucumber and halve the tomatoes. Add to the salad bowl with the olives.

3 To make the dressing, drain the anchovies and put in a blender with the mustard, garlic, olive oil, lemon juice, 2 tablespoons of hot water, and black pepper. Mix together until smooth and thickened.

4 To make the croutons, cut the bread into ½-inch cubes. Heat the oil in a skillet, add the bread cubes, and cook for 3 minutes, turning frequently until golden. Remove and drain on absorbent paper towels.

5 Drizzle half the anchovy dressing over the prepared salad and toss to coat. Arrange the endive and chicory leaves around the edge, then drizzle over the remaining dressing. Sprinkle with the croutons and serve immediately.

INGREDIENTS
Serves 4

1 small head endive
1 small head chicory
1 fennel bulb
14-oz. can artichokes, drained and rinsed
½ cucumber
1 cup cherry tomatoes
½ cup ripe olives

FOR THE ANCHOVY DRESSING:
2-oz. can anchovy fillets
1 tsp. mustard
1 small garlic clove, peeled and crushed
4 tbsp. olive oil
1 tbsp. lemon juice
freshly ground black pepper

FOR THE CIABATTA CROUTONS:
2 thick slices ciabatta or similar-style bread
2 tbsp. olive oil

Helpful Hint

To reduce the fat in the croutons, cut the bread into cubes as above and toss in a large bowl with 2–3 teaspoons of olive oil. Cook in a preheated oven at 350° F for 15–20 minutes or until just golden and crisp. Serve as above.

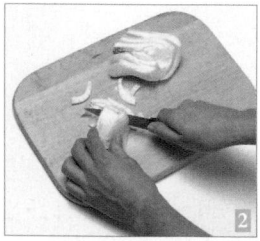
2

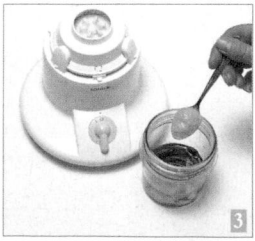
3

4

Rice-Filled Bell Peppers

1 Preheat the oven to 400° F. Put the tomatoes in a small bowl, and add boiling water to cover. Leave for 1 minute, then drain. Plunge the tomatoes into cold water to cool, then peel off the skins. Quarter, remove the seeds, and chop.

2 Heat the olive oil in a skillet, and cook the onion gently for 10 minutes until softened. Add the garlic, chopped tomatoes, and sugar.

3 Gently cook the tomato mixture for 10 minutes until thickened. Remove from the heat and stir the rice, pine nuts, and oregano into the sauce. Season to taste with salt and pepper.

4 Halve the bell peppers lengthwise, cutting through and leaving the stem on. Remove the seeds and cores, then put the bell peppers in a lightly greased roasting pan, cut-side down, and cook in the preheated oven for 10 minutes.

5 Turn the bell peppers so they are cut-side up. Spoon in the filling, then cover with foil. Return to the oven for 15 minutes or until the bell peppers are very tender, removing the foil for the last 5 minutes to allow the tops to brown a little.

6 Serve 1 red and 1 yellow bell pepper half to each person, along with a mixed salad and crusty bread.

INGREDIENTS
Serves 4

8 ripe tomatoes
2 tbsp. olive oil
1 onion, peeled and chopped
1 garlic clove, peeled and crushed
½ tsp. dark brown sugar
1½ cups cooked long-grain rice
½ cup pine nuts, toasted
1 tbsp. freshly chopped oregano
salt and freshly ground black pepper
2 large red bell peppers
2 large yellow bell peppers

TO SERVE:
mixed salad
crusty bread

Helpful Hint

It may be necessary to take a very thin slice from the bottom of the bell peppers to enable them to stand on the baking sheet. Be careful not to cut right through.

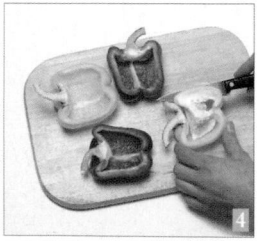

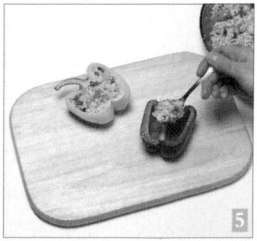

Pasta with Spicy Red Bell Pepper Sauce

1 Preheat the broiler. Broil the bell peppers, turning frequently for 10 minutes until the skins are blackened and blistered.

2 Put the peppers in a plastic container, and leave until cool enough to handle. Peel off the skin, then halve the peppers and scrape away the seeds. Chop the pepper flesh coarsely, and put in a food processor or blender.

3 Heat the olive oil in a large saucepan and cook the onion for 5 minutes. Stir in the garlic, anchovies, and chili, and cook for an additional 5 minutes, stirring. Add to the food processor and blend until fairly smooth.

4 Return the mixture to the saucepan with the tomatoes, and stir in the lemon rind and juice. Season to taste with salt and pepper. Add 2–3 tablespoons of vegetable stock if the sauce is a little thick. Bring to a boil and bubble for 1–2 minutes.

5 Meanwhile, bring a large saucepan of lightly salted water to a boil, and cook the pasta for 10 minutes or until al dente. Drain thoroughly. Add the sauce, and toss well to coat thoroughly.

6 Tip into a warmed serving dish or onto individual plates. Sprinkle with shavings of Parmesan cheese and a few basil leaves before serving.

INGREDIENTS
Serves 4

2 red bell peppers
2 tbsp. olive oil
1 onion, peeled and chopped
2 garlic cloves, peeled and crushed
4 anchovy fillets
1 red chili, seeded and finely chopped
7-oz. can chopped tomatoes
2 tsp. finely grated lemon rind
1 tbsp. lemon juice
salt and freshly ground black pepper
2–3 tbsp. vegetable stock (optional)
5¼ cups dried pasta, such as tagliatelle, linguine, or shells

TO GARNISH:
shaved Parmesan cheese
fresh basil leaves

Tasty Tip

If you prefer a chunkier sauce, do not put the bell peppers through the food processor, but finely chop instead. Add to the saucepan with the onion mixture and continue from Step 4.

Rigatoni with Oven-Dried Cherry Tomatoes & Mascarpone

1 Preheat the oven to 275° F. Halve the cherry tomatoes and place close together on a nonstick baking sheet, cut-side up. Sprinkle lightly with the sugar, and then with a little salt and pepper. Cook in the preheated oven for 1¼ hours or until dry but not beginning to brown. Let cool on the baking sheet. Put in a bowl, drizzle over the olive oil, and toss to coat.

2 Bring a large saucepan of lightly salted water to a boil, and cook the pasta for about 10 minutes or until al dente. Add the frozen peas 2–3 minutes before the end of the cooking time. Drain thoroughly and return the pasta and the peas to the saucepan.

3 Add the mascarpone to the saucepan. When melted, add the tomatoes, mint, parsley, and a little black pepper. Toss gently together, then transfer to a warmed serving dish or individual plates, and garnish with sprigs of fresh mint. Serve immediately.

INGREDIENTS
Serves 4

3 cups red cherry tomatoes
1 tsp. sugar
salt and freshly ground black pepper
2 tbsp. olive oil
5¼ cups dried rigatoni
1 cup frozen peas
2 tbsp. mascarpone cheese
1 tbsp. freshly chopped mint
1 tbsp. freshly chopped parsley
sprigs of fresh mint, to garnish

Tasty Tip

Double the quantity of tomatoes. When cooked, pack tightly into a sterilized jar layered up with fresh herbs and garlic. Cover with olive oil and leave in the refrigerator for a few days. Use as above or serve as an antipasto with bread, cold meats, and olives. Do not keep for longer than 2 weeks.

Red Bell Pepper & Basil Tart

1 Preheat the oven to 400° F. Sift the flour and salt into a bowl. Make a well in the center. Stir together the egg, oil, and 1 tablespoon of tepid water. Add to the dry ingredients, drop in the olives, and mix to a dough. Knead on a lightly floured surface for a few seconds until smooth, then wrap in plastic wrap and chill in the refrigerator for 30 minutes.

2 Roll out the pastry and use to line a 9-inch springform fluted flan pan. Lightly prick the base with a fork. Cover and chill in the refrigerator for 20 minutes.

3 Cook the bell peppers under a hot broiler for 10 minutes or until the skins are blackened and blistered. Put the peppers in a plastic container, cool for 10 minutes, then remove the skin and slice.

4 Line the pastry case with foil or waxed paper weighed down with baking beans and bake blind for 10 minutes. Remove the foil and beans, and cook for an additional 5 minutes. Reduce the oven temperature to 350° F.

5 Beat the mascarpone cheese until smooth. Gradually add the milk and eggs. Stir in the peppers and basil, and season to taste with salt and pepper. Spoon into the flan shell and cook for 25–30 minutes or until lightly set. Garnish with a sprig of fresh basil and serve immediately with a mixed salad.

Helpful Hint

Baking the pastry shell before filling it is an important step in making any kind of quiche or pie with a moist filling. It ensures that the pastry will not become soggy and that it will be cooked through.

INGREDIENTS
Serves 4–6

FOR THE OLIVE PASTRY:

2 cups all-purpose flour
pinch of salt
5 tbsp. pitted ripe olives, finely chopped
1 medium egg, lightly beaten, plus 1 egg yolk
3 tbsp. olive oil

FOR THE FILLING:

2 large red bell peppers, seeded and quartered
¼ cup mascarpone cheese
4 tbsp. milk
2 medium eggs
3 tbsp. freshly chopped basil
salt and freshly ground black pepper
sprig of fresh basil, to garnish
mixed salad, to serve

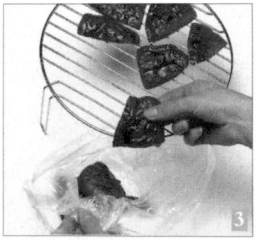

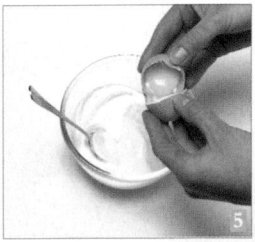

Spinach Dumplings with Rich Tomato Sauce

1 To make the tomato sauce, heat the olive oil in a large saucepan, and cook the onion for 5 minutes. Add the garlic and chili, and cook for an additional 5 minutes until softened.

2 Stir in the wine, chopped tomatoes, and lemon rind. Bring to a boil, cover, and simmer for 20 minutes, then uncover and simmer for 15 minutes or until the sauce has thickened. Remove the lemon rind and season to taste with salt and pepper.

3 To make the spinach dumplings, wash the spinach thoroughly and remove any tough stalks. Cover and cook in a large saucepan over a low heat with just the water clinging to the leaves. Drain, then squeeze out all the excess water. Finely chop and put in a large bowl.

4 Add the ricotta, bread crumbs, Parmesan cheese, and egg yolk to the spinach. Season with nutmeg, salt, and pepper. Mix together and shape into 20 walnut-size balls.

5 Toss the spinach balls in the flour. Heat the olive oil in a large nonstick skillet, and cook the balls gently for 5–6 minutes, turning occasionally. Garnish with fresh basil leaves, and serve immediately with the tomato sauce and tagliatelle.

Helpful Hint

It is very important to squeeze out all the excess water from the cooked spinach, otherwise the dumplings will fall apart when they are cooked.

INGREDIENTS
Serves 4

FOR THE SAUCE:
2 tbsp. olive oil
1 onion, peeled and chopped
1 garlic clove, peeled and crushed
1 red chili, seeded and chopped
⅔ cup dry white wine
14-oz. can tomatoes
pared strip of lemon rind

FOR THE DUMPLINGS:
10 cups fresh spinach leaves
¼ cup ricotta cheese
¼ cup fresh white bread crumbs
¼ cup Parmesan cheese, shredded
1 medium egg yolk
¼ tsp. freshly grated nutmeg
salt and freshly ground black pepper
5 tbsp. all-purpose flour
2 tbsp. olive oil, for cooking
fresh basil leaves, to garnish
freshly cooked tagliatelle, to serve

Venetian-Style Vegetables & Beans

1 Put the beans in a bowl, cover with plenty of cold water, and allow to soak for at least 8 hours or overnight.

2 Drain and rinse the beans. Put in a large saucepan with 5 cups cold water. Tie the parsley and rosemary in cheesecloth and add to the beans with the olive oil. Boil rapidly for 10 minutes, then lower the heat and simmer for 20 minutes with the saucepan half covered. Stir in the tomatoes and shallots, and simmer for an additional 10–15 minutes or until the beans are cooked.

3 Meanwhile, slice the red and white onions into rings, and finely dice the carrot and celery. Heat the olive oil in a saucepan and cook the onions over a very low heat for about 10 minutes. Add the carrot, celery, and bay leaves to the saucepan, and cook for an additional 10 minutes, stirring frequently, until the vegetables are tender. Sprinkle with sugar, stir, and cook for 1 minute.

4 Stir in the vinegar. Cook for 1 minute, then remove from the heat. Drain the beans through a strainer, discarding all the herbs, then add the beans to the onion mixture, and season well with salt and pepper. Mix, then tip the beans into a large serving bowl. Let cool, then serve at room temperature.

Helpful Hint

If time is short, put the beans into a large saucepan and cover with cold water. Bring to a boil, and boil rapidly for 10 minutes. Turn off the heat and allow to stand for 2 hours. Drain well and cover with fresh water. Cook as above.

INGREDIENTS
Serves 4

1½ cups dried pinto beans
3 sprigs of fresh parsley
1 sprig of fresh rosemary
2 tbsp. olive oil
7-oz. can chopped tomatoes
2 shallots, peeled

FOR THE VEGETABLE MIXTURE:
1 large red onion, peeled
1 large white onion, peeled
1 medium carrot, peeled
2 celery stalks, trimmed
3 tbsp. olive oil
3 bay leaves
1 tsp. sugar
3 tbsp. red wine vinegar
salt and freshly ground black pepper

Roast Butternut Squash Risotto

1 Preheat the oven to 375° F. Cut the butternut squash in half, thickly peel, then scoop out the seeds and discard. Cut the flesh into ¾-inch cubes.

2 Pour the oil into a large roasting pan, and heat in the preheated oven for 5 minutes. Add the butternut squash and garlic cloves. Turn in the oil to coat, then roast in the oven for about 25–30 minutes or until golden brown and very tender, turning the vegetables halfway through the cooking time.

3 Melt the butter in a large saucepan. Add the rice and stir over a high heat for a few seconds. Add the saffron and the wine, and boil fiercely until almost totally reduced, stirring frequently. At the same time, heat the stock in a separate saucepan and keep at a steady simmer.

4 Reduce the heat under the rice to low. Add a ladleful of stock to the saucepan and simmer, stirring until absorbed. Continue adding the stock in this way until the rice is tender. This will take about 20 minutes and it may not be necessary to add all the stock.

5 Turn off the heat and stir in the herbs, Parmesan cheese, and seasoning. Cover and allow to stand for 2–3 minutes. Quickly remove the skins from the roasted garlic. Add to the risotto with the butternut squash and mix gently. Garnish with sprigs of oregano, and serve immediately with Parmesan cheese.

INGREDIENTS
Serves 4

1 medium butternut squash
2 tbsp. olive oil
1 garlic bulb, cloves separated but unpeeled
1 tbsp. unsalted butter
1¼ cups risotto rice
large pinch of saffron strands
⅔ cup dry white wine
4 cups vegetable stock
1 tbsp. freshly chopped parsley
1 tbsp. freshly chopped oregano
½ cup Parmesan cheese, finely shredded
salt and freshly ground black pepper
sprigs of fresh oregano, to garnish
extra Parmesan cheese, to serve

Helpful Hint

It is important to keep the stock simmering alongside the risotto, because this ensures that the cooking process is not interrupted.

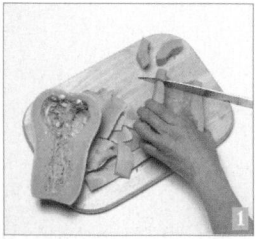

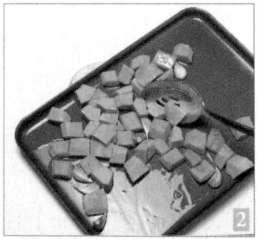

Hot Broiled Chicory & Pears

1 Preheat the broiler. Spread the chopped almonds in a single layer on the broiler pan. Broil for about 3 minutes, moving the almonds around occasionally, until lightly browned. Set aside.

2 Halve the chicory lengthwise and cut out the cores. Mix together the olive and peanut oils. Brush about 2 tablespoons all over the chicory.

3 Put the chicory in a broiler pan, cut-side up, and cook under a hot broiler for 2–3 minutes or until charred. Turn and cook for an additional 1–2 minutes, then turn again.

4 Peel, core, and thickly slice the pears. Brush with 1 tablespoon of the oils, then place the pears on top of the chicory. Broil for an additional 3–4 minutes or until both the chicory and pears are soft.

5 Transfer the chicory and pears to four warmed serving plates. Beat together the remaining oil, lemon juice, and oregano, then season to taste with salt and pepper.

6 Drizzle the dressing over the chicory and pears, and sprinkle with the almonds. Garnish with fresh oregano, and serve with ciabatta bread.

INGREDIENTS
Serves 4

½ cup unblanched almonds, coarsely chopped
4 small heads chicory
2 tbsp. olive oil
1 tbsp. peanut oil
2 firm, ripe dessert pears
2 tsp. lemon juice
1 tsp. freshly chopped oregano.
salt and freshly ground black pepper
freshly chopped oregano, to garnish
warmed ciabatta or similar-style bread, to serve

Helpful Hint

If preparing the pears ahead of time for this recipe, dip or brush them with some lemon juice to ensure that they do not discolor before cooking.

Eggplant Cannelloni with Watercress Sauce

1 Preheat the oven to 375° F. Cut the eggplants lengthwise into thin slices, discarding the side pieces. Heat 2 tablespoons of oil in a skillet, and cook the eggplant slices in a single layer in several batches, turning once until golden on both sides.

2 Mix the cheeses, basil, and seasoning together. Lay the eggplant slices on a clean surface, and spread the cheese mixture evenly between them.

3 Roll up the slices from one of the short ends to enclose the filling. Place seam-side down in a single layer in an ovenproof dish. Cook in the preheated oven for 15 minutes or until golden.

4 To make the watercress sauce, blanch the watercress leaves in boiling water for about 30 seconds. Drain the watercress well, then rinse in a strainer under cold running water and squeeze dry. Put the stock, shallot, lemon rind, and thyme in a small saucepan. Boil rapidly until reduced by half, then remove from the heat and strain.

5 Put the watercress and strained stock in a food processor and blend until fairly smooth. Return to the saucepan, stir in the sour cream and lemon juice, and season the sauce to taste with salt and pepper. Heat until the sauce is piping hot.

6 Serve a little of the sauce drizzled over the eggplants, and the rest separately in a pitcher. Garnish the cannelloni with sprigs of watercress and lemon zest. Serve immediately.

INGREDIENTS
Serves 4

4 large eggplants
½ cup olive oil
1½ cups ricotta cheese
1 cup Parmesan cheese, shredded
3 tbsp. freshly chopped basil
salt and freshly ground black pepper

FOR THE WATERCRESS SAUCE:
¼ cup watercress, trimmed
1 cup vegetable stock
1 shallot, peeled and sliced
pared strip of lemon rind
1 large sprig of thyme
3 tbsp. sour cream
1 tsp. lemon juice

TO GARNISH:
sprigs of watercress
lemon zest

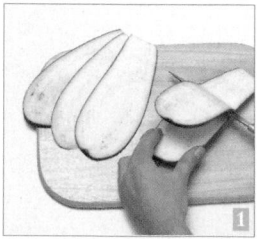

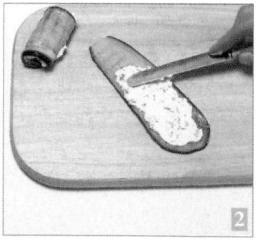

Panzanella

1 Leave the crusts on on the bread. Add 1 teaspoon of red wine vinegar to a pitcher of ice water, put the slices of bread in a bowl, and pour over the water. Make sure the bread is covered completely. Allow to soak for 3–4 minutes until just soft.

2 Remove the soaked bread from the water and squeeze it gently, first with your hands, and then in a clean dishtowel, to remove any excess water. Put the bread on a large plate, cover with a piece of plastic wrap, and chill in the refrigerator for about 1 hour.

3 Meanwhile, beat together the olive oil, the remaining red wine vinegar, and lemon juice in a large serving bowl. Add the garlic and onion, and stir to coat well.

4 Halve the cucumber and remove the seeds. Dice both the cucumber and tomatoes. Add, along with the olives, to the garlic and onions. Tear the bread into bite-sized chunks and add to the bowl, along with the fresh basil leaves. Toss, and serve immediately with a grinding of sea salt and black pepper.

INGREDIENTS
Serves 4

loaf of day-old Italian bread, about 9 thick slices
1 tbsp. red wine vinegar
4 tbsp. olive oil
1 tsp. lemon juice
1 small garlic clove, peeled and finely chopped
1 red onion, peeled and finely sliced
1 cucumber, peeled
2 medium ripe tomatoes, seeded
¾ cup pitted ripe olives
about 20 basil leaves, coarsely torn, or left whole if small
sea salt and freshly ground black pepper

Tasty Tip

Choose an open-textured Italian bread, such as ciabatta, for this classic Tuscany salad. Look in your local delicatessen for different flavored marinated olives. Try chili and garlic, or basil, garlic, and orange.

2

3

4

Vegetable Frittata

1 Preheat the broiler just before cooking. Lightly beat the eggs with the parsley, tarragon, and half the cheese. Season to taste with pepper and set aside. Salt is not needed, as the pecorino is very salty.

2 Bring a large saucepan of lightly salted water to a boil. Add the new potatoes and cook for 8 minutes. Add the carrots and cook for 4 minutes. Then add the broccoli florets and the zucchini, and cook for an additional 3–4 minutes or until all the vegetables are barely tender. Drain well.

3 Heat the oil in an 8-inch heavy skillet. Add the scallions and cook for 3–4 minutes or until softened. Add all the vegetables, cook for a few seconds, then pour in the beaten egg mixture.

4 Stir gently for about a minute, then cook for an additional 1–2 minutes or until the bottom of the frittata is set and golden brown.

5 Place the skillet under a hot broiler for 1 minute or until almost set and just beginning to brown. Sprinkle with the remaining cheese, and broil for an additional 1 minute or until it is lightly browned.

6 Loosen the edges and slide out of the skillet. Cut into wedges and serve hot or warm with a mixed green salad and crusty Italian bread.

INGREDIENTS
Serves 2

6 medium eggs
2 tbsp. freshly chopped parsley
1 tbsp. freshly chopped tarragon
¼ cup pecorino or Parmesan cheese, finely shredded
freshly ground black pepper
1¼ cups tiny new potatoes
2 small carrots, peeled and sliced
1¼ cups broccoli, cut into small florets
1 zucchini, about ¼ cup, sliced
2 tbsp. olive oil
4 scallions, trimmed and thinly sliced

TO SERVE:
mixed green salad
crusty Italian bread

Food Fact

A frittata is a heavy omelette, usually with a vegetable, meat, or cheese filling that is cooked slowly and often finished in the oven or under the broiler. It is closer to a Spanish tortilla than to a classic French omelette.

Panzerotti

1 Sift the flour and salt into a bowl. Stir in the yeast. Make a well in the center. Add the oil and the warm water, and mix to a soft dough. Knead on a lightly floured surface until smooth and elastic. Put in a greased bowl, cover, and leave in a warm place to rise while making the filling.

2 To make the filling, heat the oil in a skillet and cook the onion for 5 minutes. Add the garlic, yellow bell pepper, and zucchini. Cook for 5 minutes or until the vegetables are tender. Tip into a bowl and leave to cool slightly. Stir in the olives, mozzarella cheese, and season to taste with salt and pepper.

3 Briefly reknead the dough. Divide into 16 equal pieces. Roll out each to a circle about 4 inches in diameter. Mix together the tomato paste and dried herbs, then spread about 1 teaspoon on each circle, leaving a ¾-inch border around the edge.

4 Divide the filling equally among the circles. Be careful not to overfill, as they will leak during cooking. Brush the edges with water, then fold in half to enclose the filling. Press to seal, then crimp the edges.

5 Heat the oil to 350° F. Deep-fry the panzerotti in batches for 3 minutes or until golden. Drain on absorbent paper towels, and keep warm in a low oven until ready to serve with fresh arugula.

Helpful Hint

Make sure to allow the panzerotti to cool before serving. The filling will be very hot when freshly cooked.

INGREDIENTS
Serves 16

4 cups high-gluten bread flour
pinch of salt
1 tsp. rapid-rise active dry yeast
2 tbsp. olive oil
1¼ cups warm water
fresh arugula, to serve

FOR THE FILLING:
1 tbsp. olive oil
1 small red onion, peeled and finely chopped
2 garlic cloves, peeled and crushed
½ yellow bell pepper, seeded and chopped
1 small zucchini, trimmed and chopped
5 tbsp. pitted ripe olives, quartered
1 cup mozzarella cheese, cut into tiny cubes
salt and freshly ground black pepper
5–6 tbsp. tomato paste
1 tsp. dried mixed herbs
oil for deep-frying

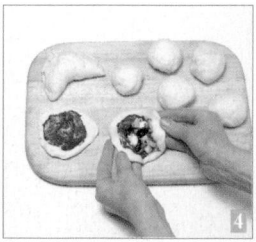

Pasta Primavera

1 Trim and halve the green beans. Bring a large saucepan of lightly salted water to a boil, and cook the beans for 4–5 minutes, adding the peas after 2 minutes. Drain the beans and peas, and briefly rinse under cold running water.

2 Heat the butter and oil in a large nonstick skillet. Add the carrots and cook for 2 minutes, then stir in the zucchini and leeks and cook for 10 minutes, stirring, until the vegetables are almost tender.

3 Stir the cream and lemon rind into the vegetables and boil over a gentle heat until the sauce is slightly reduced and the vegetables are cooked.

4 Meanwhile, bring a large saucepan of lightly salted water to a boil and cook the tagliatelle for 10 minutes or until al dente.

5 Add the beans, peas, Parmesan cheese, and herbs to the sauce. Stir for 30 seconds or until the cheese has melted and the vegetables are hot.

6 Drain the tagliatelle, add the vegetables and sauce, toss gently to mix, and season to taste with salt and pepper. Spoon into a warmed serving bowl, garnish with a few sprigs of dill, and serve immediately.

INGREDIENTS
Serves 4

1 cup fine green beans
1 cup peas
½ stick butter
1 tsp. olive oil
1 cup baby carrots, scrubbed
2 zucchini, trimmed and thinly sliced
¼ cup baby leeks, trimmed and cut into 1-inch lengths
1 cup heavy cream
1 tsp. finely grated lemon rind
4 cups dried tagliatelle
¼ cup Parmesan cheese, shredded
1 tbsp. freshly cut chives
1 tbsp. freshly chopped dill
salt and freshly ground black pepper
sprigs of fresh dill, to garnish

Food Fact

Primavera means "spring," and this dish is classically made with spring vegetables. At other times, use available vegetables.

Spaghetti with Pesto

1 To make the pesto, place the Parmesan cheese in a food processor with the basil leaves, pine nuts, and garlic, and process until well-blended.

2 With the motor running, gradually pour in the extra-virgin olive oil until a thick sauce forms. Add a little more oil if the sauce seems too thick. Season to taste with salt and pepper. Transfer to a bowl and cover, then store in the refrigerator until required.

3 Bring a large pan of lightly salted water to a rolling boil. Add the spaghetti and cook according to the package directions or until al dente.

4 Drain the spaghetti thoroughly and return to the pan. Stir in the pesto and toss lightly. Heat through gently, then spoon the pasta into a warmed serving dish or onto individual plates. Garnish with basil leaves and serve immediately with extra Parmesan cheese.

INGREDIENTS
Serves 4

1¼ cups freshly grated Parmesan cheese, plus extra to serve
½ cup fresh basil leaves, plus extra to garnish
6 tbsp. pine nuts
3 large garlic cloves, peeled
¼ cup extra-virgin olive oil, plus more if necessary
salt and freshly ground pepper
14 oz. spaghetti

Helpful Hint

You can still make pesto if you do not have a food processor. Tear the basil leaves and place them in a mortar with the garlic, pine nuts, and a tablespoonful of the oil. Pound to a paste using a pestle, gradually working in the rest of the oil. Transfer to a bowl and stir in the cheese. Season to taste with salt and pepper. Pesto will keep for 2–3 days if stored in the refrigerator.

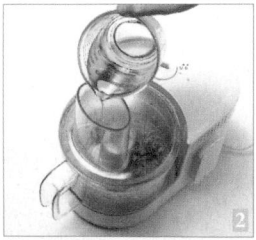

Pasta Shells with Broccoli & Capers

1 Bring a large pan of lightly salted water to a rolling boil. Add the conchiglie, then return to a boil and cook for 2 minutes. Add the broccoli to the pan. Return to a boil and continue cooking for 8–10 minutes or until the conchiglie is al dente.

2 Meanwhile, heat the olive oil in a large skillet, then add the onion and cook for 5 minutes or until softened, stirring frequently. Stir in the capers and chili flakes, and cook for an additional 2 minutes.

3 Drain the pasta and broccoli and add to the skillet. Toss the ingredients to mix thoroughly. Sprinkle over the cheeses, then stir until the cheeses have just melted. Season to taste with salt and pepper, then spoon into a warmed serving dish. Garnish with chopped parsley and serve immediately with extra Parmesan cheese.

INGREDIENTS
Serves 4

3½ cups conchiglie (shells)
1 lb. broccoli florets, cut into small pieces
5 tbsp. olive oil
1 large onion, peeled and finely chopped
4 tbsp. capers in brine, rinsed and drained
½ tsp. dried chili flakes (optional)
¼ cup freshly grated Parmesan cheese, plus extra to serve
¼ cup grated pecorino cheese
salt and freshly ground black pepper
2 tbsp. freshly chopped Italian parsley, to garnish

Helpful Hint

Chili flakes are made from dried, crushed chilies and add a pungent hot spiciness to this dish. There are lots of other chili products that you could use instead. For instance, substitute a tablespoonful of chili oil for one of the tablespoons of olive oil, or add a dash of hot sauce at the end of cooking.

Venetian Herb Orzo

1 Rinse the spinach leaves in cold water several times and set aside. Finely chop the arugula leaves with the parsley and mint. Thinly slice the green of the scallions.

2 Bring a large pan of water to a boil, then add the spinach leaves, herbs, and scallions, and cook for about 10 seconds. Remove and rinse under cold running water. Drain well, and using your hands, squeeze out all the excess moisture.

3 Place the spinach, herbs, and scallions in a food processor. Blend for 1 minute. Then, with the motor running, gradually pour in the olive oil until the sauce is well-blended.

4 Meanwhile, bring a large pan of lightly salted water to a rolling boil. Add the pasta and cook according to the package directions or until al dente. Drain thoroughly and place in a large, warmed bowl.

5 Add the spinach sauce to the orzo and stir lightly until the orzo is well-coated. Stir in an extra tablespoon of olive oil if the mixture seems too thick. Season well with salt and pepper. Serve immediately on warmed plates or let cool to room temperature.

INGREDIENTS
Serves 4–6

2½ cups baby spinach leaves
1½ cups arugula leaves
⅔ cup Italian parsley
few leaves of fresh mint
6 scallions, trimmed
3 tbsp. extra-virgin olive oil, plus more if required
1 lb. orzo
salt and freshly ground black pepper

Food Fact

Also called "rocket," arugula adds a peppery flavor to many dishes. The tender tiny leaves have the most delicate flavor, and as they grow in size, the flavor becomes more pronounced.

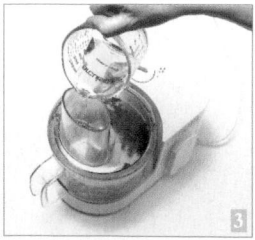

Cheesy Pasta with Tomatoes & Cream

1 Place the ricotta cheese in a bowl and beat until smooth, then add the remaining cheeses with the eggs, herbs, and seasoning to taste. Beat well until creamy and smooth.

2 Cut the prepared pasta dough into quarters. Working with one quarter at a time and covering the remaining quarters with a clean, damp dishtowel, roll out the pasta very thinly. Using a 4-inch pastry cutter or small saucer, cut out as many rounds as possible.

3 Place a small tablespoonful of the filling mixture slightly below the center of each round. Lightly moisten the edge of the round with water and fold in half to form a filled half-moon shape. Using a dinner fork, press the edges together firmly.

4 Transfer to a lightly floured cookie sheet and continue filling the remaining pasta. Leave to dry for 15 minutes.

5 Heat the oil in a large pan, then add the onions and cook for 3–4 minutes or until beginning to soften. Add the garlic and cook for 1–2 minutes, then add the tomatoes, vermouth, and cream, and bring to a boil. Simmer for 10–15 minutes or until thickened and reduced.

6 Bring a large pan of salted water to a boil. Add the filled pasta and return to a boil. Cook, stirring frequently to prevent sticking, for 5 minutes or until al dente. Drain and return to the pan. Pour over the tomato and cream sauce. Garnish with basil leaves and serve immediately.

INGREDIENTS
Serves 4

Fresh pasta (see Fresh Tagliatelle with Zucchini, page 70)
1 cup fresh ricotta cheese
2 cups grated, smoked mozzarella (use normal if smoked is unavailable)
1 cup freshly grated pecorino or Parmesan cheese
2 medium eggs, lightly beaten
2–3 tbsp. finely chopped mint, basil, or parsley
salt and freshly ground black pepper

FOR THE SAUCE:
2 tbsp. olive oil
1 small onion, peeled and finely chopped
2 garlic cloves, peeled and finely chopped
1 lb. ripe plum tomatoes, peeled, deseeded, and finely chopped
¼ cup white vermouth
1 cup heavy cream
fresh basil leaves, to garnish

1

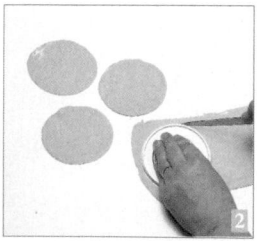
2

3

Pasta-Stuffed Bell Peppers

1 Preheat the oven to 375° F. Bring a pan of water to a boil. Trim the bottom of each bell pepper so it sits straight. Blanch the bell peppers for 2–3 minutes, then drain on paper towels.

2 Return the water to a boil. Add ½ teaspoon of salt and the pasta, and cook for 3–4 minutes or until al dente. Drain thoroughly, saving the water. Rinse under cold running water, then drain again and set aside.

3 Heat 2 tablespoons of the olive oil in a large skillet, then add the onion and cook for 3–4 minutes. Add the garlic and cook for 1 minute. Stir in the tomatoes and wine, and cook for 5 minutes, stirring frequently. Add the olives, herbs, mozzarella cheese, and half the Parmesan cheese. Season to taste with salt and pepper. Remove from the heat and stir in the pasta.

4 Dry the insides of the bell peppers with paper towels, then season lightly. Arrange the bell peppers in a lightly greased, shallow baking dish and fill with the pasta mixture. Sprinkle with the remaining Parmesan cheese and drizzle the remaining oil over the peppers. Pour in boiling water to ½ inch up the sides of the dish. Cook in the preheated oven for 25 minutes or until cooked. Serve immediately with freshly made tomato sauce.

INGREDIENTS
Serves 6

6 red, yellow, or orange bell peppers, tops cut off and deseeded
salt and freshly ground black pepper
1½ cups tiny pasta shapes
4 tbsp. olive oil
1 onion, peeled and finely chopped
2 garlic cloves, peeled and finely chopped
3 ripe plum tomatoes, skinned, deseeded, and chopped
¼ cup dry white wine
8 pitted black olives, chopped
4 tbsp. freshly chopped mixed herbs, such as parsley, basil, oregano, or marjoram
1 cup diced mozzarella cheese
4 tbsp. grated Parmesan cheese
fresh tomato sauce, preferably homemade, to serve

Tasty Tip

For a rich tomato sauce, chop 2 lbs. ripe tomatoes, then place in a pan with 1 crushed garlic clove, 1 tablespoon olive oil, and 2 tablespoons Worcestershire sauce. Cook until soft. Sieve or purée and serve with the bell peppers.

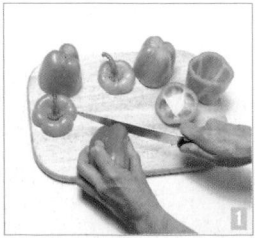

Fusilli with Zucchini & Sun-Dried Tomatoes

1 Heat 2 tablespoons of the olive oil in a large skillet, then add the onion and cook for 5-7 minutes or until softened. Add the chopped garlic and zucchini slices, and cook for an additional 5 minutes, stirring occasionally.

2 Stir the chopped tomatoes and the sun-dried tomatoes into the skillet, and season to taste with salt and pepper. Cook until the zucchini are just tender and the sauce is slightly thickened.

3 Bring a large pan of lightly salted water to a rolling boil. Add the fusilli and cook according to the package directions or until al dente.

4 Drain the fusilli thoroughly and return to the pan. Add the butter and remaining oil, and toss to coat. Stir the chopped basil or parsley into the zucchini mixture and pour over the fusilli. Toss and spoon into a warmed serving dish. Serve with grated Parmesan or pecorino cheese.

INGREDIENTS
Serves 6

5 tbsp. olive oil
1 large onion, peeled and thinly sliced
2 garlic cloves, peeled and finely chopped
1½ lbs. zucchini, trimmed and sliced
14-oz. can chopped plum tomatoes
12 sun-dried tomatoes, cut into thin strips
salt and freshly ground black pepper
4 cups fusilli
2 tbsp. butter, diced
2 tbsp. freshly chopped basil or Italian parsley
grated Parmesan or pecorino cheese, for serving

Food Fact

Sun-dried tomatoes come in jars with olive oil or simply dried in packages, in which case they will need rehydrating. The latter are better for this recipe, as they will soak up the juices from the chopped tomatoes and zucchini and help to thicken the sauce.

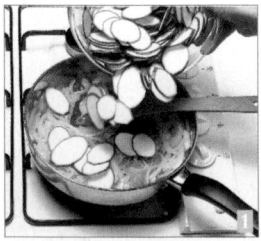

Linguine with Walnut Pesto

1 Bring a pan of water to a boil. Add the walnut halves and simmer for about 1 minute. Drain and turn onto a clean dishtowel. Using the towel, rub the nuts gently to loosen the skins, then turn into a coarse sieve or colander and shake to separate the skins. Discard the skins and coarsely chop the nuts.

2 With the the food processor running, drop in the garlic cloves and chop finely. Remove the lid, then add the walnuts, bread crumbs, olive and walnut oils, and the parsley. Blend to a paste with a crumbly texture.

3 Scrape the nut mixture into a bowl, then add the softened butter and, using a wooden spoon, cream them together. Gradually beat in the cream and the Parmesan cheese. Season the walnut pesto to taste with salt and pepper.

4 Bring a large pan of lightly salted water to a rolling boil. Add the linguine and cook according to the package instructions or until al dente.

5 Drain the linguine thoroughly, setting aside 1–2 tablespoons of the cooking water. Return the linguine and water to the pan. Add the walnut pesto, 1 tablespoon at a time, tossing and stirring until well-coated. Tip into a warmed serving dish or spoon onto individual plates. Serve immediately with the extra grated Parmesan cheese.

INGREDIENTS
Serves 4

1 cup walnut halves
1–2 garlic cloves, peeled and coarsely chopped
⅓ cup dried bread crumbs
3 tbsp. extra-virgin olive oil
1 tbsp. walnut oil
3–4 tbsp. freshly chopped parsley
½ stick butter, softened
2 tbsp. heavy cream
¼ cup grated Parmesan cheese, plus extra to serve
salt and freshly ground black pepper
1 lb. linguine

Helpful Hint

It is important to use dried bread crumbs for this recipe. Avoid the bright orange variety, which are unsuitable. Spread about 1 cup fresh bread crumbs on a cookie sheet and bake in a very low oven for about 20–25 minutes, stirring occasionally, until dry but not colored.

Four-Cheese Tagliatelle

1 Place the whipping cream with the garlic cloves in a medium pan, and heat gently until small bubbles begin to form around the edge of the pan. Using a slotted spoon, remove and discard the garlic cloves.

2 Add all the cheeses to the pan and stir until melted. Season with a little salt and a lot of black pepper. Keep the sauce warm over a low heat, but do not let it come to a boil.

3 Meanwhile, bring a large pan of lightly salted water to a boil. Add the tagliatelle, then return to a boil and cook for 2–3 minutes or until al dente.

4 Drain the pasta and return it to the pan. Pour the sauce over the pasta, then add the chives and toss lightly until well-coated. Spoon into a warmed serving dish or spoon onto individual plates. Garnish with a few basil leaves and serve immediately with extra Parmesan cheese.

INGREDIENTS
Serves 4

1¼ cups whipping cream
4 garlic cloves, peeled and lightly bruised
¼ cup diced fontina cheese
¾ cup grated Gruyère cheese
¾ cup diced mozzarella cheese
¼ cup grated Parmesan cheese, plus extra to serve
salt and freshly ground black pepper
10 oz. fresh green tagliatelle
1–2 tbsp. freshly cut chives
fresh basil leaves, to garnish

Helpful Hint

Fresh pasta takes much less time to cook than dried pasta and 2–3 minutes is usually long enough for it to be al dente, but check the package for cooking directions. Tagliatelle comes from Bologna, where it is usually served with a meat sauce. Green tagliatelle is generally flavored with spinach, but it is also available flavored with fresh herbs, which would go particularly well with the rich cheese sauce in this recipe.

Spaghetti alla Puttanesca

1 Heat the olive oil in a large skillet, then add the anchovies and cook, stirring with a wooden spoon and crushing the anchovies until they disintegrate. Add the garlic and dried chilies, and cook for 1 minute, stirring frequently.

2 Add the tomatoes, olives, capers, oregano, and tomato paste, and cook, stirring occasionally, for 15 minutes or until the liquid has evaporated and the sauce is thickened. Season the tomato sauce to taste with salt and pepper.

3 Meanwhile, bring a large pan of lightly salted water to a boil. Add the spaghetti and cook according to the package directions or until al dente.

4 Drain the spaghetti thoroughly, setting aside 1–2 tablespoons of the the cooking water. Return the spaghetti with the reserved water to the pan. Pour the tomato sauce over the spaghetti, then add the chopped parsley and toss to coat. Spoon into a warmed serving dish or onto individual plates and serve immediately.

INGREDIENTS
Serves 4

4 tbsp. olive oil
2 oz. anchovy fillets in olive oil, drained and coarsely chopped
2 garlic cloves, peeled and finely chopped
½ tsp. crushed dried chilies
14-oz. can chopped plum tomatoes
1 cup pitted black olives, cut in half
2 tbsp. capers, rinsed and drained
1 tsp. freshly chopped oregano
1 tbsp. tomato paste
salt and freshly ground black pepper
14 oz. spaghetti
2 tbsp. freshly chopped parsley

Helpful Hint

Anchovies are heavily salted after filleting to preserve them, so should be used only in small quantities. For a less-salty dish, drain them and soak in a little milk for about 20 minutes before using. You can, of course, omit the anchovies to make a vegetarian version of this recipe.

Tagliatelle Primavera

1 Bring a medium pan of salted water to a boil. Add the asparagus and blanch for 1–2 minutes or until just beginning to soften. Using a slotted spoon, transfer to a colander and rinse under cold running water. Repeat with the carrots and zucchini. Add the snow peas and return to a boil, then drain, rinse immediately, and drain again. Set aside the blanched vegetables.

2 Heat the butter in a large skillet. Add the onion and red bell pepper and cook for 5 minutes or until they begin to soften and color. Pour in the dry vermouth; it will bubble, steam, and evaporate almost immediately. Stir in the cream and simmer over a medium-low heat until reduced by about half. Add the blanched vegetables with the leeks, peas, and seasoning, and heat through for 2 minutes.

3 Meanwhile, bring a large pan of lightly salted water to a boil, then add the tagliatelle and return to a boil. Cook for 2-3 minutes or until al dente. Drain and return to the pan.

4 Stir the chopped parsley into the cream and vegetable sauce, then pour over the pasta and toss to coat thoroughly. Sprinkle with the grated Parmesan cheese and toss lightly. Spoon into a warmed serving bowl or spoon onto individual plates and serve immediately.

Helpful Hint

If using thin asparagus spears, there is no need to peel the stems. This is only necessary on the long spears that can have a woody stalk as the season progresses.

INGREDIENTS
Serves 4

4 oz. asparagus, lightly peeled and cut into 2½ in. lengths
2 carrots, peeled and cut into julienne strips
2 zucchini, trimmed and cut into julienne strips
⅓ cup small snow peas
½ cup butter
1 small onion, peeled and finely chopped
1 small red bell pepper, deseeded and finely chopped
¼ cup dry vermouth
1 cup heavy cream
1 small leek, trimmed and julienned
¼ cup fresh green peas (or frozen, thawed)
salt and freshly ground black pepper
14 oz. fresh tagliatelle
2 tbsp. freshly chopped Italian parsley
¼ cup grated Parmesan cheese

Eggplant & Ravioli Parmigiana

1 Preheat the oven to 350° F. Heat 2 tablespoons of the olive oil in a large, heavy-based pan, then add the onion and cook for 6–7 minutes or until softened. Add the garlic, then cook for 1 minute. Stir in the tomatoes, sugar, bay leaf, dried oregano, and basil, then bring to a boil, stirring frequently. Simmer for 30–35 minutes or until thickened and reduced, stirring occasionally. Stir in the fresh basil and season to taste with salt and pepper. Remove the tomato sauce from the heat and set aside.

2 Heat the remaining olive oil in a large, heavy-based skillet over a high heat. Dip the eggplant slices in the egg mixture, then in the bread crumbs. Cook in batches until golden on both sides. Drain on paper towels. Add more oil between batches if necessary.

3 Spoon a little tomato sauce into the base of a lightly greased large baking dish. Cover with a layer of eggplant slices, a sprinkling of Parmesan cheese, a layer of mozzarella cheese, then more sauce. Repeat the layers, then cover the sauce with a layer of cooked ravioli. Continue to layer in this way, ending with a layer of mozzarella cheese. Sprinkle the top with Parmesan cheese.

4 Drizzle with a little extra olive oil if desired, then bake in the preheated oven for 30 minutes or until golden brown and bubbling. Serve immediately.

Helpful Hint

Eggplants absorb a huge amount of oil during cooking, so use a good nonstick skillet and gradually add oil as required. You can use baby eggplants for this recipe if you prefer. Trim off the stalk ends, then cut them lengthwise into ½-inch strips.

INGREDIENTS
Serves 6

4 tbsp. olive oil
1 large onion, peeled and finely chopped
2–3 garlic cloves, peeled and crushed
2 14-oz. cans chopped tomatoes
2 tsp. brown sugar
1 dried bay leaf
1 tsp. dried oregano
1 tsp. dried basil
2 tbsp. freshly shredded basil
salt and freshly ground black pepper
2–3 medium eggplants, sliced crosswise ½ in. thick
2 medium eggs, beaten with 1 tbsp. water
1 cup dried bread crumbs
3/4 cup freshly grated Parmesan cheese
14 oz. mozzarella cheese, thinly sliced
9 oz. cheese-filled ravioli, cooked and drained

Zucchini Lasagna

1 Preheat the oven to 400° F. Heat the oil in a large skillet, then add the onion and cook for 3–5 minutes. Add the mushrooms and cook for 2 minutes. Add the zucchini and cook for an additional 3–4 minutes, or until tender. Stir in the garlic, thyme, and basil or parsley, then season to taste with salt and pepper. Remove from the heat and set aside.

2 Spoon one third of the white sauce onto the base of a lightly greased large baking dish. Arrange a layer of lasagna over the sauce. Spread half the zucchini mixture over the pasta, then sprinkle with some of the mozzarella and some of the Parmesan cheese. Repeat with more white sauce and another layer of lasagna, then cover with half the drained tomatoes.

3 Cover the tomatoes with lasagna, the remaining zucchini mixture, and some mozzarella and Parmesan cheese. Repeat the layers, ending with a layer of lasagna sheets, white sauce, and the remaining Parmesan cheese. Bake in the preheated oven for 35 minutes or until golden. Serve immediately.

INGREDIENTS
Serves 8

2 tbsp. olive oil
1 medium onion, peeled and finely chopped
4 cups mushrooms, wiped and thinly sliced
3–4 zucchini, trimmed and thinly sliced
2 garlic cloves, peeled and finely chopped
½ tsp. dried thyme
1–2 tbsp. freshly chopped basil or Italian parsley
salt and freshly ground black pepper
1 quantity prepared white sauce, (see page 232)
12 oz. lasagna sheets, cooked
2 cups grated mozzarella cheese
½ cup grated Parmesan cheese
14-oz. canned chopped tomatoes, drained

Helpful Hint

There is now a huge range of canned tomatoes available. Look for canned cherry tomatoes, which have a much sweeter flavor, or those with added ingredients and flavorings. Tomatoes with chopped bell peppers, garlic, or fresh herbs would all work well here and add extra flavor.

1

2

3

Baked Macaroni and Cheese

1 Preheat the oven to 375 °F. Bring a large heavy-based pan of lightly salted water to a rolling boil. Add the macaroni and cook according to the package directions or until al dente. Drain the pasta thoroughly and set aside.

2 Meanwhile, melt ½ cup of the butter in a large, heavy-based pan, then add the onion and cook, stirring frequently, for 5–7 minutes or until softened. Sprinkle in the flour and cook, stirring constantly, for about 2 minutes. Remove the pan from the heat and stir in the milk, then return to the heat and cook, stirring, until a smooth sauce has formed.

3 Add the bay leaf and thyme to the sauce, and season to taste with salt, pepper, cayenne pepper, and freshly grated nutmeg. Simmer for about 15 minutes, stirring frequently, until thickened and smooth.

4 Remove the sauce from the heat. Add the leeks, mustard, and cheddar cheese, and stir until the cheese has melted. Stir in the macaroni, then spoon into a lightly greased baking dish.

5 Sprinkle the bread crumbs and Parmesan cheese over the macaroni. Dot with the remaining butter, then bake in the preheated oven for 1 hour or until golden. Garnish with a basil sprig and serve immediately.

INGREDIENTS
Serves 8

4 cups macaroni
¼ cup butter
1 onion, peeled and finely chopped
3 tbsp. all-purpose flour
4 cups milk
1–2 dried bay leaves
½ tsp. dried thyme
salt and freshly ground black pepper
cayenne pepper
freshly grated nutmeg
2 small leeks, trimmed, finely chopped, cooked, and drained
1 tbsp. Dijon mustard
3½ cups grated cheddar cheese
2 tbsp. dried bread crumbs
2 tbsp. freshly grated Parmesan cheese
basil sprig, to garnish

Helpful Hint

Make sure that you simmer the macaroni only until just al dente and drain immediately, as it will continue to cook in the oven, where it needs to soak up the flavors of the sauce. For a more substantial dish, stir some chopped, lean smoked bacon into the macaroni before baking.

Penne with Vodka & Caviar

1 Bring a large pan of lightly salted water to a rolling boil. Add the penne and cook according to the package directions or until al dente. Drain thoroughly and set aside.

2 Heat the butter in a large skillet or wok, then add the scallions and stir-fry for 1 minute. Stir in the garlic and cook for an additional minute. Pour the vodka into the pan; it will bubble and steam. Cook until the vodka is reduced by about half, then add the heavy cream and return to a boil. Simmer gently for 2–3 minutes or until the sauce has thickened slightly.

3 Stir in the tomatoes, then stir in all but 1 tablespoon of the caviar and season to taste with salt and pepper. Add the penne and toss lightly to coat. Cook for 1 minute or until heated through. Divide the mixture among four warmed pasta bowls and garnish with the remaining caviar. Serve immediately.

INGREDIENTS
Serves 4

3½ cups penne
2 tbsp. butter
4–6 scallions, trimmed and thinly sliced
1 garlic clove, peeled and finely chopped
½ cup vodka
¾ cup heavy cream
1–2 ripe plum tomatoes, skinned, deseeded, and chopped
3 oz. caviar
salt and freshly ground black pepper

Food Fact

Authentic sturgeon caviar is very expensive. Red caviar from salmon, or black or red lumpfish roe, can be substituted. Alternatively, 6 oz. of thinly sliced smoked salmon pieces can also be substituted. Sturgeon caviar has a salty flavor, so always check the taste before adding salt. Smoked salmon and lumpfish roe have a much saltier taste, however, so no additional salt would be necessary.

Rigatoni with Gorgonzola & Walnuts

1 Bring a large pan of lightly salted water to a rolling boil. Add the rigatoni and cook according to the package directions or until al dente. Drain the pasta thoroughly, then set aside and keep warm.

2 Melt the butter in a large pan or wok over a medium heat. Add the Gorgonzola cheese and stir until just melted. Add the brandy (if desired) and cook for 30 seconds, then pour in the whipping or heavy cream and cook for 1–2 minutes, stirring until the sauce is smooth.

3 Stir in the walnut pieces, basil, and half the Parmesan cheese, then add the rigatoni. Season with salt and pepper. Return to the heat, stirring frequently, until heated through. Divide the pasta among four warmed bowls, then sprinkle with the remaining Parmesan cheese and serve immediately with cherry tomatoes and fresh green salad leaves.

INGREDIENTS
Serves 4

3½ cups rigatoni
½ stick butter
1 cup crumbled Gorgonzola cheese
2 tbsp. brandy, optional
¼ cup whipping or heavy cream
½ cup walnut pieces, lightly toasted and coarsely chopped
1 tbsp. freshly chopped basil
½ cup freshly grated Parmesan cheese
salt and freshly ground black pepper

TO SERVE:
cherry tomatoes
fresh green salad leaves

Tasty Tip

This blue cheese sauce is also very good with pappardelle or lasagnette, both very wide egg pasta noodles. Either whipping or heavy cream may be used here; heavy cream is higher in fat, so will give a richer, creamier finish to the sauce. If preferred, you could use sour cream, but it must be heated gently since it can curdle at high temperatures.

Pumpkin-Filled Pasta with Butter & Sage

1 Mix together the ingredients for the filling in a bowl, seasoning to taste with freshly grated nutmeg, salt, and pepper. If the mixture seems too wet, add a few more bread crumbs to bind.

2 Cut the pasta dough into quarters. Work with one quarter at a time, covering the remaining quarters with a damp dishtowel. Roll out the dough very thinly into a strip 4 inches wide. Drop spoonfuls of the filling along the strip 2½ inches apart, in two rows about 2 inches apart. Moisten the outside edges and the spaces between the filling with water.

3 Roll out another strip of pasta and lay it over the filled strip. Press down gently along both edges and between the filled sections. Using a fluted pastry wheel, cut along both long sides, down the center, and between the fillings to form cushions. Transfer the cushions to a lightly floured cookie sheet. Continue making cushions and let dry for 30 minutes.

4 Bring a large pan of lightly salted water to a boil. Add the pasta cushions and return to a boil. Cook, stirring frequently, for 4–5 minutes or until al dente. Drain carefully.

5 Heat the butter in a pan, then stir in the shredded sage leaves and cook for 30 seconds. Add the pasta cushions and stir gently, then spoon into serving bowls. Sprinkle with the grated Parmesan cheese and serve immediately.

INGREDIENTS
Serves 6–8

1 quantity fresh pasta dough (see page 70)
1 cup butter
2 tbsp. freshly shredded sage leaves
½ cup freshly grated Parmesan cheese, to serve

FOR THE FILLING:
about 1 cup freshly cooked pumpkin or sweet potato flesh, mashed and cooled
⅓ cup dried bread crumbs
1 cup freshly grated Parmesan cheese
1 medium egg yolk
½ tsp. soft brown sugar
2 tbsp. freshly chopped parsley
freshly grated nutmeg
salt and freshly ground black pepper

1

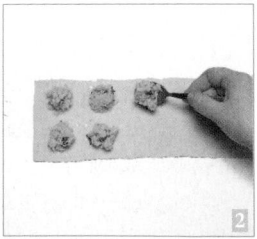
2

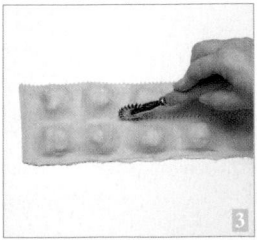
3

Cold Sesame Noodles

1 Bring a large pan of lightly salted water to a rolling boil. Add the noodles or spaghetti and cook according to the package directions or until al dente. Drain. Rinse and drain again, then toss in the sesame oil and set aside.

2 Heat the peanut oil in a wok or large skillet over a high heat. Add the green bell pepper, daikon, and snow peas or green beans, and stir-fry for 1 minute. Stir in the garlic and cook for 30 seconds.

3 Add the soy sauce to the pan with the vinegar, chili sauce, sugar, peanut butter, and ¼ cup of hot water. Simmer, stirring constantly, until the peanut butter is smooth, adding a little more water if necessary and adjusting the seasoning to taste.

4 Add the scallions and the noodles or spaghetti to the peanut sauce and cook, stirring, for 2–3 minutes or until heated through. Spoon the mixture into a large serving bowl and leave to cool to room temperature, stirring occasionally. Garnish with the toasted sesame seeds and cucumber julienne strips before serving.

Food Fact

Daikon, also known as "Japanese radish," resembles a white carrot in shape. It has a very fresh, peppery flavor and is often used in salads, either peeled or grated. Because it has a high water content, it should be sprinkled with salt and drained in a sieve over a bowl for about 30 minutes after preparing. Rinse well under cold running water and pat dry on paper towels before stir-frying.

INGREDIENTS
Serves 4–8

1 lb. buckwheat (soba) noodles or whole-wheat spaghetti
salt
1 tbsp. sesame oil
1 tbsp. peanut oil
1 green bell pepper, deseeded and thinly sliced
4 oz. daikon, julienned
¼ cup trimmed and sliced snow peas or green beans
2 garlic cloves, peeled and finely chopped
2 tbsp. soy sauce, or to taste
1 tbsp. cider vinegar
2 tbsp. sweet chili sauce, or to taste
2 tsp. sugar
½ cup peanut butter
6–8 scallions, trimmed and diagonally sliced

GARNISH:
toasted sesame seeds
julienned strips of cucumber

Singapore Noodles

1 Bring a large pan of lightly salted water to a rolling boil. Add the noodles and cook according to the package directions or until al dente. Drain thoroughly and toss with 1 tablespoon of the oil.

2 Heat the remaining oil in a wok or large skillet over high heat. Add the mushrooms, ginger, chili, and red bell pepper, and stir-fry for 2 minutes. Add the garlic, zucchini, scallions, and garden peas, and stir lightly.

3 Push the vegetables to one side and add the curry paste, ketchup, and about ½ cup hot water. Season to taste with salt or a few drops of soy sauce and let boil vigorously, stirring until the paste is smooth.

4 Stir the egg noodles and the bean sprouts into the vegetable mixture, and stir-fry until coated with the paste and completely heated through. Season with more soy sauce if necessary, then turn into a large warmed serving bowl or spoon onto individual plates. Garnish the noodles with sesame seeds and cilantro leaves. Serve immediately.

INGREDIENTS
Serves 4

8 oz. thin, round egg noodles
3 tbsp. peanut or vegetable oil
2 cups field mushrooms, thinly sliced
1-in. piece ginger, peeled and finely chopped
1 red chili, deseeded and thinly sliced
1 red bell pepper, deseeded and thinly sliced
2 garlic cloves, peeled and crushed
1 medium zucchini, cut in half lengthwise and diagonally sliced
4–6 scallions, trimmed and thinly sliced
½ cup frozen garden peas, thawed
1 tbsp. curry paste
2 tbsp. ketchup
salt or soy sauce
1 cup bean sprouts, rinsed and drained

TO GARNISH:
sesame seeds
fresh cilantro leaves

Helpful Hint

There is a huge range of curry pastes available, varying from very mild to extremely hot. Obviously, the choice here depends very much on your personal preference, but try to select one with Asian rather than Indian overtones—Thai green or red curry paste would be a good choice.

Tortellini, Cherry Tomato, & Mozzarella Skewers

1 Preheat the broiler and line a broiler pan with foil, just before cooking. Bring a large pan of lightly salted water to a rolling boil. Add the tortellini and cook according to the package directions or until al dente. Drain and rinse under cold running water. Drain again and toss with 2 tablespoons of the olive oil and set aside.

2 Pour the remaining olive oil into a small bowl. Add the crushed garlic and thyme or basil, then blend well. Season to taste with salt and black pepper and set aside.

3 To assemble the skewers, thread the tortellini alternately with the cherry tomatoes and cubes of mozzarella. Arrange the skewers on the broiler pan and brush generously on all sides with the olive oil mixture.

4 Cook the skewers under the preheated broiler for about 5 minutes or until they begin to turn golden, turning them halfway through cooking. Arrange 2 skewers on each plate and garnish with a few basil leaves. Serve immediately with dressed lettuce leaves.

INGREDIENTS
Serves 6

9 oz. mixed green and plain cheese- or vegetable-filled fresh tortellini
⅔ cup extra-virgin olive oil
2 garlic cloves, peeled and crushed
pinch dried thyme or basil
salt and freshly ground black pepper
8 oz. cherry tomatoes
1 lb. mozzarella, cut into 1-in. cubes
basil leaves, to garnish
dressed lettuce leaves, to serve

Helpful Hint

These skewers make an ideal starter for a barbecue. Alternatively, a small quantity of the prepared ingredients can be threaded onto smaller skewers and served as canapés. If using wooden skewers for this recipe, soak them in cold water for at least 30 minutes before cooking to keep them from scorching under the broiler. The tips of the skewers may be protected with small pieces of foil.

2

3

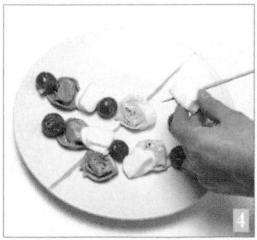
4

Tortellini & Summer Vegetable Salad

1 Bring a large pan of lightly salted water to a rolling boil. Add the tortellini and cook according to the package directions or until al dente.

2 Using a large slotted spoon, transfer the tortellini to a colander to drain. Rinse under cold running water and drain again. Transfer to a large bowl and toss with 2 tablespoons of the olive oil.

3 Return the pasta water to a boil and drop in the green beans and broccoli florets; blanch them for 2 minutes or until just beginning to soften. Drain, then rinse under cold running water and drain again thoroughly. Add the vegetables to the tortellini.

4 Add the bell pepper, onion, artichoke hearts, capers, and olives to the bowl; stir lightly.

5 Whisk together the vinegar, mustard, and brown sugar in a bowl, and season to taste with salt and pepper. Slowly whisk in the remaining olive oil to form a thick, creamy dressing. Pour over the tortellini and vegetables, add the chopped basil or parsley, and stir until lightly coated. Transfer to a shallow serving dish or salad bowl. Garnish with the hard-boiled egg quarters and serve.

Food Fact

Black olives are picked when fully ripe and a brownish pink color, then fermented and oxidized until they become black. Dry-cured black olives can be bought from Italian food shops or the delicatessen counter of some large supermarkets, but if you are unable to get them, use ordinary small black olives instead.

INGREDIENTS
Serves 6

12 oz. mixed green and plain cheese-filled fresh tortellini
⅔ cup extra-virgin olive oil
1½ cups trimmed fine green beans
6 oz. broccoli florets
1 yellow or red bell pepper, deseeded and thinly sliced
1 red onion, peeled and sliced
6 oz. jar marinated artichoke hearts, drained and halved
2 tbsp. capers
½ cup dry-cured pitted black olives
3 tbsp. raspberry or balsamic vinegar
1 tbsp. Dijon mustard
1 tsp. soft brown sugar
salt and freshly ground black pepper
2 tbsp. freshly chopped basil or Italian parsley
2 quartered hard-boiled eggs, to garnish

3

4

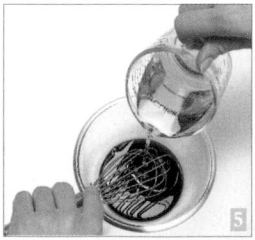
5

Fettuccine with Calf's Liver & Calvados

1 Season the flour with the salt, black pepper, and paprika, then toss the liver in the flour until well-coated.

2 Melt half the butter and 1 tablespoon of the olive oil in a large skillet and fry the liver in batches for 1 minute or until just browned but still slightly pink inside. Remove using a slotted spoon and place in a warmed dish.

3 Add the remaining butter to the pan. Stir in 1 tablespoon of the seasoned flour and cook for 1 minute. Pour in the Calvados and cider, and cook over a high heat for 30 seconds. Stir the cream into the sauce and simmer for 1 minute to thicken slightly, then season to taste. Return the liver to the pan and heat through.

4 Bring a large pan of lightly salted water to a rolling boil. Add the fettuccine and cook according to the package directions, about 3–4 minutes or until al dente.

5 Drain the fettuccine thoroughly, then return to the pan and toss in the remaining olive oil. Divide among four warmed plates, and spoon the liver and sauce over the pasta. Garnish with thyme sprigs and serve immediately.

INGREDIENTS
Serves 4

½ cup all-purpose flour
salt and freshly ground black pepper
1 tsp. paprika
1 lb. calf's liver, trimmed and thinly sliced
½ stick butter
1½ tbsp. olive oil
2 tbsp. Calvados
¾ cup cider
⅔ cup whipping cream
12 oz. fresh fettuccine
fresh thyme sprigs, to garnish

Helpful Hint

Calvados is made from apples and adds a fruity taste to this dish, although you can, of course, use ordinary brandy instead. Calf's liver is very tender with a delicate flavor. It should be cooked over a high heat until the outside is brown and crusty and the center still slightly pink. Take care not to overcook the liver, or you will spoil its taste and texture.

Tagliatelle with Stuffed Pork Escalopes

1 Preheat the oven to 350° F. Mix the broccoli with the mozzarella cheese, garlic, and beaten eggs. Season to taste with salt and pepper, and set aside until needed.

2 Using a meat mallet or rolling pin, pound the escalopes on a sheet of waxed paper until ¼ inch thick. Divide the broccoli mixture between the escalopes, and roll each one up from the shortest side. Place the pork rolls in a lightly greased ovenproof dish, then drizzle the olive oil over the rolls and bake in the preheated oven for 40–50 minutes, or until cooked.

3 Meanwhile, melt the butter in a heavy-based pan, then stir in the flour and cook for 2 minutes. Remove from the heat and whisk in the milk and stock. Season to taste, then stir in the mustard and cook until smooth and thickened. Keep warm.

4 Bring a large pan of lightly salted water to a rolling boil. Add the tagliatelle and cook according to the package directions, about 3–4 minutes or until al dente. Drain thoroughly and spoon into a warmed serving dish. Slice each pork roll into 3, place on top of the pasta, and pour the sauce over. Garnish with sage leaves and serve immediately.

INGREDIENTS
Serves 4

¼ cup broccoli florets, finely chopped and blanched
1 cup grated mozzarella cheese
1 garlic clove, peeled and crushed
2 large eggs, beaten
salt and freshly ground black pepper
4 thin pork escalopes, weighing about 3½ oz. each
1 tbsp. olive oil
2 tbsp. butter
2 tbsp. flour
⅔ cup milk
⅔ cup chicken stock
1 tbsp. Dijon mustard
8 oz. fresh tagliatelle
sage leaves, to garnish

Helpful Hint

Pounding the pork escalopes makes them thinner, but tenderizes the meat. Brush with a little oil to keep them from sticking to the mallet or rolling pin, or pound (with the blunt side of the mallet) between two sheets of greased waxed paper or plastic wrap. Take care not to tear the fibers.

Spicy Chicken with Open Ravioli & Tomato Sauce

1 Heat the oil in a skillet, add the onion, and cook gently for 2–3 minutes. Add the cumin, paprika, and cinnamon, and cook for an additional minute. Add the chicken, season to taste with salt and pepper, and cook for 3–4 minutes or until tender. Add the peanut butter and stir well. Set aside.

2 Melt the butter in the skillet, then add the shallot and cook for 2 minutes. Add the tomatoes and garlic, and season to taste. Simmer gently for 20 minutes, or until thickened, then keep the sauce warm.

3 Cut each sheet of lasagna into 6 squares. Bring a large pan of lightly salted water to a rolling boil. Add the lasagna squares, and cook according to the package directions, about 3–4 minutes or until al dente. Drain the lasagna pieces thoroughly, then set aside and keep warm.

4 Layer the pasta squares with the spicy filling on individual warmed plates. Pour over a little of the hot tomato sauce and sprinkle with chopped cilantro. Serve immediately.

INGREDIENTS
Serves 2–3

2 tbsp. olive oil
1 onion, peeled and finely chopped
1 tsp. ground cumin
1 tsp. hot paprika
1 tsp. ground cinnamon
⅔ cup chopped boneless and skinless chicken breasts
salt and freshly ground black pepper
1 tbsp. smooth peanut butter
½ stick butter
1 shallot, peeled and finely chopped
14-oz. can chopped tomatoes
2 garlic cloves, peeled and crushed
4 oz. fresh egg lasagna
2 tbsp. freshly chopped cilantro

Helpful Hint

Remember that fresh pasta should be exactly that; buy no more than two days ahead and preferably on the day that you plan to cook it. Since it contains fresh eggs, it should always be stored in the refrigerator, kept in its package or wrapped in nonstick baking parchment, then in plastic wrap.

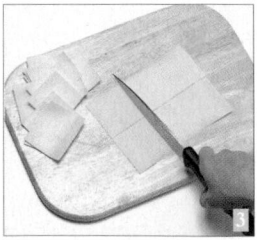

Farfalle & Chicken in White Wine Sauce

1 Place the chicken breasts between two sheets of waxed paper and, using a meat mallet or wooden rolling pin, pound as thinly as possible. Season with salt and pepper and set aside.

2 Mash the feta cheese with a fork and blend with the egg and half the tarragon. Divide the mixture between the chicken breasts and roll up each piece. Secure with toothpicks.

3 Heat half the butter and all the olive oil in a skillet, then add the onion and cook for 2–3 minutes. Remove, using a slotted spoon, and set aside. Add the chicken to the skillet and cook for 3–4 minutes or until browned.

4 Pour in the wine and stock, and stir in the remaining tarragon. Cover and simmer gently for 10–15 minutes or until the chicken is cooked.

5 Meanwhile, bring a large pan of lightly salted water to a rolling boil. Add the farfalle and cook according to the package directions, about 3–4 minutes or until al dente. Drain, then toss in the remaining butter and tip into a warm serving dish.

6 Cut each chicken roll into four slices and place on the pasta. Whisk the sauce until smooth, then stir in the sour cream and onions. Heat the sauce gently, then pour over the chicken. Sprinkle with the parsley and serve immediately.

INGREDIENTS
Serves 4

4 boneless and skinless chicken breasts, about 1 lb. in total weight
salt and freshly ground black pepper
4 oz. feta cheese
1 small egg, beaten
2 tbsp. freshly chopped tarragon
½ stick butter
1 tbsp. olive oil
1 onion, peeled and sliced into rings
⅔ cup white wine
⅔ cup chicken stock
12 oz. fresh farfalle
3–4 tbsp. sour cream
2 tbsp. freshly chopped parsley

Food Fact

Feta is a Greek cheese, traditionally made from ewe's milk, but now more often from cow's milk. It is preserved in brine, which gives it a salty flavor; always drain feta before using.

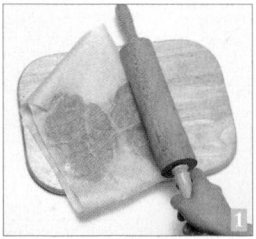

Polenta Roulade with Mozzarella & Spinach

1 Preheat the oven to 475 °F. Oil and line a large jelly roll pan (9 x 13 in.) with nonstick baking parchment.

2 Pour the milk into a heavy-based pan and whisk in the semolina. Bring to a boil, then simmer, stirring continuously with a wooden spoon, for 3–4 minutes or until very thick. Remove from heat and stir in the butter and cheddar cheese until melted. Whisk in the egg yolks and season to taste with salt and pepper. Pour into the lined jelly roll pan. Cover and leave to cool for 1 hour.

3 Cook the baby spinach in batches in a large pan with 1 teaspoon of water for 3–4 minutes or until wilted. Drain thoroughly and season to taste with salt, pepper, and nutmeg, then leave to cool.

4 Spread the spinach over the cooled semolina mixture and sprinkle ¾ cup of the mozzarella and half the Parmesan cheese on top. Bake in the preheated oven for 20 minutes or until golden.

5 Leave to cool, then roll up like a jelly roll. Sprinkle with the remaining mozzarella and Parmesan cheese, then bake for another 15–20 minutes or until golden. Serve immediately with freshly made tomato sauce.

INGREDIENTS
Serves 8

2 ½ cups milk
⅔ cup fine semolina or polenta
2 tbsp. butter
¼ cup grated cheddar cheese
2 medium egg yolks
salt and freshly ground black pepper
1½ lbs. baby spinach leaves
½ tsp. freshly grated nutmeg
1 ¼ cups grated mozzarella cheese
2 tbsp. freshly grated Parmesan cheese
freshly made tomato sauce, to serve

Helpful Hint

It is important to use the correct size of pan for this dish, so that the polenta mixture is thin enough to roll up. Do not be tempted to put it in the refrigerator to cool, or it will become too hard and crack when rolled.

Penne with Mixed Bell Peppers & Garlic

1 Preheat the broiler and line the broiler rack with foil. Cut the bell peppers in half, then deseed and place cut side down on the broiler rack. Cook under the broiler until the skins become blistered and black all over. Place the bell peppers in a plastic bag and let cool, then discard the skin and slice thinly.

2 Heat the olive oil in a heavy-based pan. Add the onion, celery, garlic, and bacon and cook for 4–5 minutes or until the onion has softened. Add the bell peppers and cook for 1 minute. Pour in the chicken stock and season to taste with salt and pepper. Cover and simmer for about 20 minutes.

3 Meanwhile, bring a large pan of lightly salted water to a rolling boil. Add the penne and cook according to the package directions, about 3–4 minutes or until al dente. Drain thoroughly and return to the pan.

4 Pour the bell pepper sauce over the pasta and toss lightly. Spoon into a warmed serving dish and sprinkle with the chopped parsley and grated pecorino cheese. Serve immediately with a green salad and warm whole-wheat bread.

Helpful Hint

Broiling brings out all the delicious flavor of bell peppers. Make sure that they are blackened and blistered so that the skins simply slip off. You could also roast the bell peppers in the oven, if preferred. Place them in a roasting pan, then brush with a little olive oil and cook at 400° F for 25 minutes or until the skins are slightly charred.

INGREDIENTS
Serves 4

1 lb. green, red, and yellow bell peppers
2 tbsp. olive oil
1 large onion, peeled and sliced
1 celery stalk, trimmed and finely chopped
2 garlic cloves, peeled and crushed
4 slices smoked bacon, finely chopped
1¼ cups chicken stock
salt and freshly ground black pepper
3 cups fresh penne
2 tbsp. freshly chopped parsley
2 tbsp. finely grated pecorino cheese

TO SERVE:
green salad
warm whole-wheat bread

Angel-Hair Pasta with Smoked Salmon & Jumbo Shrimp

1 Cook the baby spinach leaves in a large pan with 1 teaspoon of water for 3–4 minutes or until wilted. Drain thoroughly, then season to taste with salt, pepper, and nutmeg, and keep warm. Remove the shells from all but four of the jumbo shrimp and set aside.

2 Bring a large pan of lightly salted water to a rolling boil. Add the pasta and cook according to the package directions, about 3–4 minutes or until al dente. Drain thoroughly and return to the pan. Stir in the butter and the shelled shrimp, then cover and keep warm.

3 Beat the eggs with the dill and season well, then stir into the spaghetti and shrimp. Return the pan to the heat briefly, just long enough to lightly scramble the eggs, then remove from the heat. Carefully mix in the smoked salmon strips and the cooked spinach. Toss gently to mix. Tip into a warmed serving dish and garnish with the shrimp and dill sprigs. Serve immediately with grated Parmesan cheese.

INGREDIENTS
Serves 4

8 oz. baby spinach leaves
salt and freshly ground black pepper
pinch of freshly grated nutmeg
8 oz. cooked jumbo shrimp in their shells
1 lb. fresh angel-hair pasta
½ stick butter
3 medium eggs
1 tbsp. freshly chopped dill, plus extra to garnish
4 oz. smoked salmon, cut into strips
dill sprigs, to garnish
2 tbsp. grated Parmesan cheese, to serve

Helpful Hint

Make sure that you use cooked and not raw jumbo shrimp for this dish. If you buy them raw, remove the heads and shells, then briefly sauté in a little olive oil until just pink and opaque. This will take only 3–4 minutes; take care not to overcook them or they will toughen.

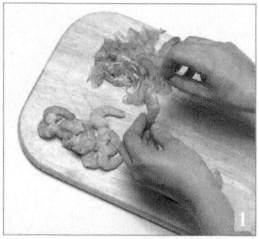
1

2

3

Pasta Ring with Chicken & Sun-Dried Tomatoes

1 Preheat the oven to 375° F. Lightly brush an 8-inch ring mold with a little melted butter and dust with the bread crumbs.

2 Melt ½ stick of the butter in a heavy-based pan. Add the flour and cook for 1 minute. Whisk in the milk and cook, stirring until thickened. Add the chopped onion, season with salt and pepper, and set aside.

3 Bring a large pan of lightly salted water to a rolling boil. Add the tagliatelle and cook according to the package directions, about 3–4 minutes or until al dente. Drain thoroughly and stir into the white sauce. Pour the pasta mixture into the prepared mold and bake in the preheated oven for 25–30 minutes.

4 Melt the remaining butter in a skillet, then add the chicken and cook for 4–5 minutes or until cooked. Pour in the wine and cook over a high heat for 30 seconds. Blend the cornstarch with 1 teaspoon of water and stir into the pan. Add 1 tablespoon chopped tarragon and the tomatoes. Season well, then cook for a few minutes until thickened.

5 Allow the pasta to cool for 5 minutes, then unmold onto a large plate. Fill the center with the chicken sauce. Garnish with the remaining tarragon and serve immediately.

INGREDIENTS
Serves 6

1 stick butter, plus extra for brushing
2 tbsp. natural white bread crumbs
3 tbsp. flour
about 1¼ cups milk
1 small onion, peeled and very finely chopped
salt and freshly ground black pepper
8 oz. fresh tagliatelle
1 lb. chicken breast fillets, skinned and cut into strips
¼ cup white wine
1 tsp. cornstarch
2 tbsp. freshly chopped tarragon
2 tbsp. chopped sun-dried tomatoes

Helpful Hint

To ensure that the pasta turns out easily, brush the ring mold with melted butter, then put in the freezer for 3–4 minutes to harden. Brush again with butter before dusting with the bread crumbs, making sure it is well coated.

1

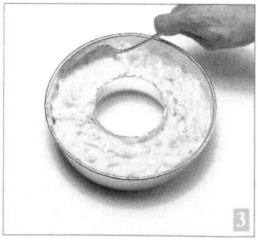
3

4

Salmon & Mushroom Linguine

1 Preheat the oven to 375° F. Place the salmon in a shallow pan and cover with water. Season well with salt and pepper and bring to a boil, then lower the heat and simmer for 6–8 minutes or until cooked. Drain and keep warm.

2 Melt ½ stick of the butter in a heavy-based pan. Stir in the flour and cook for 1 minute, then whisk in the chicken stock. Simmer gently until thickened. Stir in the cream and season to taste with salt and pepper. Keep the sauce warm.

3 Melt the remaining butter in a pan, then add the sliced mushrooms and cook for 2–3 minutes. Stir the mushrooms into the white sauce.

4 Bring a large pan of lightly salted water to a rolling boil. Add the linguine and cook according to the package directions or until al dente.

5 Drain the pasta thoroughly and return to the pan. Stir in half the sauce, then spoon into a lightly greased, 1¼-quart, shallow ovenproof dish. Flake the salmon and add to the remaining sauce, then pour over the pasta. Sprinkle with the cheese and bread crumbs, then bake in the preheated oven for 15–20 minutes or until golden. Garnish with the parsley and serve immediately.

INGREDIENTS
Serves 4

1 lb. salmon fillets, skinned
salt and freshly ground black pepper
¾ stick butter
3 tbsp. flour
1¼ cups chicken stock
⅔ cup whipping cream
2½ cups mushrooms, wiped and sliced
12 oz. linguine
½ cup grated cheddar cheese
1 cup fresh white bread crumbs
2 tbsp. freshly chopped parsley, to garnish

Helpful Hint

When cooking the salmon, the poaching liquid should be just simmering and not boiling rapidly. Add extra flavor if you like by putting in a bay leaf and a sprig of fresh thyme or a thinly pared strip of lemon rind. The salmon should be slightly undercooked in this recipe, as it will then be baked in the oven.

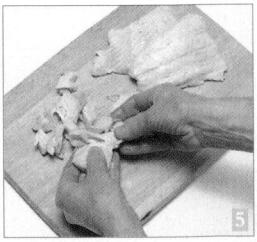

Spaghetti with Hot Chili Mussels

1 Scrub the mussels and remove any beards. Discard any that do not close when tapped. Place in a large pan with the white wine and half the crushed garlic. Cover and cook over a high heat for 5 minutes, shaking the pan from time to time. When the mussels have opened, drain, setting aside the juices and straining them through a cheesecloth-lined sieve. Discard any mussels that have not opened and keep the rest warm.

2 Heat the oil in a heavy-based pan, then add the remaining garlic with the chilies and cook for about 30 seconds. Stir in the chopped tomatoes and ⅓ cup of the cooking liquid and simmer for 15–20 minutes. Season to taste with salt and pepper.

3 Meanwhile, bring a large pan of lightly salted water to a rolling boil. Add the spaghetti and cook according to the package directions, about 3–4 minutes or until al dente.

4 Drain the spaghetti thoroughly and return to the pan. Add the mussels and tomato sauce to the pasta and toss lightly to cover, then spoon into a warmed serving dish or onto individual plates. Garnish with chopped parsley and serve immediately with warm crusty bread.

INGREDIENTS
Serves 4

2 lb. fresh live mussels
1¼ cups white wine
3–4 garlic cloves, peeled and crushed
2 tbsp. olive oil
1–2 bird's eye chilies, deseeded and chopped
2 14-oz. cans chopped tomatoes
salt and freshly ground black pepper
12 oz. fresh spaghetti
2 tbsp. freshly chopped parsley, to garnish
warm, crusty bread, to serve

Food Fact

Mussels are bivalves (which means they have two shells hinged together) with blue-black colored shells. They attach themselves to rocks on the seabed and take up to two years to mature. They are usually sold in netted bags, either by weight or volume. If you buy by volume, you will need 1 quart for this recipe.

Conchiglioni with Crab au Gratin

1 Preheat the oven to 400° F. Bring a large pan of lightly salted water to a rolling boil. Add the pasta shells and cook according to the package directions or until al dente. Drain the pasta thoroughly and allow it to dry completely.

2 Melt half the butter in a heavy-based pan. Add the shallots and chili, and cook for 2 minutes, then stir in the crabmeat. Stuff the cooled shells with the crab mixture and set aside.

3 Melt the remaining butter in a small pan and stir in the flour. Cook for about 1 minute, then whisk in the wine and milk and cook, stirring until thickened. Stir in the crème fraîche and grated cheese and season with salt and pepper.

4 Place the crab-filled shells in a lightly greased, large, shallow baking dish or tray, and spoon a little of the sauce on top. Toss the bread crumbs in the melted butter or oil, then sprinkle over the pasta shells. Bake in the preheated oven for 10 minutes. Serve immediately with a cheese or tomato sauce and a tossed green salad or cooked baby vegetables.

INGREDIENTS
Serves 4

6 oz. large pasta shells
½ stick butter
1 shallot, peeled and finely chopped
1 bird's eye chili, deseeded and finely chopped
2 7-oz. cans crabmeat, drained
3 tbsp. all-purpose flour
¼ cup white wine
¼ cup milk
3 tbsp. crème fraîche
1½ tbsp. grated cheddar cheese
salt and freshly ground black pepper
1 tbsp. oil or melted butter
1 cup fresh white bread crumbs

TO SERVE:
cheese or tomato sauce
tossed green salad or freshly cooked baby vegetables

Helpful Hint

Canned crabmeat is preserved in brine, so drain well and do not add too much salt when seasoning. Crab is in season between April and December and is least expensive during these months, so consider buying fresh white crabmeat for this recipe; you will need a medium-sized crab that weighs about 12 oz.

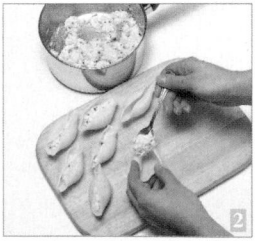

Pappardelle with Spicy Lamb & Bell Peppers

1 Preheat the broiler just before cooking. Fry the ground lamb in a skillet until browned. Heat the olive oil in a heavy-based pan, then add the onion, garlic, and all the chopped bell peppers and cook gently for 3–4 minutes or until softened. Add the browned ground lamb to the pan and cook, stirring, until the onions have softened, then drain off any remaining oil.

2 Stir the chili powder and cumin into the pan and cook gently for 2 minutes. Add the tomato paste, then pour in the wine and season to taste with salt and pepper. Reduce the heat and simmer for 10–15 minutes or until the sauce has reduced.

3 Meanwhile, bring a large pan of lightly salted water to a rolling boil. Add the papardelle and cook according to the package directions or until al dente. Drain thoroughly, then return to the pan and stir the meat sauce into the pasta. Keep warm.

4 Meanwhile, place the bread crumbs on a cookie sheet, drizzle the melted butter over the bread crumbs, and place under the preheated broiler for 3–4 minutes or until golden and crispy. Let cool, then mix with the grated cheddar cheese. Spoon the pasta mixture into a warmed serving dish, then sprinkle with the bread crumbs and parsley. Serve immediately.

INGREDIENTS
Serves 4

1 lb. fresh ground lamb
2 tbsp. olive oil
1 onion, peeled and finely chopped
2 garlic cloves, peeled and crushed
1 green bell pepper, deseeded and chopped
1 yellow bell pepper, deseeded and chopped
½ tsp. hot chili powder
1 tsp. ground cumin
1 tbsp. tomato paste
⅔ cup red wine
salt and freshly ground black pepper
12 oz. pappardelle
1 cup fresh white bread crumbs
2 tbsp. butter, melted
¼ cup grated cheddar cheese
1 tbsp. freshly chopped parsley

Tasty Tip

Choose very lean ground lamb for this dish. To add extra flavor, add a fresh bay leaf or a sprig of fresh rosemary to the pan when frying the ground lamb and remove at the end of step 2, when the sauce has reduced.

Farfalle with Zucchini & Mushrooms

1 Heat the butter and olive oil in a large pan. Add the onion, garlic, and bacon lardons, and cook for 3–4 minutes or until the onion has softened. Add the zucchini and cook, stirring, for 3–4 minutes. Add the mushrooms, then lower the heat and cook covered for 4–5 minutes.

2 Meanwhile, bring a large pan of lightly salted water to a rolling boil. Add the farfalle and cook according to the package directions or until al dente. Drain thoroughly, then return to the pan and keep warm.

3 Season the mushroom mixture to taste, then stir in the crème fraîche and half the chopped parsley. Simmer for 2–3 minutes or until the sauce is thick and creamy.

4 Pour the sauce over the cooked pasta. Toss lightly, then reheat for 2 minutes or until piping hot. Spoon into a warmed serving dish and sprinkle over the chopped parsley. Garnish with pecorino cheese shavings and serve immediately with mixed salad leaves and crusty bread.

INGREDIENTS
Serves 4

2 tbsp. butter
2 tsp. olive oil
1 small onion, peeled and finely chopped
2 garlic cloves, peeled and crushed
scant ½ cup bacon lardons
2½ cups zucchini, trimmed and diced
2 cups button mushrooms, wiped and roughly chopped
3 cups farfalle
salt and freshly ground black pepper
1 cup crème fraîche
2 tbsp. freshly chopped parsley
shaved pecorino cheese, to garnish

TO SERVE:
mixed salad leaves
crusty bread

Helpful Hint

To shave pecorino or Parmesan cheese, use a sharp knife or a vegetable peeler. If you find this difficult, you could coarsely grate the cheese instead. Avoid tubs of ready-grated pecorino and Parmesan; they tend to be powdery and flavorless, and are a poor substitute for fresh cheese.

Cannelloni with Tomato & Red Wine Sauce

1 Preheat the oven to 400° F. Heat the oil in a heavy-based pan, then add the onion and garlic and cook for 2–3 minutes. Cool slightly, then stir in the ricotta cheese and pine nuts. Season the filling to taste with salt, pepper, and the nutmeg.

2 Cut each lasagna sheet in half. Put a little of the ricotta filling on each piece and roll up like a cigar to resemble cannelloni tubes. Arrange the cannelloni, seam-side down, in a single layer, in a lightly greased, 2-quart shallow oven-proof dish.

3 Melt the butter in a pan, then add the shallot and cook for 2 minutes. Pour in the red wine, tomatoes, and sugar and season well. Bring to a boil, then lower the heat and simmer for about 20 minutes or until thickened. Add a little more sugar if desired. Transfer to a food processor and blend until a smooth sauce is formed.

4 Pour the warm tomato sauce over the cannelloni and sprinkle with the grated mozzarella cheese. Bake in the preheated oven for about 30 minutes or until golden and bubbling. Garnish and serve immediately with a green salad.

Food Fact

Mozzarella is the Italian cheese often used to top pizzas, as it is elastic and stringy when cooked. It is a soft, kneaded, brilliantly white cheese with a delicate, almost spongy texture. Traditionally, it was made from buffalo milk, but now cow's milk is more often used.

INGREDIENTS
Serves 6

2 tbsp. olive oil
1 onion, peeled and finely chopped
1 garlic clove, peeled and crushed
1 cup ricotta cheese
scant ⅓ cup pine nuts
salt and freshly ground black pepper
pinch freshly grated nutmeg
9 oz. fresh spinach lasagna
2 tbsp. butter
1 shallot, peeled and finely chopped
⅔ cup red wine
2 14-oz. cans chopped tomatoes
½ tsp. sugar
½ cup grated mozzarella cheese, plus extra to serve
1 tbsp. freshly chopped parsley, to garnish
fresh green salad, to serve

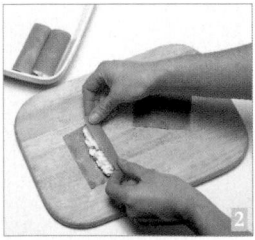

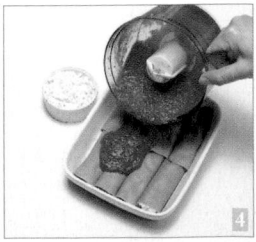

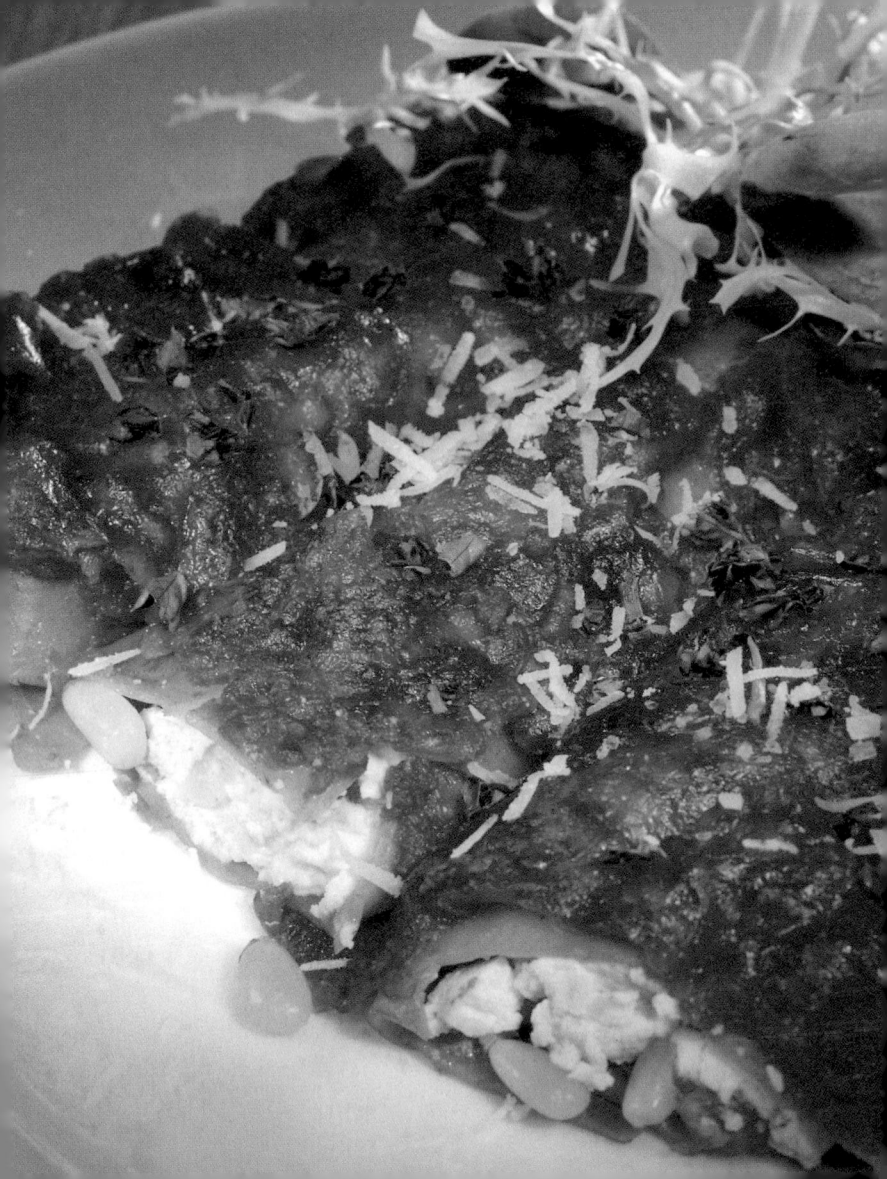

Pasta Triangles with Pesto & Walnut Dressing

1 Preheat the broiler to high. Cut the lasagna sheets in half, then into triangles, and set aside. Mix the pesto and ricotta cheese together, and warm gently in a pan.

2 Toast the walnuts under the preheated broiler until golden. Rub off the skins. Place the nuts in a food processor with the bread and grind finely.

3 Mix the sour cream with the mascarpone cheese in a bowl. Add the ground walnuts and pecorino cheese, and season to taste with salt and pepper. Whisk in the olive oil. Pour into a pan and warm gently.

4 Bring a large pan of lightly salted water to a rolling boil. Add the pasta triangles and cook, according to the package directions, about 3–4 minutes or until al dente.

5 Drain the pasta thoroughly and arrange a few triangles on each serving plate. Top each one with a spoonful of the pesto mixture, then place another triangle on top. Continue to layer the pasta and pesto mixture, then spoon a little of the walnut sauce on top of each stack. Garnish with dill, basil, or parsley, and serve immediately with a freshly dressed tomato and cucumber salad.

INGREDIENTS
Serves 6

1 lb. fresh egg lasagna
4 tbsp. pesto
4 tbsp. ricotta cheese
1 cup shelled walnuts
1 slice white bread, crusts removed
⅔ cup sour cream
½ cup mascarpone cheese
¼ cup grated pecorino cheese
salt and freshly ground black pepper
1 tbsp. olive oil
sprig of dill or freshly chopped basil or parsley, to garnish
tomato and cucumber salad, to serve

Tasty Tip

For a simple tomato and cucumber salad, arrange overlapping thin slices of cucumbers and tomatoes on a large plate. Drizzle on top a dressing made with 1 teaspoon Dijon mustard, 4 tablespoons extra-virgin olive oil, 1 tablespoon lemon juice, and a pinch each of sugar, salt, and pepper. Leave at room temperature for 15 minutes before serving.

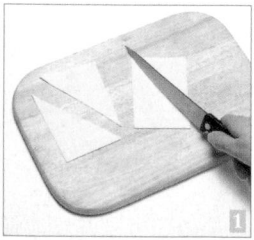
1

2

3

Eggplant & Tomato Layer

1 Preheat the oven to 375° F. Brush the eggplant slices with 5 tablespoons of the olive oil and place on a cookie sheet. Bake in the preheated oven for 20 minutes or until tender. Remove from the oven and increase the temperature to 400° F.

2 Heat the remaining oil in a heavy-based pan. Add the onion and garlic. Cook for 2–3 minutes, then add the tomatoes, wine, and sugar. Season to taste with salt and pepper, then simmer for 20 minutes.

3 Melt the butter in another pan. Stir in the flour and cook for 2 minutes, then whisk in the milk. Cook for 2–3 minutes or until thickened. Season to taste.

4 Pour a little white sauce into a lightly greased baking dish. Cover with a layer of lasagna and spread with tomato sauce, then add some of the eggplant. Cover thinly with white sauce and sprinkle with a little mozzarella cheese. Continue to layer in this way, finishing with a layer of lasagna.

5 Beat together the eggs and yogurt. Season, then pour over the lasagna. Sprinkle with the remaining cheese and bake in the preheated oven for 25–30 minutes or until golden. Garnish with basil leaves and serve.

INGREDIENTS
Serves 4

2 eggplants, about 1½ lb., trimmed and thinly sliced
6 tbsp. olive oil
1 onion, peeled and finely sliced
1 garlic clove, peeled and crushed
14-oz. can chopped tomatoes
¼ cup red wine
½ tsp. sugar
salt and freshly ground black pepper
½ stick butter
3 tbsp. flour
1¼ cups milk
8 oz. fresh egg lasagna
2 medium eggs, beaten
¼ cup plain yogurt
1¼ cups grated mozzarella cheese
fresh basil leaves, to garnish

Food Fact

Technically a fruit, but generally classified as a vegetable, eggplants originated in India. Eggplants are now grown throughout the world, and are widely used in a variety of regional cuisines.

Cannelloni with Gorgonzola Sauce

1 Preheat the oven to 375° F. Melt the salted butter in a heavy-based pan, then add the shallot and bacon, and cook for about 4–5 minutes.

2 Add the mushrooms to the pan and cook for 5–6 minutes or until the mushrooms are very soft. Stir in the flour and cook for 1 minute, then stir in the heavy cream and cook gently for an additional 2 minutes. Let cool.

3 Cut each sheet of lasagna in half. Spoon some filling onto each piece and roll up from the longest side to resemble cannelloni. Arrange the cannelloni in a lightly greased, shallow 1¼-quart ovenproof dish.

4 Heat the unsalted butter very slowly in a pan, and when it is melted, add the Gorgonzola cheese. Stir until the cheese has melted, then stir in the whipping cream. Bring to a boil slowly, then simmer gently for about 5 minutes or until thickened.

5 Pour the cream sauce over the cannelloni. Place in the preheated oven and bake for 20 minutes or until golden and completely heated through. Serve immediately with assorted salad leaves.

INGREDIENTS
Serves 2–3

½ stick salted butter
1 shallot, peeled and finely chopped
2 slices bacon, rind removed and chopped
4 cups wiped and finely chopped mushrooms
2 tbsp. all-purpose flour
½ cup heavy cream
4 oz. fresh egg lasagna, 6 sheets in total
3 tbsp. unsalted butter
1¼ cups diced Gorgonzola cheese
⅔ cup whipping cream
assorted lettuce leaves, to serve

Tasty Tip

Gorgonzola cheese is very salty. As it is combined in this recipe with bacon, which is also salty, some of the butter used here is unsalted in order to balance the flavor. Italians use a wide range of mushrooms in their cooking, so for extra taste, you could use chestnut or large open-field mushrooms instead of ordinary button mushrooms.

2

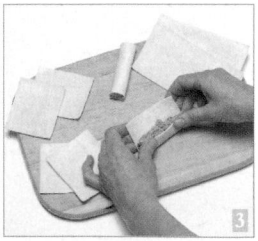
3

4

Ratatouille & Pasta Bake

1 Preheat the oven to 375° F. Heat the olive oil in a heavy-based pan, then add half the onion and cook gently for 2–3 minutes. Stir in the tomatoes and wine, then simmer for 20 minutes or until a thick consistency is formed. Add the sugar and season to taste with salt and pepper. Set aside.

2 Meanwhile, melt the butter in another pan, then add the remaining onion, the garlic, mushrooms, and zucchini, and cook for 10 minutes or until softened.

3 Spread a little tomato sauce in the base of a lightly greased baking dish. Top with a layer of lasagna and spoon over half the mushroom and zucchini mixture. Repeat the layers, finishing with a layer of lasagna.

4 Beat the eggs and cream together, then pour over the lasagna. Mix the mozzarella and pecorino cheeses together, then sprinkle on top of the lasagna. Place in the preheated oven and cook for about 20 minutes or until golden brown. Serve immediately with a green salad.

INGREDIENTS
Serves 4

1 tbsp. olive oil
2 large onions, peeled and finely chopped
14-oz. can chopped tomatoes
7 tbsp. white wine
½ tsp. sugar
salt and freshly ground black pepper
3 tbsp. butter
2 garlic cloves, peeled and crushed
2 cups mushrooms, wiped and thickly sliced
1½ lbs. zucchini, trimmed and thickly sliced
4 oz. fresh spinach lasagna
2 large eggs
2 tbsp. heavy cream
¼ cup grated mozzarella cheese
¼ cup grated pecorino cheese
green salad, to serve

Tasty Tip

For speed and simplicity, this recipe is a simplified version of ratatouille. If preferred, it can be made more traditionally by substituting a small chopped eggplant and a deseeded and chopped green or red bell pepper for some of the zucchini.

Lamb & Pasta Pie

1 Preheat the oven to 375° F. Lightly grease an 8-inch spring-form cake pan. Blend the flour, salt, margarine, and white vegetable fat in a food processor and add sufficient cold water to make a smooth, pliable dough. Knead on a lightly floured surface, then roll out two thirds to line the base and sides of the tin. Brush the pastry with egg white and set aside.

2 Melt the butter in a heavy-based pan, stir in the flour, and cook for 2 minutes. Stir in the milk and cook, stirring, until a smooth, thick sauce is formed. Season to taste with salt and pepper and set aside.

3 Bring a large pan of lightly salted water to a rolling boil. Add the macaroni and cook according to the package directions or until al dente. Drain, then stir into the white sauce with the grated cheese.

4 Heat the oil in a skillet. Add the onion, garlic, celery, and ground lamb and cook, stirring, for 5–6 minutes. Stir in the tomato paste and tomatoes and cook for 10 minutes. Cool slightly.

5 Place half the pasta mixture, then all the ground lamb in the pastry-lined tin. Top with a layer of pasta. Roll out the remaining pastry and cut out a lid. Brush the edge with water, then place over the filling and pinch the edges together. Use trimmings to decorate the top.

6 Brush the pie with beaten egg yolk and bake in the preheated oven for 50–60 minutes; cover the top with tin foil if it browns too quickly. Stand for 15 minutes before turning out. Serve immediately.

INGREDIENTS
Serves 8
2⅔ cup all-purpose flour
about ½ cup margarine
about ½ cup vegetable shortening
pinch of salt
1 small egg, separated
½ stick butter
⅓ cup flour
1¼ cups milk
salt and freshly ground black pepper
2 cups macaroni
½ cup grated cheddar cheese
1 tbsp. vegetable oil
1 onion, peeled and chopped
1 garlic clove, peeled and crushed
2 celery stalks, trimmed and chopped
1 lb. ground lamb
1 tbsp. tomato paste
14-oz. can chopped tomatoes

Baked Macaroni with Mushrooms & Leeks

1 Preheat the oven to 425° F. Heat 1 tablespoon of the olive oil in a large skillet, then add the onion and garlic and cook for 2 minutes. Add the leeks, mushrooms, and 2 tablespoons of the butter, then cook for 5 minutes. Pour in the white wine and cook for 2 minutes, then stir in the crème fraîche or cream. Season to taste with salt and pepper.

2 Meanwhile, bring a large pan of lightly salted water to a rolling boil. Add the macaroni and cook according to the package directions or until al dente.

3 Melt 2 tablespoons of the butter with the remaining oil in a small skillet. Add the bread crumbs and fry until just beginning to turn golden brown. Drain on paper towels.

4 Drain the pasta thoroughly. Toss in the remaining butter, then spoon into a lightly greased shallow baking dish. Cover the pasta with the leek and mushroom mixture, then sprinkle with the fried bread crumbs. Bake in the preheated oven for 5–10 minutes or until golden and crisp. Garnish with chopped parsley and serve.

INGREDIENTS
Serves 4

2 tbsp. olive oil
1 onion, peeled and finely chopped
1 garlic clove, peeled and crushed
2 small leeks, trimmed and chopped
1 lb. assorted wild mushrooms, trimmed
¼ stick butter
¼ cup white wine
⅔ cup crème fraîche or whipping cream
salt and freshly ground black pepper
3 cups short-cut macaroni
1½ cups fresh white bread crumbs
1 tbsp. freshly chopped parsley, to garnish

Helpful Hint

Some wild mushrooms are more tender and cook faster than others. Chestnut, porcini, portabella, enoki, and shiitake would all be good for this recipe. If you use chanterelles or oyster mushrooms, sauté them with the leeks for 1 minute only, as they are fairly delicate.

Vanilla & Lemon Panna Cotta with Raspberry Sauce

1 Put the cream, vanilla pod, and sugar into a saucepan. Bring to a boil, then simmer for 10 minutes until slightly reduced, stirring to prevent scalding. Remove from the heat, stir in the lemon zest, and remove the vanilla pod.

2 Soak the gelatin in the milk for 5 minutes or until softened. Squeeze out any excess milk and add to the hot cream. Stir well until dissolved.

3 Pour the cream mixture into 6 ramekins or mini pudding molds and leave in the refrigerator for 4 hours or until set.

4 Meanwhile, put 1½ cups of the raspberries, the confectioners' sugar, and lemon juice in a food processor. Blend to a purée, then pass the mixture through a strainer. Fold in the remaining raspberries with a metal spoon or rubber spatula, and chill in the refrigerator until ready to serve.

5 To serve, dip each of the molds into hot water for a few seconds, then turn out onto 6 individual serving plates. Spoon some of the raspberry sauce over and around the panna cotta, decorate with extra lemon zest, and serve.

INGREDIENTS
Serves 6

3 cups heavy cream
1 vanilla pod, split
½ cup sugar
1 tbsp. lemon zest
3 sheets gelatin
5 tbsp. milk
3 cups raspberries
3–4 tbsp. confectioners' sugar
1 tbsp. lemon juice
extra lemon zest, to decorate

Tasty Tip

Sheet gelatin is readily available from large supermarkets. It is much easier to measure and use than powdered gelatin and also gives a glossier finish to clear gelatin.

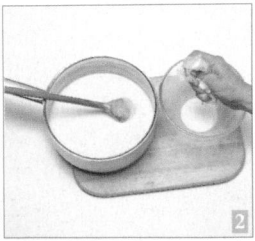

Ricotta Cheesecake with Strawberry Coulis

1 Preheat the oven to 325° F. Line an 8-inch springform pan with baking parchment. Place the dried candied peel into a food processor, and blend until the peel is chopped. Mix the cookie crumbs and the peel together, add 4 tablespoons of the melted butter, and process until mixed. Tip into the pan and spread over the bottom. Press firmly into place and set aside.

2 Blend together the sour cream, ricotta cheese, sugar, vanilla seeds, and eggs in a food processor. With the motor running, add the remaining melted butter and blend for a few seconds. Pour the mixture onto the base. Transfer to the preheated oven and cook for about 1 hour until set and risen around the edges but slightly wobbly in the center. Turn off the oven and let cool there. Chill in the refrigerator for at least 8 hours or preferably overnight.

3 Wash and drain the strawberries. Hull the fruit and remove any soft spots. Put into the food processor along with 2 tablespoons of the sugar, the orange zest, and the juice. Blend until smooth. Add the remaining sugar. Pass through a strainer to remove seeds and chill in the refrigerator until needed.

4 Cut the cheesecake into wedges, spoon over some of the strawberry coulis, and serve.

INGREDIENTS
Serves 6–8

¼ cup dried candied peel, chopped
1½ cups graham cracker crumbs
6 tbsp. butter, melted
⅔ cup sour cream
1¼ cups ricotta cheese
½ cup sugar
1 vanilla pod, seeds only
2 large eggs
2 cups strawberries
2–4 tbsp. sugar, or to taste
1 tbsp. orange zest
⅓ cup orange juice

Tasty Tip

This cheesecake has a soft, creamy texture compared to some cooked cheesecakes. This is because of the addition of sour cream. If ricotta is unavailable, substitute cream cheese.

1

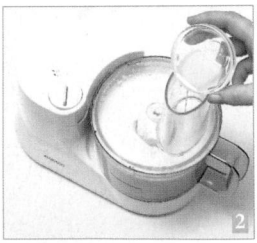
2

3

Cantuccini

1 Preheat the oven to 350° F. Line a large baking sheet with nonstick baking parchment. Place the flour, sugar, baking powder, vanilla extract, whole eggs, and one of the egg yolks into a food processor, and blend until the mixture forms a ball, scraping down the sides once or twice. Turn the mixture out onto a lightly floured surface, and knead in the chopped nuts and aniseed.

2 Divide the paste into 3 pieces and roll into logs about 1½ inches wide. Place the logs onto the baking sheet at least 2 inches apart. Brush lightly with the other egg yolk beaten with 1 tablespoon of water, and cook in the preheated oven for 30–35 minutes.

3 Remove from the oven and reduce the oven temperature to 300° F. Cut the logs diagonally into 1-inch slices and lay cut-side down on the baking sheet. Return to the oven for an additional 30–40 minutes or until dry and firm. Cool the cookies on a wire rack, and store in a large airtight container. Serve with Vin Santo or coffee.

INGREDIENTS
Makes 24 cookies

2¼ cups all-purpose flour
1 cup sugar
½ tsp. baking powder
½ tsp. vanilla extract
2 medium eggs
1 medium egg yolk
5 tbsp. mixed almonds and hazelnuts, toasted and coarsely chopped
1 tsp. whole aniseed
1 medium egg yolk mixed with 1 tbsp. water, to glaze
Vin Santo or coffee, to serve

Food Fact

Cantuccini are simply small cookies, traditionally served with Vin Santo, a sweet dessert wine. Cantucci are large cookies that are made in the same way.

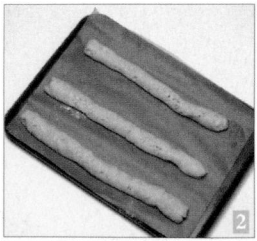

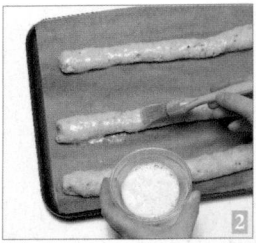

Almond & Pistachio Biscotti

1 Preheat the oven to 350° F. Line a large baking sheet with nonstick baking parchment. Toast the ground almonds and whole nuts lightly, and set aside until cool.

2 Beat together the eggs, egg yolk, and confectioners' sugar until thick, then beat in the flour, baking powder, and salt. Add the lemon zest, ground almonds, and nuts, and mix to form a slightly sticky dough.

3 Turn the dough onto a lightly floured surface, and using lightly floured hands, form into a log measuring approximately 12 inches long. Place down the center of the prepared baking sheet and transfer to the preheated oven. Cook for 20 minutes.

4 Remove from the oven and increase the oven temperature to 400° F. Cut the log diagonally into 1 inch slices. Return to the baking sheet cut-side down, and cook for an additional 10–15 minutes until golden, turning once after 10 minutes. Allow to cool on a wire rack, and store in a large airtight container.

INGREDIENTS
Makes 12 cookies

1 cup ground almonds
½ cup shelled pistachios
½ cup blanched almonds
2 medium eggs
1 medium egg yolk
⅔ cup confectioners' sugar
2 cups all-purpose flour
1 tsp. baking powder
pinch of salt
3 tsp. lemon zest

Tasty Tip

These cookies are also delicious made with a single kind of nut—try hazelnuts or just almonds. When toasting nuts, spread them out on a baking sheet, then place in a preheated oven at 400° F. Leave for 5–10 minutes, stirring occasionally. If using a lower temperature, leave for a few more minutes.

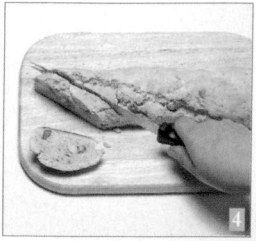

Hazelnut, Chocolate, & Chestnut Meringue Torte

1 Preheat the oven to 250° F. Line 3 baking sheets with nonstick baking parchment and draw an 8-inch circle on each.

2 Beat 1 egg white until stiff peaks form. Add 2 tablespoons of the sugar, and beat until shiny. Mix the cocoa with the remaining sugar, adding 1 tablespoon at a time, beating after each addition until all the sugar is added and the mixture is stiff and glossy. Spread onto 1 of the baking sheets within the circle drawn on the underside.

3 Put the hazelnuts in a food processor and blend until chopped. In a clean bowl, beat the 2 egg whites until stiff. Add 4 tablespoons of the sugar and beat. Add the remaining sugar, 1 tablespoon at a time, beating after each addition until all the sugar is added and the mixture is stiff and glossy.

4 Set 2 tablespoons of the nuts aside, then fold in the remainder and divide between the 2 remaining baking sheets. Sprinkle one of the hazelnut meringues with the hazelnuts, and transfer all the baking sheets to the oven. Cook in the preheated oven for 1½ hours. Turn the oven off and leave in the oven until cool.

5 Whip the cream until thick. Beat the chestnut purée in another bowl until soft. Add a spoonful of the cream and fold together before adding the remaining cream and melted chocolate, and fold together.

6 Place the plain hazelnut meringue on a large plate. Top with half the cream and chestnut mixture. Add the chocolate meringue, and top with remaining cream. Add the final meringue. Sprinkle with the grated chocolate and serve.

INGREDIENTS
Serves 8–10

FOR THE CHOCOLATE MERINGUE:
1 medium egg white
¼ cup sugar
2 tbsp. cocoa

FOR THE HAZELNUT MERINGUE:
¼ cup hazelnuts, toasted
2 medium egg whites
½ cup sugar

FOR THE FILLING:
1 cup heavy cream
9-oz. can sweetened chestnut purée
2 squares unsweetened chocolate, melted
1 square unsweetened chocolate, grated

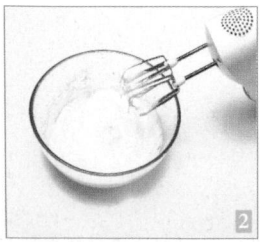

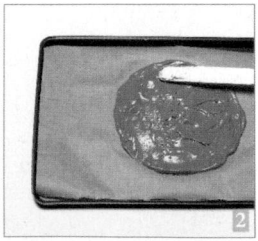

Bomba Siciliana

1 Melt the unsweetened chocolate in bowl set over a saucepan of simmering water until smooth, then cool. Beat together the crème anglaise with the whipping cream and slightly cooled chocolate. Spoon the mixture into a shallow container and freeze. Every 2 hours, remove from the freezer, and using an electric whisk or balloon whisk, beat thoroughly. Repeat 3 times, then leave until frozen solid. Soak the dried candied peel, cherries, and golden raisins in the rum, and leave until needed.

2 Chill a 4-cup pudding mold in the freezer for about 30 minutes. Remove the chocolate ice cream from the freezer to soften, then spoon the ice cream into the mold and press down well, smoothing around the edges and leaving a hollow in the center. Return the ice cream to the freezer for 1 hour or until frozen hard.

3 Remove the vanilla ice cream from the freezer to soften. Spoon the softened vanilla ice cream into the hollow, making sure to leave another hollow for the cream. Return to the freezer again, and freeze until hard.

4 Whip the cream and sugar until it is just holding its shape, then fold in the soaked fruit. Remove the mold from the freezer and spoon in the cream mixture. Return to the freezer for at least another hour.

5 When ready to serve, remove the mold from the freezer, dip into hot water for a few seconds, then turn onto a large serving plate. Dip a knife into hot water and cut into wedges to serve.

INGREDIENTS
Serves 6–8

3½ squares unsweetened chocolate, broken into pieces
1 cup fresh chilled crème anglaise
½ cup whipping cream
2 tbsp. dried candied peel, finely chopped
1 tbsp. glacé cherries, chopped
2 tbsp. golden raisins
3 tbsp. rum
2 cups good-quality vanilla ice cream
½ cup heavy cream
3 tbsp. sugar

Tasty Tip

For the best flavor, buy whole candied peel. Cut it into strips using kitchen scissors, then chop crosswise into small pieces.

Summer Fruit Semifreddo

1 Wash and remove the stalks from the fruits, as necessary, then put them into a food processor or blender with the confectioners' sugar and lemon juice. Blend to a purée, pour into a jug, and chill in the refrigerator until needed.

2 Remove the seeds from the vanilla pod by opening the pod and scraping with the back of a knife. Add the seeds to the sugar, and beat with the egg yolks until pale and thick.

3 In another bowl, whip the cream until soft peaks form. Do not overwhip. In a third bowl, beat the egg whites with the salt until stiff peaks form.

4 Using a large metal spoon—to avoid knocking any air from the mixture—fold together the fruit purée, egg yolk mixture, cream, and egg whites. Transfer the mixture to a round, shallow container, and put into the freezer until almost frozen. If the mixture freezes solid, thaw in the refrigerator until semifrozen. Turn out the semifrozen mixture, cut into wedges, and serve decorated with red currants. If the mixture thaws completely, eat immediately and do not refreeze.

INGREDIENTS
Serves 6–8

2 cups raspberries
1 cup blueberries
1 cup red currants
½ cup confectioners' sugar
2 tbsp. lemon juice
1 vanilla pod, split
¼ cup sugar
4 large eggs, separated
2 cups heavy cream
pinch of salt
fresh red currants, to decorate

Tasty Tip

Use the egg and cream mixture as the basis for a host of other flavors, such as praline, chocolate, or fall berries.

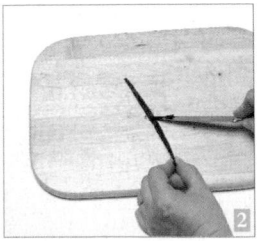

Cassatta

1 Line a 3 x 4 x 6 inch loaf pan with plastic wrap. Place in the freezer. Melt 3½ squares of the chocolate into a heatproof bowl set over a saucepan of simmering water, stir until smooth, then cool. Place the crème anglaise into a bowl. Stir in the cream and the chocolate, and stir until mixed. Spoon into a shallow container, and transfer to the freezer. Every 2 hours, remove from the freezer and beat thoroughly. Repeat 3 times, then leave until frozen solid.

2 Remove the chocolate ice cream from the freezer and let it soften. Remove the loaf pan from the freezer and press the chocolate ice cream into the bottom of the pan, letting it come up the sides. Return the ice cream to the freezer, and leave until solid.

3 Soften the pistachio ice cream, then beat in the pistachios, candied peel, and cherries. Spoon into the pan, pressing down well and smoothing the top. Return to the freezer until hard. Soften the strawberry ice cream and spread onto the pistachio ice cream. Smooth the top. Return to the freezer for at least 1 hour or until completely solid.

4 Meanwhile, melt the remaining chocolate, stir until smooth, and cool slightly. Remove the loaf pan from the freezer. Dip into hot water and turn onto a serving dish. Using a teaspoon, drizzle the chocolate over the ice cream in a haphazard pattern. Return the cassatta to the freezer until the chocolate has set. Dip a knife in hot water and use to slice the cassatta. Serve immediately.

INGREDIENTS
Serves 6–8

11 squares unsweetened chocolate, broken into pieces
1 cup fresh chilled crème anglaise
½ cup whipping cream
2½ cups good quality pistachio ice cream
¼ cup shelled pistachios, toasted
½ cup dried candied peel, finely chopped
1 tbsp. glacé cherries, finely chopped
2½ cups good-quality strawberry ice cream

Tasty Tip

To make your own pistachio ice cream, toast ½ cup of shelled pistachios, and when cool, chop finely. Follow the recipe for chocolate ice cream, omitting the chocolate and folding in the nuts with the cream. Add a few drops of green food coloring, if desired.

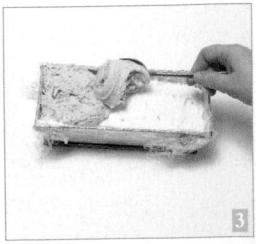

Marzipan Cake

1 Grind the blanched almonds in a food processor until fairly fine. Mix with 1¾ cups of the confectioners' sugar. Beat the egg whites until stiff, then using a metal spoon or rubber spatula, fold into the almond mixture to form a stiff dough. It will still be quite sticky but will firm up as it rests. Leave for 30 minutes.

2 Dust a work surface very generously with some of the remaining confectioners' sugar. Roll out two thirds of the marzipan into a large sheet to a thickness of ¼ inch. Use to line a sloping-sided baking dish with a base measuring 8 x 10 inches. Trim the edges and put any trimmings with the remainder of the marzipan.

3 Cut the Madeira cake into thin slices, and make a layer of sponge to cover the bottom of the marzipan. Sprinkle with the Marsala wine. Beat the ricotta with the sugar, and add the lemon zest, candied peel, and cherries. Spread this over the sponge. Slice the peaches and put them on top of the ricotta. Whip the cream and spread it over the peaches. Roll out the remaining marzipan, and lay it over the cream to seal the whole cake, pressing down gently to remove any air. Press the edges of the marzipan together. Chill in the refrigerator for 2 hours.

4 Turn the cake out onto a serving plate, and dust generously with confectioners' sugar. Slice thickly and serve.

INGREDIENTS
Serves 12–14

4 cups blanched almonds
2¼ cups confectioners' sugar (includes sugar for dusting and rolling)
4 medium egg whites
1 small Madeira or plain sponge cake
2 tbsp. Marsala or Italian fortified wine
1 cup ricotta cheese
¼ cup sugar
2 tsp. grated lemon zest
½ cup dried candied peel, chopped
1 tbsp. glacé cherries, finely chopped
15-oz. can peach halves, drained
1 cup heavy cream

Helpful Hint

Homemade marzipan is stickier than commercially prepared versions. Use plenty of confectioners' sugar when rolling it, as well as sprinkling the dish liberally with it.

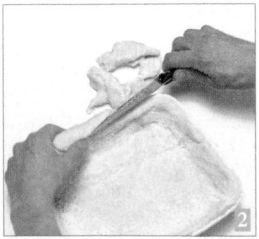

Chestnut Cake

1 Preheat the oven to 300° F. Grease and line a 9-inch springform pan. Beat together the butter and sugar until light and fluffy. Add the chestnut purée and beat. Gradually add the eggs, beating after each addition. Sift in the flour with the baking powder and cloves. Add the fennel seeds and beat. The mixture should drop easily from a wooden spoon when tapped against the side of the bowl. If not, add some milk.

2 Beat in the raisins and pine nuts. Spoon the mixture into the prepared pan and smooth the top. Transfer to the center of the oven and cook in the preheated oven for 55–60 minutes or until a toothpick inserted in the center of the cake comes out clean. Remove from the oven and leave in the pan.

3 Meanwhile, mix together the confectioners' sugar and lemon juice in a small saucepan until smooth. Heat gently until hot but not boiling. Using a toothpick, poke holes all over the cake. Pour the hot syrup evenly on top, and let it soak into the cake. Decorate with pared strips of lemon and serve.

INGREDIENTS
Serves 8–10

1¼ sticks butter, softened
¼ cup sugar
9-oz. can sweetened chestnut purée
3 medium eggs, lightly beaten
1½ cups all-purpose flour
1 tsp. baking powder
pinch of ground cloves
1 tsp. fennel seeds, crushed
½ cup raisins
½ cup pine nuts, toasted
¼ cup confectioners' sugar
5 tbsp. lemon juice
pared strips of lemon rind, to decorate

Tasty Tip

There are two methods for toasting pine nuts. Tip the nuts into a hot, dry skillet and stir often until the nuts have browned on both sides. Tip immediately onto a large plate and allow to cool. Or, spread the pine nuts onto a large baking sheet and transfer to a preheated oven and cook at 400° F for about 3–5 minutes, checking often, as they burn very easily. Remove the toasted pine nuts from the oven, tip onto a plate, and allow to cool, then use as required.

Sauternes & Olive Oil Cake

1 Preheat the oven to 275° F. Grease and line a 10-inch springform pan. Sift the flour onto a large sheet of waxed paper and set aside. Using a freestanding electric mixer, beat the eggs and sugar together until pale and stiff. Add the lemon and orange zest.

2 Turn the speed to low, and pour the flour from the paper in a slow, steady stream onto the egg and sugar mixture. Immediately add the wine and olive oil, and switch the machine off, as the olive oil should not be incorporated completely.

3 Using a rubber spatula, fold the mixture very gently 3 or 4 times so that the ingredients are just incorporated. Pour the mixture immediately into the prepared pan, and cook in the preheated oven for 20–25 minutes, without opening the door for at least 15 minutes. Test if cooked by pressing the top lightly with a clean finger—if it springs back, remove from the oven. If not, cook for longer.

4 Let the cake cool in the pan on a wire rack. Remove the cake from the pan when cool enough to handle.

5 Meanwhile, peel the peaches and cut into segments. Toss with the brown sugar and lemon juice, and set aside. When the cake is cold, dust with confectioners' sugar, cut into wedges, and serve with the peaches.

INGREDIENTS
Serves 8–10

1 cup all-purpose flour, plus extra for dusting
4 medium eggs
½ cup sugar
2 tsp. grated lemon zest
2 tsp. grated orange zest
2 tbsp. Sauternes or other sweet dessert wine
3 tbsp. good-quality extra-virgin olive oil
4 ripe peaches
1–2 tsp. soft brown sugar, or to taste
1 tbsp. lemon juice
confectioners' sugar, to dust

Helpful Hint

Be careful not to overmix in Step 3 when folding the mixture together, or the finished cake will be very heavy.

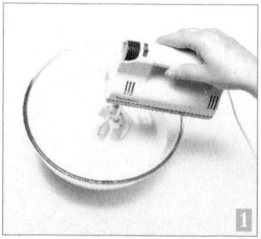

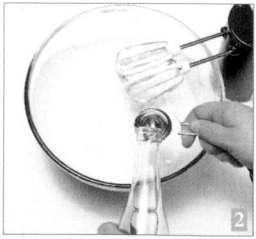

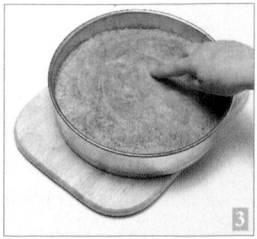

Frozen Amaretto Soufflé with Strawberries

1 Wrap a collar of waxed paper around a 3-cup soufflé dish or 6–8 individual ramekin dishes to extend at least 2 inches above the rim and secure with kitchen string. Break the Amaretto cookies into a bowl. Sprinkle with ¼ cup of the Amaretto liqueur and let soak.

2 Put the lemon zest and juice into a small heatproof bowl, and sprinkle with the gelatin. Leave for 5 minutes, then put the bowl over a saucepan of simmering water, ensuring that the base of the bowl does not touch the water. Stir occasionally until the gelatin has dissolved completely.

3 In a clean bowl, beat the egg yolks and sugar until pale and thick, then stir in the gelatin and the soaked cookies. In another bowl, lightly whip 1¼ cups of the cream, and using a large metal spoon or rubber spatula, fold into the mixture. In a third clean bowl, beat the egg whites until stiff, then fold into the soufflé mixture. Transfer to the prepared dish or individual ramekin dishes, and level the top. Freeze for at least 8 hours or overnight.

4 Put the strawberries into a bowl with the vanilla pod and seeds, sugar, and remaining Amaretto liqueur. Leave overnight in the refrigerator, then allow to come to room temperature before serving.

5 Place the soufflé in the refrigerator for about 1 hour. Whip the remaining cream and use to decorate the soufflé, then sprinkle a few finely crushed Amaretto cookies on the top, and serve with the strawberries.

INGREDIENTS
Serves 6–8

1 cup Amaretto cookies or macaroons
½ cup Amaretto liqueur
1 tbsp. grated lemon zest
2 tbsp. lemon juice
1 tbsp. powdered gelatin
6 medium eggs, separated
¼ cup soft brown sugar
2 cups heavy cream
4 cups fresh strawberries, halved if large
1 vanilla pod, split and seeds scraped out
2 tbsp. sugar
few finely crushed Amaretto cookies or macaroons, to decorate

Helpful Hint

When making ice cream, it is important to keep the freezer at a low temperature and leave the door closed, so that proper freezing can occur.

Baked Stuffed Amaretto Peaches

1 Preheat the oven to 350° F. Halve the peaches and remove the pits. Take a very thin slice from the bottom of each peach half so that it will sit flat on the baking sheet. Dip the peach halves in lemon juice and arrange on a baking sheet.

2 Crush the Amaretto cookies or macaroons lightly, and put into a large bowl. Add the almonds, pine nuts, sugar, lemon zest, and butter. Work with your fingertips until the mixture resembles coarse bread crumbs. Add the egg yolk and mix well.

3 Divide the Amaretto and nut mixture among the peach halves, pressing down lightly. Cook in the preheated oven for 15 minutes or until the peaches are tender and the filling is golden. Remove from the oven and drizzle with the honey.

4 Place 2 peach halves on each serving plate, and spoon over some sour cream or plain yogurt, then serve.

INGREDIENTS
Serves 4

4 ripe peaches
1 tbsp. grated lemon zest
2 tbsp. lemon juice
¼ cup Amaretto cookies or macaroons
½ cup chopped blanched almonds, toasted
½ cup pine nuts, toasted
3 tbsp. golden brown sugar, firmly packed
½ stick butter
1 medium egg yolk
2 tsp. honey
sour cream or plain yogurt, to serve

Tasty Tip

If fresh peaches are unavailable, use nectarines. Alternatively, use drained, canned peach halves that have been packed in juice, rather than syrup. You can vary the filling according to personal preference—try ground almonds, sugar, crumbled trifle sponge cakes, and lemon rind moistened with medium sherry.

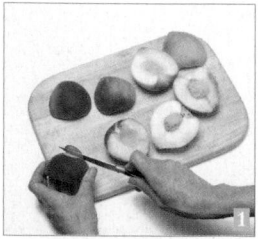
1

2

3

Almond & Pine Nut Pie

1 Preheat the oven to 400° F. Roll out the pastry, and use to line a 9-inch fluted flan pan. Chill in the refrigerator for 10 minutes, then line with waxed paper and baking beans, and bake blind in the preheated oven for 10 minutes. Remove the paper and beans, and cook for an additional 10–12 minutes until cooked. Allow to cool, then reduce the oven temperature to 375° F.

2 Grind the almonds in a food processor until fine. Add the sugar, salt, eggs, and vanilla and almond extracts, and blend. Add the butter, flour, and baking powder, and blend until smooth.

3 Spread a thick layer of the raspberry jelly over the cooled pastry shell, then pour in the almond filling. Sprinkle the pine nuts evenly over the top, and cook for 30 minutes until firm and browned.

4 Remove the pie from the oven and let cool. Dust generously with confectioners' sugar, and serve cut into wedges with whipped cream.

INGREDIENTS
Serves 6

1¼ cups sweet short-crust pastry
¼ cup blanched almonds
½ cup sugar
pinch of salt
2 medium eggs
1 tsp. vanilla extract
2–3 drops almond extract
1 stick unsalted butter, softened
2 tbsp. flour
½ tsp. baking powder
3–4 tbsp. raspberry jelly
½ cup pine nuts
confectioners' sugar, to decorate
whipped cream, to serve

Tasty Tip

Blend 1½ cups all-purpose flour and ¾ stick diced, cold butter together in a food processor until they resemble coarse bread crumbs. Add 2 tablespoons sugar, and blend briefly to mix. Beat together 1 medium egg yolk with 2 tablespoons of cold water and add to the food processor. Pulse until the mixture begins to form a ball, adding a little more cold water if necessary. Tip onto a floured surface and knead briefly until smooth. Wrap and refrigerate for at least 30 minutes.

1

2

3

Coffee Ricotta

1 Preheat the oven to 425° F. Beat the ricotta and cream together until smooth. Stir in the ground coffee beans, sugar, and brandy. Cover and refrigerate for at least 2 hours (the longer it stands, the better the flavor). Meanwhile, grease 2 baking sheets and line with nonstick baking parchment.

2 Cream together the butter and sugar until fluffy. gradually beat in the egg, a little at a time. In a bowl, sift the flour, then fold into the butter mixture to form a soft dough. Spoon the mixture into a piping bag fitted with a ½-inch plain tip. Pipe 3-inch lengths of the mixture, spaced well apart, onto the baking sheet. Use a sharp knife to cut the dough off cleanly at the tip.

3 Cook in the preheated oven for 6–8 minutes until just golden at the edges. Cool on the baking sheet for 5 minutes before transferring to a wire rack to cool completely.

4 To serve, spoon the coffee and ricotta mixture into small coffee cups. Serve with the cookies.

INGREDIENTS
Serves 6

3 cups fresh ricotta cheese
½ cup heavy cream
2 tbsp. espresso beans, freshly ground
4 tbsp. sugar
3 tbsp. brandy
½ stick butter, softened
½ cup sugar
1 medium egg, beaten
½ cup all-purpose flour

Helpful Hint

When making the cookies, spoon the mixture very carefully into the piping bag to avoid getting large air bubbles in the mixture. This will help you pipe the cookies smoothly onto the baking sheet.

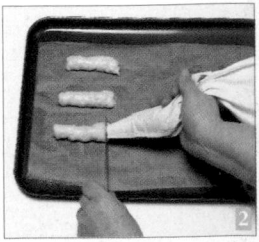

Zabaglione with Rum-Soaked Raisin Compote

1 Put the raisins in a small bowl with the lemon zest and ground cinnamon. Pour over the Marsala wine to cover, and leave to macerate for at least 1 hour. When the raisins are plump, lift out of the Marsala wine, and set the raisins and wine aside. Discard the lemon zest.

2 In a large heatproof bowl, mix together the egg yolks and sugar. Add the white wine and Marsala wine, and stir well to combine. Put the bowl over a saucepan of simmering water, ensuring that the bottom of the bowl does not touch the water. Beat constantly until the mixture doubles in bulk.

3 Remove from the heat and continue beating for about 5 minutes until the mixture has cooled slightly. Fold in the raisins and then immediately fold in the whipped cream. Spoon into dessert glasses or goblets, and serve with crisp cookies.

INGREDIENTS
Serves 6

2 tbsp. raisins
1 strip thinly pared lemon zest
½ tsp. ground cinnamon
3 tbsp. Marsala or Italian fortified wine
3 medium egg yolks
3 tbsp. sugar
½ cup dry white wine
½ cup heavy cream, lightly whipped
crisp cookies, to serve

Food Fact

Zabaglione, an Italian concoction of eggs, sugar, and wine is virtually identical to sabayon—the French dessert of eggs, sugar, and wine. Make the zabaglione as above, and omit the raisins. Serve with poached pears, summer fruits, or on its own in stemmed glasses.

Raspberry & Almond Pie

1 Preheat the oven to 400° F. Blend the flour, salt, and butter in a food processor until the mixture resembles bread crumbs. Add the sugar and lemon zest, and blend again for 1 minute. Mix the egg yolk with 2 tablespoons of cold water, and add to the mixture. Blend until the mixture starts to come together, adding a little more water if necessary, then tip out onto a lightly floured surface. Knead until smooth, wrap in plastic wrap, and chill in the refrigerator for 30 minutes.

2 Roll the dough out thinly on a lightly floured surface, and use to line a 9-inch fluted pan pie. Chill in the refrigerator for 10 minutes. Line the pastry shell with waxed paper and baking beans. Cook for 10 minutes, then remove the paper and beans, and return to the oven for an additional 10–12 minutes until cooked. Allow to cool slightly, then reduce the oven temperature to 375° F.

3 Blend together the butter, sugar, ground almonds, and eggs until smooth. Spread the raspberries over the base of the pastry, then cover with the almond mixture. Cook for 15 minutes. Remove from the oven, sprinkle with the slivered or flaked almonds, and dust generously with confectioners' sugar. Cook for an additional 15–20 minutes until firm and golden brown. Let cool, then serve.

INGREDIENTS
Serves 6–8

FOR THE PIE CRUST:
2 cups all-purpose flour
pinch of salt
1 stick butter, cut into pieces
4 tbsp. sugar
2 tsp. grated lemon zest
1 medium egg yolk

FOR THE FILLING:
¼ stick butter
½ cup sugar
¼ cup ground almonds
2 medium eggs
2 cups raspberries, thawed if frozen
2 tbsp. slivered or flaked almonds
confectioners' sugar, for dusting

Tasty Tip

Omit the raspberries in the above pie. Spread the almond mixture over the base of the pastry shell, and top with poached or drained canned pear halves. Sprinkle with slivered almonds and cook as above.

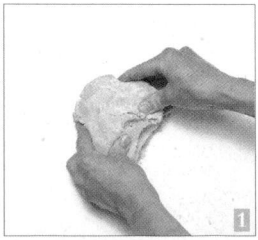
1

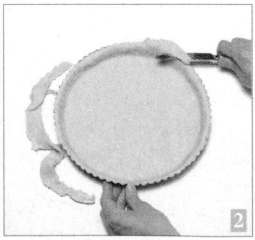
2

3

Goat Cheese & Lemon Pie

1 Preheat the oven to 400° F. Rub the butter into the all-purpose flour and salt until the mixture resembles bread crumbs, then stir in the sugar. Beat the egg yolk with 2 tablespoons of cold water and add to the mixture. Mix together until a dough is formed, then turn the dough out onto a lightly floured surface and knead until smooth. Chill in the refrigerator for 30 minutes.

2 Roll the dough out thinly on a lightly floured surface and use to line a 1½-inch-deep, 9-inch fluted flan pan. Chill in the refrigerator for 10 minutes. Line the pastry shell with waxed paper and baking beans, and bake blind in the preheated oven for 10 minutes. Remove the paper and beans. Return to the oven for an additional 12–15 minutes until cooked. Allow to cool slightly, then reduce the oven temperature to 300° F.

3 Beat the goat cheese until smooth. Beat in the eggs, sugar, lemon rind, and juice. Add the cream and mix well.

4 Carefully pour the cheese mixture into the pastry shell, and return to the oven. Cook in the oven for 35–40 minutes or until just set. If it begins to brown or swell, open the oven door for 2 minutes, then reduce the temperature to 250° F and leave the pie to cool in the oven. Chill in the refrigerator until cold. Decorate and serve with fresh raspberries.

INGREDIENTS
Serves 8–10

FOR THE PIE CRUST:
1 stick butter, cut into small pieces
2 cups all-purpose flour
pinch of salt
4 tbsp. sugar
1 medium egg yolk

FOR THE FILLING:
1½ cups mild fresh goat cheese
3 medium eggs, beaten
½ cup sugar
3 tbsp. grated lemon rind
½ cup lemon juice
2 cups heavy cream
fresh raspberries, to decorate and serve

Tasty Tip

The goat cheese adds a certain unusual piquancy to this pie. Substitute cream cheese or ricotta, if preferred.

Tiramisu

1 Lightly grease and line a 3 x 5 x 9 inch loaf pan with a piece of plastic wrap. Put the mascarpone cheese and confectioners' sugar into a large bowl, and using a rubber spatula, beat until smooth. Stir in 2 tablespoons of chilled coffee and mix thoroughly.

2 Whip the cream with 1 tablespoon of the coffee liqueur until just thickened. Stir a spoonful of the whipped cream into the mascarpone mixture, then fold in the rest. Spoon half of the mascarpone mixture into the prepared loaf pan, and smooth the top.

3 Put the remaining coffee and coffee liqueur into a shallow dish just bigger than the ladyfingers. Using half of the ladyfingers, dip one side of each ladyfinger into the coffee mixture, then arrange on top of the mascarpone mixture in a single layer. Spoon the rest of the mascarpone mixture over the ladyfingers, and smooth the top.

4 Dip the remaining ladyfingers in the coffee mixture, and arrange on top of the mascarpone mixture. Drizzle with any remaining coffee mixture. Cover with plastic wrap and chill for 4 hours.

5 Turn the tiramisu out onto a large serving plate, and sprinkle with the grated chocolate or chocolate curls. Dust with cocoa, cut into slices, and serve with summer berries.

INGREDIENTS
Serves 4

1 cup mascarpone cheese
¼ cup confectioners' sugar, sifted
⅔ cup strong brewed coffee, chilled
1 cup heavy cream
3 tbsp. coffee liqueur
1 cup Savoiardi or ladyfingers
2 squares unsweetened chocolate, grated or made into small curls
cocoa, for dusting
assorted summer berries, to serve

Food Fact

This now-classic Italian dessert appears in all kinds of forms in most Italian cookbooks. The name literally means "pick me up."

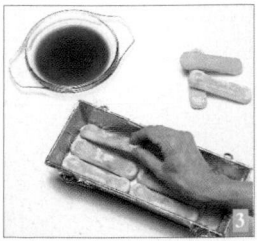

Cannoli with Ricotta Cheese

1 In a large bowl, beat together the butter and the sugar until light and fluffy. Add the white wine and salt, and mix together well. Fold in the flour, and knead to form a soft dough. Set aside for 2 hours.

2 Lightly flour a work surface and roll the dough out to a thickness of about ¼ inch. Cut into 5-inch squares. Wrap the pastry around the cannoli or cream-horn molds, using the beaten egg to seal. Make 3–4 at a time.

3 Heat the vegetable oil to 350° F in a deep-fat fryer, and cook the cannoli for 1–2 minutes or until puffed and golden. Drain well on absorbent paper towels, and allow to cool. Remove the molds when the cannoli are cool enough to handle. Repeat until all the cannoli are cooked.

4 Beat the ricotta cheese with the sugar, orange water, and vanilla extract until creamy. Add the cherries, angelica, dried candied peel, and chopped chocolate. Fill each cannoli using a piping bag with a large plain tip, or a small spoon. Dust with confectioners' sugar and serve when cool.

INGREDIENTS
Makes 24

FOR THE PIECRUST:
2 tbsp. butter
2 tbsp. sugar
3 tbsp. dry white wine
pinch of salt
1¼ cups all-purpose flour
1 medium egg, lightly beaten
vegetable oil, for deep-frying

FOR THE FILLING:
2 cups ricotta cheese
½ cup sugar
2 tbsp. orange water
1 tsp. vanilla extract
2 tbsp. glacé cherries, chopped
2 tbsp. angelica, chopped
⅔ cup dried candied peel, chopped
3 squares unsweetened chocolate, finely chopped
confectioners' sugar, for dusting

Helpful Hint

Cannoli molds are difficult to come by outside Italy. Substitute cream-horn molds for lengths of 1-inch thick bamboo or cane (washed thoroughly).

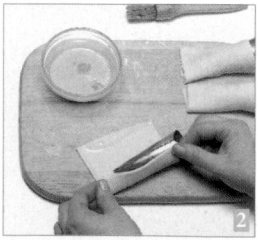

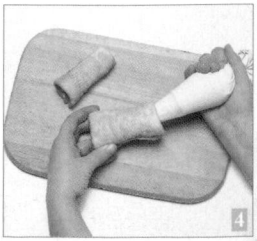

Index

almonds:
Almond & Pine Nut Pie 496
Almond & Pistachio Biscotti 476
Marzipan Cake 486
Raspberry & Almond Tart 502
Amaretto Soufflé with Strawberries, Frozen 492
Angel-hair Pasta with Smoked Salmon & Jumbo Shrimip 442
Antipasti with Focaccia 46
Antipasto Penne 194
Arugula & Potato Soup with Garlic Croutons 38
Asparagus, Chicken &, with Tagliatelle 302

beans:
Pasta & Bean Soup 98
Venetian-Style Vegetables & Beans 374
White Bean Soup with Parmesan Croutons 30
beef:
Chinese Beef with Angel Hair Pasta 256
Fillet Steaks with Tomato & Garlic Sauce 216
Gnocchi with Tuscan Beef Ragù 268
Italian Pot Roast 224
Meatballs with Olives 212
Pan-Fried Beef with Creamy Mushrooms 198
Pasta with Beef, Capers, & Olives 252
Spicy Chili Beef 242
Beet Ravioli with Dill Cream Sauce 72
bell peppers:
Braised Mixed Bell Peppers 62
Pappardelle with Spicy Lamb & Bell Peppers 452
Pasta & Bell Pepper Salad 328
Pasta with Spicy Red Bell Pepper Sauce 366
Pasta-Stuffed Bell Peppers 398
Penne with Mixed Bell Peppers & Garlic 440
Red Bell Pepper & Basil Tart 370
Rice-Filled Bell Peppers 364
Salmon & Roasted Red bell Pepper Pasta 90
Bomba Siciliana 480
Bread & Tomato Soup 36
Broccoli & Capers, Pasta Shells with 392
Bruschetta with Pecorino, Garlic, & Tomatoes 52

Calamari, Stuffed, with Romesco Sauce 112
Cannelloni 220
Creamy Chicken 290
Crispy Cod 172
Eggplant, with Watercress Sauce 380
with Gorgonzola Sauce 462
with Spicy Bolognese Filling 234
with Tomato & Red Wine Sauce 456
Tuna 130
Cannoli with Ricotta Cheese 508
Cantuccini 474
Cassatta 484
cheese:
Cannelloni with Gorgonzola Sauce 462
Cannoli with Ricotta Cheese 508
Cheesy Baked Chicken Macaroni 340
Cheesy Pasta with Tomatoes & Cream 396
Coffee Ricotta 498
Four-Cheese Tagliatelle 404
Goat Cheese & Lemon Pie 504
Mozzarella Frittata with Tomato & Basil Salad 48
Mozzarella Pockets with Cranberry Relish 68
Parmesan & Garlic Lobster 120
Polenta Roulade with Mozzarella & Spinach 438
Prosciutto & Gruyère Carbonara 266
Rigatoni with Oven-Dried Cherry Tomatoes & Mascarpone 368
Spinach & Ricotta Gnocchi with Butter & Parmesan 76
Tiramisu 506
Tortellini, Cherry Tomato, & Mozzarella Skewers 426
Cheesecake, Ricotta, with Strawberry Coulis 472
Chestnut Cake 488
chicken:
Braised Chicken with Red Bell Peppers 306
Cheesy Baked Chicken Macaroni 340
Chicken & Asparagus with Tagliatelle 302
Chicken & Pasta Salad 308
Chicken & Shrimp-Stacked Ravioli 346
Chicken Cacciatore 278
Chicken, Gorgonzola & Mushroom Macaroni 336
Chicken Marengo 330
Chicken en Papillote with Zucchini & pasta 298
Chicken with Porcini Mushrooms & Cream 282
Chicken Tagliatelle 312
Chicken Under a Brick 300
Creamy Chicken & Sausage Penne 318
Creamy Chicken Cannelloni 290
Farfalle & Chicken in White Wine Sauce 436
Herb-Baked Chicken with Tagliatelle 316
Lemon Chicken with Basil & Linguine 286
Lemon Chicken with Potatoes, Rosemary, & Olives 280
Mini Chicken Balls with Tagliatelle 326
Mixed Vegetable & Chicken Pasta 314
Pasta Ring with Chicken & Sun-Dried Tomatoes 444
Penne with Pan-Fried Chicken & Capers 348
Pesto Chicken Tagliatelle 344
Poached Chicken with Salsa Verde Herb Sauce 296
Prosciutto-Wrapped Chicken with Ribbon Pasta 322
Saffron Roast Chicken with Crispy Onions 270
Spicy Chicken & Pasta Salad 334
Spicy Chicken with Open Ravioli & Tomato Sauce 434
Spicy Mexican Chicken 342
chicken livers:
Chicken Liver & Tomato Sauce with Tagliolini 288
Crostini with Chicken Livers 54
Chicory, Hot Broiled, & Pears 378
Chorizo with Pasta in a Tomato Sauce 238
clams:
Red Pesto & Clam Spaghetti 116
Spaghetti alle Vongole 174
cod:
Crispy Cod Cannelloni 172
Roasted Cod with Saffron Aioli 122
Saucy Cod & Pasta Bake 158
Coffee Ricotta 498
Conchiglioni with Crab au Gratin 450
Crab au Gratin, Conchiglioni with 450
Cranberry Relish 68
Crostini with Chicken Livers 54

duck:
Duck Lasagna with Porcini & Basil 292
Hot Duck Pasta Salad 310

eggplant:
Eggplant & Ravioli Parmigiana 410
Eggplant & Tomato Layer 460
Eggplant Cannelloni with Watercress Sauce 380
Baked Eggplant with Tomato & Mozzarella 324
Melanzane Parmigiana 356

farfalle:
& Chicken in White Wine Sauce 436
with Zucchini & Mushrooms 454
with Smoked Trout in a Dill & Vodka Sauce 150
fettuccine:
with Calf's Liver & Calvados 430
with Sardines & Spinach 184
with Wild Mushrooms & Prosciutto 104

fish:
Foil-Baked Fish 124
Mediterranean Fish Stew 134
Sweet-&-Sour Fish with Crispy Noodles 186
Flounder with Parmesan & Anchovies 136
fusilli:
with Zucchini & Sun-Dried Tomatoes 400
with Tomato & Chorizo Sauce with Roasted Bell Peppers 94

game hen:
Game Hen with Mushrooms & Red Wine Gravy 272
Game Hen with Sage & Blueberries 274
Marinated Game Hen Breasts with Broiled Polenta 304
Game Hens, with Garlic Sage Butter 276
Gnocchetti with Broccoli & Bacon Sauce 100
gnocchi:
& Prosciutto Bake 254
with Broiled Cherry Tomato Sauce 74
Spinach & Ricotta, with Butter & Parmesan 76
with Tuscan Beef Ragù 268
Grape Leaves, Sardines in 118

Haddock (Smoked) & Blue Cheese Sauce, Pappardelle with 152
ham:
Gnocchi & Prosciutto Bake 254
Prosciutto-Wrapped Chicken with Ribbon Pasta 322
Prosciutto & Gruyère Carbonara 266
Ham Steak with Red Wine Sauce & pasta 264
Hazelnut, Chocolate, & Chestnut Meringue Torte 478
Herring, Fried, with Arugula Salad 50

lamb:
Braised Lamb with Fava Beans 208
Creamed Lamb & Wild Mushroom Pasta 260
Lamb & Pasta Pie 466
Lamb Arrabbiata 258
Pappardelle with Spicy Lamb & Bell Peppers 452
Roasted Lamb with Rosemary & Garlic 206
Lasagna 214, 232
Duck, with Porcini & Basil 292
Special Seafood 154
Zucchini 412
Lettuce Soup 44
linguine:
with Fennel, Crab, & Chervil 108
with Walnut Pesto 402
liver:
Fettuccine with Calf's Liver & Calvados 430
Italian Calf's Liver 228
Tagliatelle with Creamy Liver & Basil 262
Lobster, Parmesan & Garlic 120

macaroni:
Baked Macaroni and Cheese 414
Baked Macaroni with Mushrooms & Leeks 468
mackerel:
Marinated Mackerel with Tomato & Basil Salad 146
Smoked Mackerel & Pasta Frittata 170
Marzipan Cake 486
meatballs:
Meatballs with Olives 212
Spaghetti & Meatballs 236
Mediterranean Fish Stew 134
Melanzane Parmigiana 356
Minestrone, Classic 40
Mixed Salad with Anchovy Dressing & Ciabatta Croutons 362
monkfish:
Roasted Monkfish with Prosciutto 126
Scallops & Monkfish Kabobs with Fennel Sauce 114
mushrooms, Wild Garlic Mushrooms with Pizza Grissini 64
mussels:
Mussels Arrabbiata 128
Mussels with Creamy Garlic & Saffron Sauce 60
Pasta & Mussels in Tomato & wine Sauce 178
Spaghetti with Hot Chili Mussels 448

noodles:
Cold Sesame 422
Hot Shrimp, with Sesame Dressing 166
Singapore 424

Panna Cotta with Raspberry Sauce 470
Panzanella 382
Panzerotti 386
pappardelle:
Pork with Brandy Sauce 248
with Smoked Haddock & Blue Cheese Sauce 152
with Spicy Lamb & Bell Peppers 452
pasta:
Cheesy Pasta with Tomatoes & Cream 396
Lamb & Pasta Pie 466
Pasta & Bean Soup 98
Pasta & Bell Pepper Salad 328
Pasta & Mussels in Tomato & wine Sauce 178
Pasta & Pork Ragù 244
Pasta with Beef, Capers, & Olives 252
Pasta Genovese with Pesto, Green Beans, & Potatoes 84
Pasta Primavera 388
Pasta Provençale 160
Pasta with Raw Fennel, Tomato, & Red Onions 80
Pasta Ring with Chicken & Sun-dried Tomatoes 444
Pasta Shells with Broccoli & Capers 392
Pasta with Spicy Red Bell Pepper Sauce 366
Pasta Triangles with Pesto & Walnut Dressing 458
Pasta with Walnut Sauce 96
Ratatouille & Pasta Bake 464
Tiny Pasta with Fresh Herb Sauce 86
Pasta-Stuffed Bell Peppers 398
Peaches, Baked Stuffed Amaretto 494
Pears, Hot Broiled Chicory & 378
peas:
Pea & Shrimp Risotto 110
Risi e Bisi 350
penne:
with Artichokes, Bacon, & Mushrooms 102
with Mixed Bell Peppers & Garlic 440
Moroccan 240
with Pan-Fried Chicken & Capers 348
with Vodka & Caviar 416
Peperonata 62
Polenta Roulade with Mozzarella & Spinach 438
pork:
Italian Meatballs in Tomato Sauce 226
Oven-Baked Pork Balls with Bell Peppers 200
Pappardelle Pork with Brandy Sauce 248
Pasta & Pork Ragù 244
Pork Chop Hotpot 202
Tagliatelle with Stuffed Pork Escalopes 432
Prosciutto & Gruyère Carbonara 266
pumpkin:
Cream of Pumpkin Soup 42
Pumpkin-Filled Pasta with Butter & Sage 420

Raspberry & Almond Pie 502
Ratatouille & Pasta Bake 464
Red Mullet, Broiled, with Orange & Anchovy Sauce 138
rice:
Italian Risotto 196
Pan-Fried Salmon with Herb Risotto 142
Pea & Shrimp Risotto 110
Rice & Vegetable Timbale 352
Rice Soup with Potato Sticks 32
Rice-Filled Bell Peppers 364
Risi e Bisi 350
Roast Butternut Squash Risotto 376
rigatoni:
with Gorgonzola & Walnuts 418

with Oven-Dried Cherry Tomatoes & Mascarpone 368
with Roasted Beets & Arugula 360
Risi e Bisi 350

Saffron Roast Chicken with Crispy Onions 270
Salami & Vegetable Gratin, Hot 192
salmon:
Angel-Hair Pasta with Smoked Salmon & Jumbo Shrimp 442
Pan-Fried Salmon with Herb Risotto 142
Salmon & Mushroom Linguine 446
Salmon & Roasted Red Bell Pepper Pasta 90
Salmon & Spaghetti in a Creamy Egg Sauce 180
Seared Salmon & Lemon Linguine 162
sardines:
Fettuccine with Sardines & Spinach 184
Sardines in Grape Leaves 118
sausages:
Creamy Chicken & Sausage Penne 318
Oven-Roasted Vegetables with Sausages 190
Sausage & Red Currant Pasta Bake 246
Tagliatelle with Spicy Sausage Ragù 250
Sauternes & Olive Oil Cake 490
scallops:
Pan-Fried Scallops & Pasta 168
Scallops & Monkfish Kabobs with Fennel Sauce 114
Sea Bass in Creamy Mustard & Prosciutto Sauce 144
seafood:
Creamy Coconut Seafood Pasta 182
Seafood Pockets with Pappardelle & Cilantro Pesto 176
Seafood Special 148
Special Seafood Lasagna 154
Sesame Noodles, Cold 422
shrimp:
Angel-Hair Pasta with Smoked Salmon & Jumbo Shrimp 442
Chicken & Shrimp-Stacked Ravioli 346
Hot Shrimp Noodles with Sesame Dressing 166
Hot Jumbo Shrimp with Prosciutto 66
Louisiana Shrimp & Fettuccine 88
Pea & Shrimp Risotto 110
Singapore Noodles 424
Snapper, Broiled, with Roasted Bell Pepper 140
spaghetti:
Bolognese 210, 230
with Fresh Tomatoes, Chili, & Potatoes 82
with Hot Chili Mussels 448
& Meatballs 236
with Pesto 390
alla Puttanesca 406
Salmon &, in a Creamy Egg Sauce 180
with Turkey & Bacon Sauce 338
alle Vongole 174
spaghettini:
with Lemon Pesto and Cheese & Herb Bread 58
with Peas, Scallions, & Mint 92
spinach:
Fettuccine with Sardines & Spinach 184
Polenta Roulade with Mozzarella & Spinach 438
Spinach & Ricotta Gnocchi with Butter & Parmesan 76
Spinach Dumplings with Rich Tomato Sauce 372
Squash (Butternut) Risotto, Roast 376
Strawberries, Frozen Amaretto Soufflé with 492
Summer Fruit Semifreddo 482
Swordfish Niçoise, Warm 188

Tagliarini with Fava Beans, Saffron, & Crème Fraîche 106
tagliatelle:
with Brown Butter, Asparagus, & Parmesan 78
with Creamy Liver & Basil 262
Fresh, with Zucchini 70
Primavera 408
with Spicy Sausage Ragù 250
with Stuffed Pork Escalopes 432
with Tuna & Anchovy Tapenade 164
Tiramisu 506
tomatoes:
Bread & Tomato Soup 36
Eggplant & Tomato Layer 460
Italian Baked Tomatoes with Curly Endive & Radicchio 56
Rich Tomato Sauce 372
Rich Tomato Soup with Roasted Red Bell Peppers 34
Rigatoni with Oven-Dried Cherry Tomatoes & Mascarpone 368
Stuffed Tomatoes with Broiled Polenta 358
Tomato Sauce 226
Tortellini, Cherry Tomato, & Mozzarella Skewers 426
tortellini:
Tortellini & Summer Vegetable Salad 428
Tortellini, Cherry Tomato, & Mozzarella Skewers 426
trout, Farfalle with Smoked Trout in a Dill & Vodka Sauce 150
tuna:
Seared Tuna with Italian Salsa 132
Tuna & Macaroni Timbales 156
Tuna Cannelloni 130
Veal in Tuna Sauce 222
turkey:
Creamy Turkey & Tomato Pasta 320
Turkey & Oven-Roasted Vegetable Salad 332
Turkey Cutlets Marsala with Wilted Watercress 284
Turkey Tetrazzini 294
Vanilla & Lemon Panna Cotta with Raspberry Sauce 470
veal:
Veal Cutlets with Marsala Sauce 218
Veal in Tuna Sauce 222
Veal Italian 204
vegetables:
Classic Minestrone 40
Hot Salami & Vegetable Gratin 192
Mixed Vegetable & Chicken Pasta 314
Oven-Roasted Vegetables with Sausages 190
Pasta Primavera 388
Rice & Vegetable Timbale 352
Tagliatelle Primavera 408
Tortellini & Summer Vegetable Salad 428
Turkey & Oven-Roasted Vegetable Salad 332
Vegetable Frittata 384
Vegetables Braised in Olive Oil & Lemon 354
Venetian-Style Vegetables & Beans 374
Vitello Tonnato 222

Zabaglione with Rum-Soaked Raisin Compote 500
zucchini:
Zucchini Lasagna 412
Farfalle with Zucchini & Mushrooms 454
Fusilli with Zucchini & Sun-Dried Tomatoes 400
Ratatouille & Pasta Bake 464